Workbook to Accompany

Mike Holt's Illustrated Guide to

Understanding the
NATIONAL
ELECTRICAL CODE®

Volume 1 • Articles 90 - 480

Based on the 2011 NEC®

Since 1974
www.MikeHolt.com

Mike Holt Enterprises, Inc.
888.NEC.CODE (632.2633) • www.MikeHolt.com • Info@MikeHolt.com

NOTICE TO THE READER

Workbook to Accompany Mike Holt's Understanding the 2011 National Electrical Code, Volume 1

First Printing: March 2011

Technical Illustrator: Mike Culbreath
Cover Design: Madalina Iordache-Levay
Layout Design and Typesetting: Cathleen Kwas

COPYRIGHT © 2011 Charles Michael Holt
ISBN 978-1-932685-70-1

For more information, call 888.NEC.CODE (632.2633), or E-mail Info@MikeHolt.com.

This logo is a registered trademark of Mike Holt Enterprises, Inc.

If you are an instructor and would like to request an examination copy of this or other Mike Holt Publications:

Call: 866.NEC.CODE (632.2633) • Fax: 352.360.0983

E-mail: Info@MikeHolt.com • Visit: www.MikeHolt.com

You can download a sample PDF of all our publications by visiting www.MikeHolt.com

I dedicate this book to the
Lord Jesus Christ,
my mentor and teacher.
Proverbs 16:3

One Team

To Our Instructors and Students:

We're committed to providing you the finest product with the fewest errors, but we're realistic and know that there'll be errors found and reported after the printing of this book. The last thing we want is for you to have problems finding, communicating, or accessing this information. It's unacceptable to us for there to be even one error in our textbooks or answer keys. For this reason, we're asking you to work together with us as One Team.

Students: Please report any errors you may find to your instructor.

Instructors: Please communicate these errors to us by sending an email to corrections@mikeholt.com.

Our Commitment:

We'll continue to list all of the corrections that come through for all of our textbooks and answer keys on our Website. The most up-to-date answer keys will always be available to instructors to download from our instructor Website. We don't want you to have problems finding this updated information, so we're outlining where to go for all of this below:

To view textbook and answer key corrections: Students and instructors go to our Website, www.MikeHolt.com, click on "Books" in the sidebar of links, and then click on "Corrections."

To download the most up-to-date answer keys: Instructors go to our Website, www.MikeHolt.com, click on "Instructors" in the sidebar of links and then click on "Answer Keys." On this page you'll find instructions for accessing and downloading these answer keys.

If you're not registered as an instructor you'll need to register. Your registration will be sent to our educational director who in turn will review and approve your registration. In your approval E-mail will be the login and password so you can have access to all of the answer keys. If you have a situation that needs immediate attention, please contact the office directly at 888.NEC.CODE (632.2633).

Call 888.NEC.CODE (632.2633) or visit us online at www.MikeHolt.com

This *Workbook to Accompany Mike Holt's Understanding the National Electrical Code, Volume 1* (2011 Edition) contains over 1,300 *NEC* practice questions that are in *Code* order. Two final exams with 210 *NEC* questions that are in random order are also included. These questions are designed to test your knowledge and comprehension of the material covered in the textbook. Text and graphics referred to in this Workbook can be found in *Mike Holt's Illustrated Guide to Understanding the 2011 National Electrical Code,* Volume 1 textbook.

How To Use This Book

All the questions in this Workbook should be answered using the *2011 National Electrical Code.*

QR Codes

QR Code

What is this? It is a QR Code and gives you the ability to use your smartphone to take a photo (using a barcode reader app) and be directed to a website. For example, the QR Code to the left when captured will direct your smartphone to the Mike Holt Enterprises website. In order to use a QR code, you will need an app for your phone that allows your phone to read this barcode. Your phone may already have the ability to scan this barcode, but if not, visit the website www.mobile-barcodes.com/qr-code-software for more information.

Workbook Errors and Corrections

Humans develop the text, graphics, and layout of this book, and since currently none of us are perfect, there may be a few errors. This can occur because the *NEC* is dramatically changed each *Code* cycle; new articles are added, some are deleted, some are relocated, and many are renumbered. We take great care in researching the *NEC* requirements to ensure this book is correct. If you believe there's an error of any kind (typographical, grammatical, technical, or anything else), no matter how insignificant, please let us know.

Any errors found after printing are listed on our Website, so if you find an error, first check to see if it's already been corrected. Go to www. MikeHolt.com, click on the "Books" link, and then the "Corrections" link (www.MikeHolt.com/bookcorrections.htm).

If you don't find the error listed on the Website, contact us by sending an E-mail to Corrections@ MikeHolt.com. Be sure to include the book title, page number, and any other pertinent information.

Technical Questions

Today as never before, you can get your technical questions answered by posting them to Mike Holt's Code Forum. Just visit www.MikeHolt. com and click on the "Code Forum" link.

You Tube

 Visit the Mike Holt channel on YouTube to see video clips that accompany this and our other 2011 books (www.youtube.com/MikeHoltNEC).

NEC Library

If you really want to understand the 2011 *NEC,* then order Mike Holt's 2011 Detailed *NEC* Library. It includes the *Understanding the National Electrical Code,* Volumes 1 and 2 textbooks, the *NEC Practice Questions* book and ten DVDs (that cover the entire *Code*). This option allows you to learn at the most cost effective price.

 Order Mike Holt's Detailed *NEC* Library by calling 888.NEC.CODE (632.2633) or visiting www.MikeHolt.com/NEC.

How to Use the
National Electrical Code

The *National Electrical Code* is written for persons who understand electrical terms, theory, safety procedures, and electrical trade practices. These individuals include electricians, electrical contractors, electrical inspectors, electrical engineers, designers, and other qualified persons. The *Code* isn't written to serve as an instructive or teaching manual for untrained individuals [90.1(C)].

Learning to use the *NEC* is like learning to play the game of chess; it's a great game if you enjoy mental warfare. When learning to play chess, you must first learn the names of the game pieces, how the pieces are placed on the board, and how each piece moves.

Once you understand the fundamentals, you're ready to start playing the game. Unfortunately, at this point all you can do is make crude moves, because you really don't understand how all the information works together. To play chess well, you'll need to learn how to use your knowledge by working on sub-tle strategies before you can work your way up to the more intriguing and complicated moves.

Not a Game

Electrical work isn't a game, and it must be taken very seriously. Learning the basics of electricity, important terms and concepts, as well as the basic layout of the *NEC* gives you just enough knowledge to be dangerous. There are thousands of specific and unique applications of electrical installations, and the *Code* doesn't cover every one of them. To safely apply the *NEC*, you must understand the purpose of a rule and how it affects the safety aspects of the installation.

NEC Terms and Concepts

The *NEC* contains many technical terms, so it's crucial for *Code* users to understand their meanings and their applications. If you don't understand a term used in a *Code* rule, it will be impossible to properly apply the *NEC* requirement. Be sure you understand that Article 100 defines the terms that apply to two or more *Code* articles. For example, the term "Dwelling Unit" is found in many articles; if you don't know what a dwelling unit is, how can you apply the requirements for it?

In addition, many articles have terms unique for that specific article and definitions of those terms are only applicable for that given article. For example, Section 250.2 contains the definitions of terms that only apply to Article 250—Grounding and Bonding.

Small Words, Grammar, and Punctuation

It's not only the technical words that require close attention, because even the simplest of words can make a big difference to the application of a rule. The word "or" can imply alternate choices for equipment wiring methods, while "and" can mean an additional requirement. Let's not forget about grammar and punctuation. The location of a comma can dramatically change the requirement of a rule.

Slang Terms or Technical Jargon

Electricians, engineers, and other trade-related professionals use slang terms or technical jargon that isn't shared by all. This makes it very difficult to communicate because not everybody understands the intent or application of those slang terms. So where possible, be sure you use the proper word, and don't use a word if you don't understand its definition and application. For example, lots of electricians use the term "pigtail" when describing the short conductor for the connection of a receptacle, switch, luminaire, or equipment. Although they may understand it, not everyone does.

NEC Style and Layout

Before we get into the details of the *NEC*, we need to take a few moments to understand its style and layout. Understanding the structure and writing style of the *Code* is very important before it can be used and applied effectively. The *National Electrical Code* is organized into ten major components.

1. Table of Contents
2. Article 90 (Introduction to the *Code*)
3. Chapters 1 through 9 (major categories)
4. Articles 90 through 840 (individual subjects)
5. Parts (divisions of an article)
6. Sections and Tables (*Code* requirements)

7. Exceptions (*Code* permissions)

8. Informational Notes (explanatory material)

9. Annexes (information)

10. Index

1. Table of Contents. The Table of Contents displays the layout of the chapters, articles, and parts as well as the page numbers. It's an excellent resource and should be referred to periodically to observe the interrelationship of the various *NEC* components. When attempting to locate the rules for a particular situation, knowledgeable *Code* users often go first to the Table of Contents to quickly find the specific *NEC* Part that applies.

2. Introduction. The *NEC* begins with Article 90, the introduction to the *Code*. It contains the purpose of the *NEC*, what's covered and what isn't covered along with how the *Code* is arranged. It also gives information on enforcement and how mandatory and permissive rules are written as well as how explanatory material is included. Article 90 also includes information on formal interpretations, examination of equipment for safety, wiring planning, and information about formatting units of measurement.

3. Chapters. There are nine chapters, each of which is divided into articles. The articles fall into one of four groupings: General Requirements (Chapters 1 through 4), Specific Requirements (Chapters 5 through 7), Communications Systems (Chapter 8), and Tables (Chapter 9).

Chapter 1 General

Chapter 2 Wiring and Protection

Chapter 3 Wiring Methods and Materials

Chapter 4 Equipment for General Use

Chapter 5 Special Occupancies

Chapter 6 Special Equipment

Chapter 7 Special Conditions

Chapter 8 Communications Systems (Telephone, Data, Satellite, Cable TV and Broadband)

Chapter 9 Tables–Conductor and Raceway Specifications

4. Articles. The *NEC* contains approximately 140 articles, each of which covers a specific subject. For example:

Article 110 General Requirements

Article 250 Grounding and Bonding

Article 300 Wiring Methods

Article 430 Motors and Motor Controllers

Article 500 Hazardous (Classified) Locations

Article 680 Swimming Pools, Fountains, and Similar Installations

Article 725 Remote-Control, Signaling, and Power-Limited Circuits

Article 800 Communications Circuits

5. Parts. Larger articles are subdivided into parts.

Because the parts of a *Code* article aren't included in the section numbers, we have a tendency to forget what "part" the *NEC* rule is relating to. For example, Table 110.34(A) contains working space clearances for electrical equipment. If we aren't careful, we might think this table applies to all electrical installations, but Table 110.34(A) is located in Part III, which only contains requirements for "Over 600 Volts, Nominal installations." The rules for working clearances for electrical equipment for systems 600V, nominal, or less are contained in Table 110.26(A)(1), which is located in Part II—600 Volts, Nominal, or Less.

6. Sections and Tables.

Sections. Each *NEC* rule is called a "*Code* Section." A *Code* section may be broken down into subsections by letters in parentheses (A), (B), and so on. Numbers in parentheses (1), (2), and so forth, may further break down a subsection, and lowercase letters (a), (b), and so on, further break the rule down to the third level. For example, the rule requiring all receptacles in a dwelling unit bathroom to be GFCI protected is contained in Section 210.8(A)(1). Section 210.8(A)(1) is located in Chapter 2, Article 210, Section 8, Subsection (A), Sub-subsection (1).

Many in the industry incorrectly use the term "Article" when referring to a *Code* section. For example, they say "Article 210.8," when they should say "Section 210.8." Section numbers in this book are shown without the word "Section," unless they begin a sentence. For example, Section 210.8(A) is shown as simply 210.8(A).

Tables. Many *Code* requirements are contained within tables, which are lists of *NEC* requirements placed in a systematic arrangement. The titles of the tables are extremely important; you must read them carefully in order to understand the contents, applications, limitations, and so forth, of each table in the *Code*. Many times notes are provided in or below a table; be sure to read them as well since they're also part of the requirement. For example, Note 1 for Table 300.5 explains how to measure the cover when burying cables and raceways, and Note 5 explains what to do if solid rock is encountered.

7. Exceptions. Exceptions are *Code* requirements or permissions that provide an alternative method to a specific requirement. There are two types of exceptions—mandatory and permissive. When a rule has several exceptions, those exceptions with mandatory requirements are listed before the permissive exceptions.

Mandatory Exceptions. A mandatory exception uses the words "shall" or "shall not." The word "shall" in an exception means that if you're using the exception, you're required to do it in a particular way. The phrase "shall not" means it isn't permitted.

Permissive Exceptions. A permissive exception uses words such as "shall be permitted," which means it's acceptable (but not mandatory) to do it in this way.

8. Informational Notes. An Informational Note contains explanatory material intended to clarify a rule or give assistance, but it isn't a *Code* requirement.

9. Annexes. Annexes aren't a part of the *NEC* requirements, and are included in the *Code* for informational purposes only.

Annex A. Product Safety Standards
Annex B. Application Information for Ampacity Calculation
Annex C. Raceway Fill Tables for Conductors and Fixture Wires of the Same Size
Annex D. Examples
Annex E. Types of Construction
Annex F. Critical Operations Power Systems (COPS)
Annex G. Supervisory Control and Data Acquisition (SCADA)
Annex H. Administration and Enforcement
Annex I. Recommended Tightening Torques

10. Index. The Index at the back of the *NEC* is helpful in locating a specific rule.

Changes to the *NEC* since the previous edition(s), are identified by shading, but rules that have been relocated aren't identified as a change. A bullet symbol "•" is located on the margin to indicate the location of a rule that was deleted from a previous edition. New articles contain a vertical line in the margin of the page.

How to Locate a Specific Requirement

How to go about finding what you're looking for in the *Code* depends, to some degree, on your experience with the *NEC*. *Code* experts typically know the requirements so well they just go to the correct rule without any outside assistance. The Table of Contents might be the only thing very experienced *NEC* users need to locate the requirement they're looking for. On the other hand, average *Code* users should use all of the tools at their disposal, including the Table of Contents and the Index.

Table of Contents. Let's work out a simple example: What *NEC* rule specifies the maximum number of disconnects permitted for a service? If you're an experienced *Code* user, you'll know Article 230 applies to "Services," and because this article is so large, it's divided up into multiple parts (actually eight parts). With this knowledge, you

can quickly go to the Table of Contents and see it lists the Service Equipment Disconnecting Means requirements in Part VI.

> **Author's Comment:** The number 70 precedes all page numbers because the *NEC* is NFPA Standard Number 70.

Index. If you use the Index, which lists subjects in alphabetical order, to look up the term "service disconnect," you'll see there's no listing. If you try "disconnecting means," then "services," you'll find that the Index specifies that the rule is located in Article 230, Part VI. Because the *NEC* doesn't give a page number in the Index, you'll need to use the Table of Contents to find the page number, or flip through the *Code* to Article 230, then continue to flip through pages until you find Part VI.

Many people complain that the *NEC* only confuses them by taking them in circles. As you gain experience in using the *Code* and deepen your understanding of words, terms, principles, and practices, you'll find the *NEC* much easier to understand and use than you originally thought.

Customizing Your *Code* Book

One way to increase your comfort level with the *Code* is to customize it to meet your needs. You can do this by highlighting and underlining important *NEC* requirements, and by attaching tabs to important pages. Be aware that if you're using your *Code* book to take an exam, some exam centers don't allow markings of any type.

Highlighting. As you read through your textbook, be sure you highlight those requirements in the *Code* that are the most important or relevant to you. Use yellow for general interest and orange for important requirements you want to find quickly. Be sure to highlight terms in the Index and the Table of Contents as you use them.

Underlining. Underline or circle key words and phrases in the *NEC* with a red pen (not a lead pencil) and use a 6-inch ruler to keep lines straight and neat. This is a very handy way to make important requirements stand out. A small 6-inch ruler also comes in handy for locating specific information in the many *Code* tables.

Tabbing the *NEC*. By placing tabs on *Code* articles, sections, and tables, it will make it easier for you to use the *NEC*. However, too many tabs will defeat the purpose. You can order a set of *Code* tabs designed by Mike Holt online at www.MikeHolt.com/NEC, or by calling 888.NEC.CODE (632.2633).

About the Author

Mike Holt

Mike Holt worked his way up through the electrical trade from an apprentice electrician to become one of the most recognized experts in the world as it relates to electrical power installations. He has worked as a journeyman electrician, master electrician, and electrical contractor. Mike's experience in the real world gives him a unique understanding of how the *NEC* relates to electrical installations from a practical standpoint. You'll find his writing style to be direct, nontechnical, and practical.

Did you know that he didn't finish high school? So if you struggled in high school or if you didn't finish it at all, don't let this get you down, you're in good company. As a matter of fact, Mike Culbreath, Master Electrician, who produces the finest electrical graphics in the history of the electrical industry, didn't finish high school either. So two high school dropouts produced the text and graphics in the textbooks! However, realizing success depends on one's continuing pursuit of education. Mike immediately attained his GED (as did Mike Culbreath) and ultimately attended the University of Miami's Graduate School for a Master's degree in Business Administration (MBA).

Mike Holt resides in Central Florida, is the father of seven children, and has many outside interests and activities. He's a six-time National Barefoot Water-Ski Champion (1988, 1999, 2005, 2006, 2007, and 2008), has set many national records, has competed in three World Championships (2006, 2008, and 2010) and continues to train and work out year-round so that he can qualify to ski in the 2012 World Barefoot Championships at the age of 61!

What sets him apart from some, is his commitment to living a balanced lifestyle; placing God first, family, career, then self.

Mike Holt—Special Acknowledgments

First, I want to thank God for my godly wife who's always by my side and my children, Belynda, Melissa, Autumn, Steven, Michael, Meghan, and Brittney.

A special thank you must be sent to the staff at the National Fire Protection Association (NFPA), publishers of the *NEC*—in particular Jeff Sargent for his assistance in answering my many *Code* questions over the years. Jeff, you're a "first class" guy, and I admire your dedication and commitment to helping others understand the *NEC*. Other former NFPA staff members I would like to thank include John Caloggero, Joe Ross, and Dick Murray for their help in the past.

A personal thank you goes to Sarina, my long-time friend and office manager. It's been wonderful working side-by-side with you for over 25 years nurturing this company's growth from its small beginnings.

Technical Reviewer—Martin Shoemaker

Martin Shoemaker has been involved in the electrical and electronics fields for over 35 years. Starting as the owner of an electronics repair shop, he's worked as a broadcast engineer, field service engineer for heavy industry controls, facilities engineer for a petrochemical complex, and instrumentation engineer for a jet engine manufacturer. Martin was registered as a Professional Engineer in 1985 and has been in private practice since 1995.

He's been happily married to Joyce for over 23 years. They have two children and seven grandchildren. Martin has been a church worship leader for many years and enjoys cheering on his grandchildren in soccer, basketball, and cross country.

Notes

Introduction to the *National Electrical Code*

INTRODUCTION TO ARTICLE 90—INTRODUCTION TO THE *NATIONAL ELECTRICAL CODE*

Many *NEC* violations and misunderstandings wouldn't occur if people doing the work simply understood Article 90. For example, many people see *Code* requirements as performance standards. In fact, the *NEC* requirements are bare minimums for safety. This is exactly the stance electrical inspectors, insurance companies, and courts take when making a decision regarding electrical design or installation.

Article 90 opens by saying the *NEC* isn't intended as a design specification or instruction manual. The *National Electrical Code* has one purpose only, and that's the "practical safeguarding of persons and property from hazards arising from the use of electricity." It goes on to indicate that the *Code* isn't intended as a design specification or instruction manual. The necessity to carefully study the *NEC* rules can't be overemphasized, and the role of textbooks such as this one is to help in that undertaking. Understanding where to find the rules in the *Code* that apply to the installation is invaluable. Rules in several different articles often apply to even a simple installation.

Article 90 then describes the scope and arrangement of the *NEC*. The balance of Article 90 provides the reader with information essential to understanding those items you do find in the *Code*.

Typically, electrical work requires you to understand the first four chapters of the *NEC* which apply generally, plus have a working knowledge of the Chapter 9 tables. That knowledge begins with Article 90. Chapters 5, 6, and 7 make up a large portion of the *Code*, but they apply to special occupancies, special equipment, or other special conditions. They build on, modify, or amend the rules in the first four chapters. Chapter 8 contains the requirements for communications systems, such as telephone systems, antenna wiring, CATV, and network-powered broadband systems. Communications systems aren't subject to the general requirements of Chapters 1 through 4, or the special requirements of Chapters 5 through 7, unless there's a specific reference in Chapter 8 to a rule in Chapters 1 through 7.

 Please use the 2011 *Code* book to answer the following questions, which are based on the 2011 *NEC*.

QUESTIONS FOR ARTICLE 90—INTRODUCTION TO THE *NATIONAL ELECTRICAL CODE*

1.   The *NEC* is _____.

    (a) intended to be a design manual
    (b) meant to be used as an instruction guide for untrained persons
    (c) for the practical safeguarding of persons and property
    (d) published by the Bureau of Standards

2.   Compliance with the provisions of the *NEC* will result in _____.

    (a) good electrical service
    (b) an efficient electrical system
    (c) an electrical system essentially free from hazard
    (d) all of these

3.   The *Code* contains provisions considered necessary for safety, which will not necessarily result in _____.

    (a) efficient use
    (b) convenience
    (c) good service or future expansion of electrical use
    (d) all of these

4. Hazards often occur because of _____.

    (a) overloading of wiring systems by methods or usage not in conformity with the *NEC*

    (b) initial wiring not providing for increases in the use of electricity

    (c) a and b

    (d) none of these

5. The *Code* isn't a design specification standard or instruction manual for the untrained and unqualified.

    (a) True

    (b) False

6. The following systems shall be installed in accordance with the *NEC* requirements:

    (a) Signaling.

    (b) Communications.

    (c) Electrical conductors, equipment, and raceways.

    (d) all of these

7. The *NEC* applies to the installation of _____.

    (a) electrical conductors and equipment within or on public and private buildings

    (b) outside conductors and equipment on the premises

    (c) optical fiber cables

    (d) all of these

8. This *Code* covers the installation of _____ for public and private premises, including buildings, structures, mobile homes, recreational vehicles, and floating buildings.

    (a) optical fiber cables

    (b) electrical equipment

    (c) raceways

    (d) all of these

9. The *NEC* does not cover electrical installations in ships, watercraft, railway rolling stock, aircraft, or automotive vehicles.

    (a) True

    (b) False

10. The *Code* covers underground mine installations and self-propelled mobile surface mining machinery and its attendant electrical trailing cable.

    (a) True

    (b) False

11. Installations of communications equipment that are under the exclusive control of communications utilities, and located outdoors or in building spaces used exclusively for such installations _____ covered by the *NEC*.

    (a) are

    (b) are sometimes

    (c) are not

    (d) may be

12. Electric utilities may include entities that install, operate, and maintain _____.

    (a) communications systems (telephone, CATV, Internet, satellite, or data services)

    (b) electric supply systems (generation, transmission, or distribution systems)

    (c) local area network wiring on the premises

    (d) a or b

13. Utilities may be subject to compliance with codes and standards covering their regulated activities as adopted under governmental law or regulation.

    (a) True

    (b) False

14. Utilities may include entities that are designated or recognized by governmental law or regulation by public service/utility commissions.

    (a) True

    (b) False

15. The *NEC* does not apply to electric utility-owned wiring and equipment _____.

    (a) installed by an electrical contractor
    (b) installed on public property
    (c) consisting of service drops or service laterals
    (d) in a utility office building

16. Chapters 1 through 4 of the *NEC* apply _____.

    (a) generally to all electrical installations
    (b) only to special occupancies and conditions
    (c) only to special equipment and material
    (d) all of these

17. Communications wiring such as telephone, antenna, and CATV wiring within a building shall not be required to comply with the installation requirements of Chapters 1 through 7, except where specifically referenced in Chapter 8.

    (a) True
    (b) False

18. The material located in the *NEC* Annexes are part of the requirements of the *Code* and shall be complied with.

    (a) True
    (b) False

19. The authority having jurisdiction shall not be allowed to enforce any requirements of Chapter 7 (Special Conditions) or Chapter 8 (Communications Systems).

    (a) True
    (b) False

20. The _____ has the responsibility for deciding on the approval of equipment and materials.

    (a) manufacturer
    (b) authority having jurisdiction
    (c) testing agency
    (d) none of these

21. By special permission, the authority having jurisdiction may waive specific requirements in this *Code* where it is assured that equivalent objectives can be achieved by establishing and maintaining effective safety.

    (a) True
    (b) False

22. The authority having jurisdiction has the responsibility for _____.

    (a) making interpretations of rules
    (b) deciding upon the approval of equipment and materials
    (c) waiving specific requirements in the *Code* and permitting alternate methods and material if safety is maintained
    (d) all of these

23. If the *NEC* requires new products that are not yet available at the time a new edition is adopted, the _____ may permit the use of the products that comply with the previous edition of the *Code* adopted by that jurisdiction.

    (a) electrical engineer
    (b) master electrician
    (c) authority having jurisdiction
    (d) permit holder

24. In the *NEC*, the words "_____" indicate a mandatory requirement.

    (a) shall
    (b) shall not
    (c) shall be permitted
    (d) a or b

25. When the *Code* uses "_____," it means the identified actions are allowed but not required, and they may be options or alternative methods.

    (a) shall
    (b) shall not
    (c) shall be permitted
    (d) a or b

26. Explanatory material, such as references to other standards, references to related sections of the *NEC*, or information related to a *Code* rule, are included in the form of Informational Notes.

    (a) True
    (b) False

27. Nonmandatory Informative Annexes contained in the back of the *Code* book _____.

    (a) are for information only
    (b) aren't enforceable as a requirement of the *Code*
    (c) are enforceable as a requirement of the *Code*
    (d) a and b

28. Factory-installed _____ wiring of listed equipment need not be inspected at the time of installation of the equipment, except to detect alterations or damage.

    (a) external
    (b) associated
    (c) internal
    (d) all of these

29. Compliance with either the metric or the inch-pound unit of measurement system shall be permitted.

    (a) True
    (b) False

CHAPTER 1

GENERAL

INTRODUCTION TO CHAPTER 1—GENERAL

A young child doesn't begin reading and writing until they have an understanding of some of the basic words of the language. Similarly, you must be familiar with a few basic rules, concepts, definitions, and requirements that apply to the rest of the *NEC* and you must maintain that familiarity as you continue to apply the *Code*.

Chapter 1 consists of two topics. Article 100 provides definitions so people can understand one another when trying to communicate about *Code*-related matters and Article 110 provides the general requirements needed to correctly apply the rest of the *NEC*.

Time spent learning this general material is a great investment. After understanding Chapter 1, some of the *Code* requirements that seem confusing to other people—those who don't understand Chapter 1—will become increasingly clear to you. The requirements will strike you as being "common sense," because you'll have the foundation from which to understand and apply them. When you read the *NEC* requirements in later chapters, you'll understand the principles upon which many of them are based, and not be surprised at all. You'll read them and feel like you already know them.

- **Article 100—Definitions.** Part I of Article 100 contains the definitions of terms used throughout the *Code* for systems that operate at 600V, nominal, or less. The definitions of terms in Part II apply to systems that operate at over 600V, nominal.

    Author's Comment: The textbook covers the requirements for systems that operate at 600V, nominal, or less.

Definitions of standard terms, such as volt, voltage drop, ampere, impedance, and resistance, aren't listed in Article 100. If the *NEC* doesn't define a term, then a dictionary suitable to the authority having jurisdiction should be consulted. A building code glossary might provide better definitions than a dictionary found at your home or school.

Definitions located at the beginning of an article apply only to that specific article. For example, the definition of a "Swimming Pool" is contained in 680.2, because this term applies only to the requirements contained in Article 680—Swimming Pools, Fountains, and Similar Installations. As soon as a defined term is used in two or more articles, its definition is included in Article 100.

- **Article 110—Requirements for Electrical Installations.** This article contains general requirements for electrical installations for the following:

    - Part I. General
    - Part II. 600V, Nominal, Or Less

Notes

INTRODUCTION TO ARTICLE 100—DEFINITIONS

Have you ever had a conversation with someone, only to discover that what you said and what he or she heard were completely different? This often happens when people in a conversation don't understand the definitions of the words being used, and that's why the definitions of key terms are located right at the beginning of the *NEC* (Article 100), or at the beginning of each article.

If we can all agree on important definitions, then we speak the same language and avoid misunderstandings. Because the *Code* exists to protect people and property, it's very important to know the definitions presented in Article 100.

Now, here are a couple of things you may not know about Article 100:

Article 100 contains many, but not all, of the terms defined by the *NEC*. In general, only those terms used in two or more articles are defined in Article 100. Those terms used only within one article are located within that article, often near the beginning of the article.

- Part I of Article 100 contains the definitions of terms used throughout the *Code* for systems that operate at 600V, nominal, or less.
- Part II of Article 100 contains only terms that apply to systems that operate at over 600V, nominal.

How can you possibly learn all of these definitions? There seem to be so many. Here are a few tips:

- Break the task down. Study a few words at a time, rather than trying to learn them all at one sitting.
- Review the graphics in the accompanying textbook. These will help you see how a term is applied.
- Relate them to your work. As you read a word, think about how it applies to the work you're doing. This will provide a natural reinforcement to the learning process.

 Please use the 2011 *Code* book to answer the following questions, which are based on the 2011 *NEC*.

QUESTIONS FOR ARTICLE 100—DEFINITIONS

1. Admitting close approach, not guarded by locked doors, elevation, or other effective means, is referred to as "_____."

   (a) accessible (as applied to equipment)
   (b) accessible (as applied to wiring methods)
   (c) accessible, readily
   (d) all of these

2. Capable of being removed or exposed without damaging the building structure or finish, or not permanently closed in by the structure or finish of the building is known as "_____."

   (a) accessible (as applied to equipment)
   (b) accessible (as applied to wiring methods)
   (c) accessible, readily
   (d) all of these

3. Capable of being reached quickly for operation, renewal, or inspections without resorting to portable ladders and such is known as "_____."

   (a) accessible (as applied to equipment)
   (b) accessible (as applied to wiring methods)
   (c) accessible, readily
   (d) all of these

4. The maximum current in amperes a conductor can carry continuously, where the temperature will not be raised in excess of the conductor's insulation temperature rating is called its "_____."

(a) short-circuit rating
(b) ground-fault rating
(c) ampacity
(d) all of these

5. "_____" means acceptable to the authority having jurisdiction.

(a) Identified
(b) Listed
(c) Approved
(d) Labeled

6. An arc-fault circuit interrupter is a device intended to de-energize the circuit when it recognizes characteristics unique to _____.

(a) overcurrent
(b) arcing
(c) ground fault
(d) harmonic fundamental

7. A device that establishes a connection between the conductors of the attached flexible cord and the conductors connected to the receptacle is called a(n) "_____."

(a) attachment plug
(b) plug cap
(c) plug
(d) any of these

8. Where no statutory requirement exists, the authority having jurisdiction can be a property owner or his/her agent, such as an architect or engineer.

(a) True
(b) False

9. According to the *Code*, "automatic" is performing a function without the necessity of _____.

(a) protection from damage
(b) human intervention
(c) mechanical linkage
(d) all of these

10. A _____ is an area that includes a basin with a toilet, urinal, tub, shower, bidet, or similar plumbing fixtures.

(a) bath area
(b) bathroom
(c) rest area
(d) none of these

11. "Bonded" can be described as _____ to establish electrical continuity and conductivity.

(a) isolated
(b) guarded
(c) connected
(d) separated

12. A reliable conductor that ensures electrical conductivity between metal parts of the electrical installation that are required to be electrically connected is called a(n) "_____."

(a) grounding electrode
(b) auxiliary ground
(c) bonding conductor or jumper
(d) tap conductor

13. The connection between the grounded conductor and the equipment grounding conductor at the service is accomplished by installing a(n) _____ bonding jumper.

(a) main
(b) system
(c) equipment
(d) circuit

14. The connection between the grounded conductor and the supply-side bonding jumper or equipment grounding conductor, or both, at a _____ is called a "system bonding jumper."

(a) service disconnect
(b) separately derived system
(c) motor control center
(d) separate building or structure disconnect

15. The conductors between the final overcurrent device protecting the circuit and the outlet(s) are known as "_____ conductors."

(a) feeder
(b) branch-circuit
(c) home run
(d) none of these

16. A(n) _____ branch circuit supplies energy to one or more outlets to which appliances are to be connected.

(a) general purpose
(b) multiwire
(c) individual
(d) appliance

17. A branch circuit that supplies only one utilization equipment is a(n) _____ branch circuit.

(a) individual
(b) general-purpose
(c) isolated
(d) special-purpose

18. For a circuit to be considered a multiwire branch circuit, it shall have _____.

(a) two or more ungrounded conductors with a voltage potential between them
(b) a grounded conductor having equal voltage potential between it and each ungrounded conductor of the circuit
(c) a grounded conductor connected to the neutral or grounded terminal of the system
(d) all of these

19. The *NEC* defines a(n) "_____" as a permanent structure having a roof and walls that stands alone or that is cut off from adjoining structures by fire walls or fire barriers, with all openings therein protected by approved fire doors and used to enclose an occupancy.

(a) unit
(b) apartment
(c) building
(d) utility

20. An enclosure for either surface mounting or flush mounting provided with a frame in which a door can be hung is called a(n) "_____."

(a) enclosure
(b) outlet box
(c) cutout box
(d) cabinet

21. A circuit breaker is a device designed to _____ the circuit automatically on a predetermined overcurrent without damage to itself when properly applied within its rating.

(a) energize
(b) reset
(c) connect
(d) open

22. "_____" is a term indicating that there is an intentional delay in the tripping action of the circuit breaker, which decreases as the magnitude of the current increases.

(a) Adverse time
(b) Inverse time
(c) Time delay
(d) Timed unit

23. A clothes closet is defined as a _____ room or space intended primarily for storage of garments and apparel.

(a) habitable
(b) non-habitable
(c) conditioned
(d) finished

24. Communications equipment includes equipment used for the transmission of _____.

   (a) audio
   (b) video
   (c) data
   (d) any of these

25. Cables are considered _____ if rendered inaccessible by the structure or finish of the building.

   (a) inaccessible
   (b) concealed
   (c) hidden
   (d) enclosed

26. A conductor encased within material of composition or thickness that is not recognized by the *NEC* as electrical insulation is considered _____.

   (a) noninsulating
   (b) bare
   (c) covered
   (d) protected

27. A separate portion of a raceway system that provides access through a removable cover to the interior of the system, defines the term "_____."

   (a) junction box
   (b) accessible raceway
   (c) conduit body
   (d) cutout box

28. A solderless pressure connector is a device that _____ between conductors or between conductors and a terminal by means of mechanical pressure.

   (a) provides access
   (b) protects the wiring
   (c) is never needed
   (d) establishes a connection

29. A load is considered to be continuous if the maximum current is expected to continue for _____ or more.

   (a) one-half hour
   (b) 1 hour
   (c) 2 hours
   (d) 3 hours

30. A _____ is a device, or group of devices that governs, in some predetermined manner, the electric power delivered to the apparatus to which it is connected.

   (a) relay
   (b) breaker
   (c) transformer
   (d) controller

31. The choice of overcurrent devices so that an overcurrent condition will be localized and restrict outages to the circuit or equipment affected, is called "_____."

   (a) overcurrent protection
   (b) interrupting capacity
   (c) selective coordination
   (d) overload protection

32. _____ are designed for surface mounting with a swinging door.

   (a) Outlet boxes
   (b) Cabinets
   (c) Cutout boxes
   (d) none of these

33. The _____ of any system is the ratio of the maximum demand of a system, or part of a system, to the total connected load of a system.

   (a) load
   (b) demand factor
   (c) minimum load
   (d) calculated factor

34. A unit of an electrical system that carries or controls electric energy as its principal function is a(n) "_____."

    (a) raceway
    (b) fitting
    (c) device
    (d) enclosure

35. A(n) _____ is a device, or group of devices by which the conductors of a circuit can be disconnected from their source of supply.

    (a) feeder
    (b) enclosure
    (c) disconnecting means
    (d) conductor interrupter

36. An enclosure or piece of equipment constructed so that dust will not enter the enclosure under specified test conditions is known as "_____."

    (a) dusttight
    (b) dustproof
    (c) dust rated
    (d) all of these

37. "Continuous duty" is defined as _____.

    (a) when the load is expected to continue for five hours or more
    (b) operation at a substantially constant load for an indefinite long time
    (c) operation at loads and for intervals of time, both of which may be subject to wide variations
    (d) operation at which the load may be subject to maximum current for six hours or more

38. "Varying duty" is defined as _____.

    (a) intermittent operation in which the load conditions are regularly recurrent
    (b) operation at a substantially constant load for an indefinite length of time
    (c) operation for alternate intervals of load and rest, or load, no load, and rest
    (d) operation at loads, and for intervals of time, both of which may be subject to wide variations

39. A _____ is a single unit that provides independent living facilities for persons, including permanent provisions for living, sleeping, cooking, and sanitation.

    (a) one-family dwelling
    (b) two-family dwelling
    (c) dwelling unit
    (d) multifamily dwelling

40. A building that contains three or more dwelling units is called a "_____."

    (a) one-family dwelling
    (b) two-family dwelling
    (c) dwelling unit
    (d) multifamily dwelling

41. A fixed, stationary, or portable self-contained, electrically illuminated equipment with words or symbols designed to convey information or attract attention describes _____.

    (a) an electric sign
    (b) equipment
    (c) appliances
    (d) none of these

42. Surrounded by a case, housing, fence, or wall(s) that prevents persons from accidentally contacting energized parts is called "_____."

    (a) guarded
    (b) covered
    (c) protection
    (d) enclosed

43. As used in the *NEC*, equipment includes _____.

    (a) fittings
    (b) appliances
    (c) machinery
    (d) all of these

44. Equipment enclosed in a case that is capable of withstanding an explosion of a specified gas or vapor that may occur within it, and of preventing the ignition of a specified gas or vapor surrounding the enclosure by sparks, flashes, or explosion of the gas or vapor within, and that operates at such an external temperature that a surrounding flammable atmosphere will not be ignited thereby defines the phrase "_____."

    (a) overcurrent device
    (b) thermal apparatus
    (c) explosionproof equipment
    (d) bomb casing

45. When the term "exposed," as it applies to live parts, is used in the *Code*, it refers to _____.

    (a) being capable of being inadvertently touched or approached nearer than a safe distance by a person
    (b) parts that are not suitably guarded, isolated, or insulated
    (c) wiring on, or attached to, the surface or behind panels designed to allow access
    (d) a and b

46. For wiring methods, "on or attached to the surface, or behind access panels designed to allow access" is known as _____.

    (a) open
    (b) uncovered
    (c) exposed
    (d) bare

47. The *NEC* defines a "_____" as all circuit conductors between the service equipment, the source of a separately derived system, or other power-supply source and the final branch-circuit overcurrent device.

    (a) service
    (b) feeder
    (c) branch circuit
    (d) all of these

48. An accessory, such as a locknut, intended to perform a mechanical function best describes _____.

    (a) a part
    (b) equipment
    (c) a device
    (d) a fitting

49. A "_____" is a building or portion of a building in which one or more self-propelled vehicles can be kept for use, sale, storage, rental, repair, exhibition, or demonstration purposes.

    (a) garage
    (b) residential garage
    (c) service garage
    (d) commercial garage

50. The word "Earth" best describes what *NEC* term?

    (a) Bonded
    (b) Ground
    (c) Effective ground-fault current path
    (d) Guarded

51. A(n) _____ is an unintentional, electrically conducting connection between an ungrounded conductor of an electrical circuit, and the normally noncurrent-carrying conductors, metallic enclosures, metallic raceways, metallic equipment, or earth.

    (a) grounded conductor
    (b) ground fault
    (c) equipment ground
    (d) bonding jumper

52. Connected to ground or to a conductive body that extends the ground connection is called "_____."

    (a) equipment grounding
    (b) bonded
    (c) grounded
    (d) all of these

53. A circuit conductor that is intentionally grounded is called a(n) "_____."

(a) grounding conductor
(b) unidentified conductor
(c) grounded conductor
(d) grounding electrode conductor

54. Connected to ground without the insertion of any resistor or impedance device is referred to as "_____."

(a) grounded
(b) solidly grounded
(c) effectively grounded
(d) grounding conductor

55. A device intended for the protection of personnel that functions to de-energize a circuit or portion thereof within an established period of time when the current to ground exceeds the values established for a Class A device, is a(n) "_____."

(a) dual-element fuse
(b) inverse time breaker
(c) ground-fault circuit interrupter
(d) safety switch

56. A Class A GFCI protection device is designed to trip when the ground-fault current to ground is _____ or higher.

(a) 4 mA
(b) 5 mA
(c) 6 mA
(d) none of these

57. A system intended to provide protection of equipment from damaging line-to-ground fault currents by opening all ungrounded conductors of the faulted circuit at current levels less than the supply circuit overcurrent device defines the phrase "_____."

(a) ground-fault protection of equipment
(b) guarded
(c) personal protection
(d) automatic protection

58. The installed conductive path(s) that connects normally noncurrent-carrying metal parts of equipment together and to the system grounded conductor or to the grounding electrode conductor, or both, is known as a(n) "_____."

(a) grounding electrode conductor
(b) grounding conductor
(c) equipment grounding conductor
(d) none of these

59. A conducting object through which a direct connection to earth is established is a "_____."

(a) bonding conductor
(b) grounding conductor
(c) grounding electrode
(d) grounded conductor

60. A conductor used to connect the system grounded conductor or the equipment to a grounding electrode or to a point on the grounding electrode system is called the "_____ conductor."

(a) main grounding
(b) common main
(c) equipment grounding
(d) grounding electrode

61. A "_____" is an accommodation that combines living, sleeping, sanitary, and storage facilities within a compartment.

(a) guest room
(b) guest suite
(c) dwelling unit
(d) single-family dwelling

62. A "_____" is an accommodation with two or more contiguous rooms comprising a compartment that provides living, sleeping, sanitary, and storage facilities.

(a) guest room
(b) guest suite
(c) dwelling unit
(d) single-family dwelling

63. A handhole enclosure is an enclosure for use in underground systems, provided with an open or closed bottom, and sized to allow personnel to _____.

(a) enter and exit freely
(b) reach into but not enter
(c) have full working space
(d) examine it visually

64. A hoistway is any _____ in which an elevator or dumbwaiter is designed to operate.

(a) hatchway or well hole
(b) vertical opening or space
(c) shaftway
(d) all of these

65. Recognized as suitable for the specific purpose, function, use, environment, and application is the definition of "_____."

(a) labeled
(b) identified (as applied to equipment)
(c) listed
(d) approved

66. Within sight means visible and not more than _____ distant from the equipment.

(a) 10 ft
(b) 20 ft
(c) 25 ft
(d) 50 ft

67. The highest current at rated voltage that a device is identified to interrupt under standard test conditions is the _____.

(a) interrupting rating
(b) manufacturer's rating
(c) interrupting capacity
(d) withstand rating

68. A device that provides a means to connect bonding conductors for _____ systems to the building grounding electrode system is an intersystem bonding termination.

(a) limited energy
(b) low-voltage
(c) communications
(d) power and lighting

69. "_____" means that an object is not readily accessible to persons unless special means for access are used.

(a) Isolated
(b) Secluded
(c) Protected
(d) Locked

70. A kitchen is defined as an area with a sink and _____ provisions for food preparation and cooking.

(a) listed
(b) labeled
(c) temporary
(d) permanent

71. Equipment or materials to which a symbol or other identifying mark of a product evaluation organization that is acceptable to the authority having jurisdiction has been attached is known as "_____."

(a) listed
(b) labeled
(c) approved
(d) identified

72. An outlet intended for the direct connection of a lampholder or a luminaire is a(n) "_____."

(a) outlet
(b) receptacle outlet
(c) lighting outlet
(d) general-purpose outlet

73. Equipment or materials included in a list published by a testing laboratory acceptable to the authority having jurisdiction is said to be "_____."

    (a) book
    (b) digest
    (c) manifest
    (d) listed

74. A _____ location will be protected from weather and not subject to saturation with water or other liquids; such locations include partially protected locations under canopies, marquees, and roofed open porches.

    (a) dry
    (b) damp
    (c) wet
    (d) moist

75. A _____ location may be temporarily subject to dampness and wetness.

    (a) dry
    (b) damp
    (c) moist
    (d) wet

76. Conduit installed underground or encased in concrete slabs that are in direct contact with the earth is considered a _____ location.

    (a) dry
    (b) damp
    (c) wet
    (d) moist

77. The term "Luminaire" includes an individual lampholder.

    (a) True
    (b) False

78. A neutral conductor is the conductor connected to the _____ of a system, which is intended to carry neutral current under normal conditions.

    (a) grounding electrode
    (b) neutral point
    (c) intersystem bonding termination
    (d) none of these

79. The common point on a wye-connection in a polyphase system describes a neutral point.

    (a) True
    (b) False

80. "Nonautomatic" is defined as requiring _____ to perform a function.

    (a) protection from damage
    (b) human intervention
    (c) mechanical linkage
    (d) all of these

81. A(n) _____ is a point on the wiring system at which current is taken to supply utilization equipment.

    (a) box
    (b) receptacle
    (c) outlet
    (d) device

82. Outline lighting may include an arrangement of _____ to outline or call attention to the shape of a building.

    (a) incandescent lamps
    (b) electric-discharge lighting
    (c) electrically powered light sources
    (d) any of these

83. Any current in excess of the rated current of equipment or the ampacity of a conductor is called "_____."

    (a) trip current
    (b) fault current
    (c) overcurrent
    (d) a short circuit

84. A(n) _____ is intended to provide limited overcurrent protection for specific applications and utilization equipment, such as luminaires and appliances. This limited protection is in addition to the protection provided by the required branch-circuit overcurrent protective device.

    (a) supplementary overcurrent device
    (b) surge protection device
    (c) arc-fault circuit interrupter
    (d) Class A GFCI

85. An overload is the same as a short circuit or ground fault.

    (a) True
    (b) False

86. A panel, including buses and automatic overcurrent devices, designed to be placed in a cabinet or cutout box and accessible only from the front is known as a "_____."

    (a) switchboard
    (b) disconnect
    (c) panelboard
    (d) switch

87. Premises wiring includes _____ wiring from the service point or power source to the outlets.

    (a) interior
    (b) exterior
    (c) underground
    (d) all of these

88. The *NEC* defines a(n) "_____" as one who has skills and knowledge related to the construction and operation of the electrical equipment and installations and has received safety training to recognize and avoid the hazards involved.

    (a) inspector
    (b) master electrician
    (c) journeyman electrician
    (d) qualified person

89. NFPA 70E—*Standard for Electrical Safety in the Workplace*, provides information to help determine the electrical safety training requirements expected of a qualified person.

    (a) True
    (b) False

90. A raceway is an enclosure designed for the installation of wires, cables, or busbars.

    (a) True
    (b) False

91. Constructed, protected, or treated so as to prevent rain from interfering with the successful operation of the apparatus under specified test conditions defines the term "_____."

    (a) raintight
    (b) waterproof
    (c) weathertight
    (d) rainproof

92. A raintight enclosure is constructed or protected so that exposure to a beating rain will not result in the entrance of water under specified test conditions.

    (a) True
    (b) False

93. A contact device installed at an outlet for the connection of an attachment plug is known as a(n) "_____."

    (a) attachment point
    (b) tap
    (c) receptacle
    (d) wall plug

94. A single receptacle is a single contact device with no other contact device on the same _____.

    (a) circuit
    (b) yoke
    (c) run
    (d) equipment

95. An opening in an outlet box where one or more receptacles have been installed is called "_____."

    (a) a device
    (b) equipment
    (c) a receptacle
    (d) a receptacle outlet

96. When one electrical circuit controls another circuit through a relay, the first circuit is called a "_____."

    (a) primary circuit
    (b) remote-control circuit
    (c) signal circuit
    (d) controller

97. Equipment enclosed with a means of sealing or locking so that live parts cannot be made accessible without opening the enclosure is said to be "_____."

    (a) guarded
    (b) protected
    (c) sealable
    (d) lockable

98. A(n) _____ system is a premises wiring system whose power is derived from a source of electric energy other than a service and has no direct electrical connection to supply conductors originating in another system other than through the earth, metallic enclosures and raceways, or equipment grounding conductors.

    (a) separately derived
    (b) classified
    (c) direct
    (d) emergency

99. The conductors and equipment from the electric utility that deliver electric energy to the wiring system of the premises is called a "_____."

    (a) branch circuit
    (b) feeder
    (c) service
    (d) none of these

100. Service conductors originate at the service point and terminate at the service disconnecting means.

    (a) True
    (b) False

101. Overhead service conductors are the conductors between the _____ and the first point of connection to the service-entrance conductors at the building or other structure.

    (a) service disconnect
    (b) service point
    (c) grounding electrode
    (d) equipment grounding conductor

102. Underground service conductors are the underground conductors between the service point and the first point of connection to the service-entrance conductors in a terminal box, meter, or other enclosure, _____ the building wall.

    (a) inside
    (b) outside
    (c) above
    (d) a or b

103. The service drop is defined as the overhead conductors between the utility electric supply system and the _____.

    (a) service equipment
    (b) service point
    (c) grounding electrode
    (d) equipment grounding conductor

104. The overhead system service-entrance conductors are the service conductors between the terminals of _____ and a point where they are joined by a tap or splice to the service drop or overhead service conductors.

(a) service equipment
(b) service point
(c) grounding electrode
(d) equipment grounding conductor

105. The underground system service-entrance conductors are the service conductors between the terminals of _____ and the point of connection to the service lateral or underground service conductors.

(a) service equipment
(b) service point
(c) grounding electrode
(d) equipment grounding conductor

106. The _____ is the necessary equipment, usually consisting of a circuit breaker(s) or switch(es) and fuse(s) and their accessories, connected to the load end of service conductors, and intended to constitute the main control and cutoff of the supply.

(a) service equipment
(b) service
(c) service disconnect
(d) service overcurrent device

107. The underground conductors between the utility electric supply system and the service point are known as the "_____."

(a) utility service
(b) service lateral
(c) service drop
(d) main service conductors

108. The _____ is the point of connection between the facilities of the serving utility and the premises wiring.

(a) service entrance
(b) service point
(c) overcurrent protection
(d) beginning of the wiring system

109. The prospective symmetrical fault current at a nominal voltage to which an apparatus or system is able to be connected without sustaining damage exceeding defined acceptance criteria is known as the "_____."

(a) short-circuit current rating
(b) arc flash rating
(c) overcurrent rating
(d) available fault current

110. A signaling circuit is any electrical circuit that energizes signaling equipment.

(a) True
(b) False

111. The combination of all components and subsystems that convert solar energy into electrical energy is called a "_____ system."

(a) solar
(b) solar voltaic
(c) separately derived source
(d) solar photovoltaic

112. Special permission is the written consent from the _____.

(a) testing laboratory
(b) manufacturer
(c) owner
(d) authority having jurisdiction

113. A structure is that which is built or constructed.

(a) True
(b) False

114. A surge protective device (SPD) intended for installation on the load side of the service disconnect overcurrent device, including SPDs located at the branch panel, is a _____ SPD.

(a) Type 1
(b) Type 2
(c) Type 3
(d) Type 4

115. A switch constructed so that it can be installed in device boxes or on box covers, or otherwise used in conjunction with wiring systems recognized by the *NEC* is called a "_____ switch."

(a) transfer
(b) motor-circuit
(c) general-use snap
(d) bypass isolation

116. An isolating switch is one that is _____.

(a) not readily accessible to persons unless special means for access are used
(b) capable of interrupting the maximum operating overload current of a motor
(c) intended for use in general distribution and branch circuits
(d) intended for isolating an electrical circuit from the source of power

117. A large single panel, frame, or assembly of panels on which switches, overcurrent and other protective devices, buses, and instruments are mounted is a "_____." They are generally accessible from the rear as well as from the front and are not intended to be installed in cabinets.

(a) switchboard
(b) panel box
(c) switch box
(d) panelboard

118. "Ungrounded" describes not connected to ground or a conductive body that extends the ground connection.

(a) True
(b) False

119. A power supply used to provide alternating current power to a load for some period of time in the event of a power failure is known as a(n) "_____."

(a) uninterruptible power supply
(b) power management system
(c) surge protective device
(d) arc fault interrupter

120. Utilization equipment is equipment that utilizes electricity for _____ purposes.

(a) electromechanical
(b) heating
(c) lighting
(d) any of these

121. The 'voltage of a circuit' is defined by the *Code* as the _____ root-mean-square (effective) difference of potential between any two conductors of the circuit concerned.

(a) lowest
(b) greatest
(c) average
(d) nominal

122. A value assigned to a circuit or system for the purpose of conveniently designating its voltage class, such as 120/240V, is called "_____ voltage."

(a) root-mean-square
(b) circuit
(c) nominal
(d) source

123. An enclosure constructed so that moisture will not enter the enclosure under specific test conditions is called "_____."

(a) watertight
(b) moistureproof
(c) waterproof
(d) rainproof

124. A(n) _____ enclosure is constructed or protected so that exposure to the weather will not interfere with successful operation.

(a) weatherproof
(b) weathertight
(c) weather-resistant
(d) all weather

ARTICLE 110

Requirements for Electrical Installations

INTRODUCTION TO ARTICLE 110—REQUIREMENTS FOR ELECTRICAL INSTALLATIONS

Article 110 sets the stage for how you'll implement the rest of the *NEC*. This article contains a few of the most important and yet neglected parts of the *Code*. For example:

- How should conductors be terminated?
- What kinds of warnings, markings, and identification does a given installation require?
- What's the right working clearance for a given installation?
- What do the temperature limitations at terminals mean?
- What are the *NEC* requirements for dealing with flash protection?

It's critical that you master Article 110, and that's exactly what the *Illustrated Guide to Understanding the National Electrical Code* is designed for. As you read this article, you're building your foundation for correctly applying the *NEC*. In fact, this article itself is a foundation for much of the *Code*. The purpose for the *National Electrical Code* is to provide a safe installation, but Article 110 is perhaps focused a little more on providing an installation that is safe for the installer and maintenance electrician, so time spent in this article is time well spent.

QUESTIONS FOR ARTICLE 110— REQUIREMENTS FOR ELECTRICAL INSTALLATIONS

1. In judging equipment for approval, considerations such as the following shall be evaluated:

   (a) Mechanical strength.
   (b) Wire-bending space.
   (c) Arcing effects.
   (d) all of these

2. Listed or labeled equipment shall be installed and used in accordance with any instructions included in the listing or labeling.

   (a) True
   (b) False

3. Conductors shall be _____ unless otherwise provided.

   (a) bare
   (b) stranded
   (c) of copper
   (d) of aluminum

4. Conductor sizes are expressed in American Wire Gage (AWG) or _____.

   (a) inches
   (b) circular mils
   (c) square inches
   (d) cubic inches

5. Wiring shall be installed so that the completed system will be free from _____, other than as required or permitted elsewhere in the *Code*.

   (a) short circuits
   (b) ground faults
   (c) connections to the earth
   (d) all of these

6. Only wiring methods recognized as _____ are included in this *Code*.

    (a) expensive
    (b) efficient
    (c) suitable
    (d) cost-effective

7. Equipment intended to interrupt current at fault levels shall have an interrupting rating not less than the nominal circuit voltage and the current that is available at the line terminals of the equipment.

    (a) True
    (b) False

8. The _____ of a circuit shall be selected and coordinated to permit the circuit protective devices to clear a fault without extensive damage to the electrical equipment of the circuit.

    (a) overcurrent devices
    (b) total circuit impedance
    (c) equipment short-circuit current ratings
    (d) all of these

9. Unless identified for use in the operating environment, no conductors or equipment shall be _____ having a deteriorating effect on the conductors or equipment.

    (a) located in damp or wet locations
    (b) exposed to fumes, vapors, liquids or gases
    (c) exposed to excessive temperatures
    (d) all of these

10. Some cleaning and lubricating compounds can cause severe deterioration of many plastic materials used for insulating and structural applications in equipment.

    (a) True
    (b) False

11. The *NEC* requires that electrical work be _____.

    (a) installed in a neat and workmanlike manner
    (b) installed under the supervision of a licensed person
    (c) completed before being inspected
    (d) all of these

12. Accepted industry workmanship practices are described in ANSI/NECA 1-2006, *Standard Practices for Good Workmanship in Electrical Contracting*, and other ANSI-approved installation standards.

    (a) True
    (b) False

13. Unused openings other than those intended for the operation of equipment, intended for mounting purposes, or permitted as part of the design for listed equipment shall be _____.

    (a) filled with cable clamps or connectors only
    (b) taped over with electrical tape
    (c) repaired only by welding or brazing in a metal slug
    (d) effectively closed to afford protection substantially equivalent to the wall of the equipment

14. Internal parts of electrical equipment, including _____, shall not be damaged or contaminated by foreign materials such as paint, plaster, cleaners, abrasives, or corrosive residues.

    (a) busbars
    (b) wiring terminals
    (c) insulators
    (d) all of these

15. Wooden plugs driven into holes in _____ or similar materials shall not be used for securing electrical equipment.

    (a) masonry
    (b) concrete
    (c) plaster
    (d) all of these

16. Electrical equipment that depends on _____ for cooling of exposed surfaces shall be installed so that airflow over such surfaces is not prevented by walls or by adjacent installed equipment.

    (a) outdoor air
    (b) natural circulation of air and convection principles
    (c) artificial cooling and circulation
    (d) magnetic induction

17. Conductor terminal and splicing devices must be _____ for the conductor material and they must be properly installed and used.

    (a) listed
    (b) approved
    (c) identified
    (d) all of these

18. Connectors and terminals for conductors more finely stranded than Class B and Class C, as shown in Table 10 of Chapter 9, must be _____ for the specific conductor class or classes.

    (a) listed
    (b) approved
    (c) identified
    (d) all of these

19. Many terminations and equipment are marked with _____.

    (a) an etching tool
    (b) a removable label
    (c) a tightening torque
    (d) the manufacturer's initials

20. Connection of conductors to terminal parts shall ensure a thoroughly good connection without damaging the conductors and shall be made by means of _____.

    (a) solder lugs
    (b) pressure connectors
    (c) splices to flexible leads
    (d) any of these

21. Connection by means of wire-binding screws, studs, or nuts having upturned lugs or the equivalent shall be permitted for _____ or smaller conductors.

    (a) 12 AWG
    (b) 10 AWG
    (c) 8 AWG
    (d) 6 AWG

22. Soldered splices shall first be spliced or joined so as to be mechanically and electrically secure without solder and then be soldered.

    (a) True
    (b) False

23. The temperature rating associated with the ampacity of a _____ shall be so selected and coordinated so as not to exceed the lowest temperature rating of any connected termination, conductor, or device.

    (a) terminal
    (b) conductor
    (c) device
    (d) all of these

24. Conductor ampacity shall be determined using the _____ column of Table 310.15(B)(16) for circuits rated 100A or less or marked for 14 AWG through 1 AWG conductors, unless the equipment terminals are listed for use with conductors that have higher temperature ratings.

    (a) 30°C
    (b) 60°C
    (c) 75°C
    (d) 90°C

25. For circuits rated 100A or less, when the equipment terminals are listed for use with 75°C conductors, the _____ column of Table 310.15(B)(16) shall be used to determine the ampacity of THHN conductors.

    (a) 30°C
    (b) 60°C
    (c) 75°C
    (d) 90°C

26. Conductors shall have their ampacity determined using the _____ column of Table 310.15(B)(16) for circuits rated over 100A, or marked for conductors larger than 1 AWG, unless the equipment terminals are listed for use with higher temperature-rated conductors.

(a) 30°C
(b) 60°C
(c) 75°C
(d) 90°C

27. Separately installed pressure connectors shall be used with conductors at the _____ not exceeding the ampacity at the listed and identified temperature rating of the connector.

(a) voltages
(b) temperatures
(c) listings
(d) ampacities

28. On a 4-wire, delta-connected system where the midpoint of one phase winding is grounded, the conductor having the higher phase voltage-to-ground shall be durably and permanently marked by an outer finish that is _____ in color.

(a) black
(b) red
(c) blue
(d) orange

29. Electrical equipment such as switchboards, panelboards, industrial control panels, meter socket enclosures, and motor control centers that are in other than dwelling units, and are likely to require _____ while energized shall be field-marked to warn qualified persons of potential electric arc flash hazards.

(a) examination
(b) adjustment
(c) servicing or maintenance
(d) any of these

30. Where required by the *Code*, markings on all electrical equipment shall contain voltage, current, wattage, or other ratings with durability to withstand _____.

(a) the voltages encountered
(b) painting and other finishes applied
(c) the environment involved
(d) any lack of planning by the installer

31. Each disconnecting means shall be legibly marked to indicate its purpose unless located and arranged so _____.

(a) that it can be locked out and tagged
(b) it is not readily accessible
(c) the purpose is evident
(d) that it operates at less than 300 volts-to-ground

32. The *NEC* requires tested series-rated installations of circuit breakers or fuses to be legibly marked in the field to indicate the equipment has been applied with a series combination rating.

(a) True
(b) False

33. _____ in other than dwelling units must be legibly field-marked with the maximum available fault current, including the date the fault current calculation was performed and be of sufficient durability to withstand the environment involved.

(a) Service equipment
(b) Sub panels
(c) Motor control centers
(d) all of these

34. When modifications to the electrical installation affect the maximum available fault current at the service, the maximum available fault current shall be verified or _____ to ensure the service equipment ratings are sufficient for the maximum available fault current at the line terminals of the equipment.

(a) recalculated
(b) increased
(c) decreased
(d) adjusted

35. Field markings of maximum available fault current at a service are not required for industrial installations where conditions of maintenance and supervision ensure that only qualified persons service the equipment.

(a) True
(b) False

36. Access and _____ shall be provided and maintained about all electrical equipment to permit ready and safe operation and maintenance of such equipment.

(a) ventilation
(b) cleanliness
(c) circulation
(d) working space

37. A minimum working space depth of _____ to live parts operating at 277 volts-to-ground is required where there are exposed live parts on one side and no live or grounded parts on the other side.

(a) 2 ft
(b) 3 ft
(c) 4 ft
(d) 6 ft

38. The minimum working space on a circuit that is 120 volts-to-ground, with exposed live parts on one side and no live or grounded parts on the other side of the working space, is _____.

(a) 1 ft
(b) 3 ft
(c) 4 ft
(d) 6 ft

39. Concrete, brick, or tile walls are considered _____, as applied to working space requirements.

(a) inconsequential
(b) in the way
(c) grounded
(d) none of these

40. The required working space for access to live parts operating at 300 volts-to-ground, where there are exposed live parts on one side and grounded parts on the other side, is _____.

(a) 3 ft
(b) 3½ ft
(c) 4 ft
(d) 4½ ft

41. The required working space for access to live parts operating at 300 volts-to-ground, where there are exposed live parts on both sides of the workspace is _____.

(a) 3 ft
(b) 3½ ft
(c) 4 ft
(d) 4½ ft

42. Working space distances for enclosed live parts shall be measured from the _____ of equipment or apparatus, if the live parts are enclosed.

(a) enclosure
(b) opening
(c) a or b
(d) none of these

43. The working space in front of the electric equipment shall not be less than _____ wide, or the width of the equipment, whichever is greater.

(a) 15 in.
(b) 30 in.
(c) 40 in.
(d) 60 in.

44. Equipment associated with the electrical installation can be located above or below other electrical equipment within their working space when the associated equipment does not extend more than _____ from the front of the electrical equipment.

(a) 3 in.
(b) 6 in.
(c) 12 in.
(d) 30 in.

45. The minimum height of working spaces about electrical equipment, switchboards, panelboards, or motor control centers operating at 600V, nominal, or less and likely to require examination, adjustment, servicing, or maintenance while energized shall be 6½ ft or the height of the equipment, whichever is greater, except for service equipment or panelboards in existing dwelling units that do not exceed 200A.

    (a) True
    (b) False

46. Working space shall not be used for _____.

    (a) storage
    (b) raceways
    (c) lighting
    (d) accessibility

47. When normally enclosed live parts are exposed for inspection or servicing, the working space, if in a passageway or general open space, shall be suitably _____.

    (a) accessible
    (b) guarded
    (c) open
    (d) enclosed

48. For equipment rated 1,200A or more and over 6 ft wide that contains overcurrent devices, switching devices, or control devices, there shall be one entrance to and egress from the required working space not less than 24 in. wide and _____ high at each end of the working space.

    (a) 5½ ft
    (b) 6 ft
    (c) 6½ ft
    (d) any of these

49. For equipment rated 1,200A or more that contains overcurrent devices, switching devices, or control devices; and where the entrance to the working space has a personnel door less than 25 ft from the working space, the door shall _____.

    (a) open either in or out with simple pressure and shall not have any lock
    (b) open in the direction of egress and be equipped with panic hardware or other devices so the door can open under simple pressure
    (c) be equipped with a locking means
    (d) be equipped with an electronic opener

50. Illumination shall be provided for all working spaces about service equipment, switchboards, panelboards, and motor control centers _____.

    (a) over 600V
    (b) located indoors
    (c) rated 1,200A or more
    (d) using automatic means of control

51. All switchboards, panelboards, and motor control centers shall be _____.

    (a) located in dedicated spaces
    (b) protected from damage
    (c) in weatherproof enclosures
    (d) a and b

52. The minimum height of dedicated equipment space for motor control centers installed indoors is _____ above the enclosure, or to the structural ceiling, whichever is lower.

    (a) 3 ft
    (b) 5 ft
    (c) 6 ft
    (d) 6½ ft

53. For indoor installations, heating, cooling, or ventilating equipment shall not be installed in the dedicated space above a panelboard or switchboard.

    (a) True
    (b) False

54. The dedicated equipment space for electrical equipment that is required for panelboards installed indoors is measured from the floor to a height of _____ above the equipment, or to the structural ceiling, whichever is lower.

    (a) 3 ft
    (b) 6 ft
    (c) 12 ft
    (d) 30 ft

55. The dedicated space above a panelboard extends to a dropped or suspended ceiling, which is considered a structural ceiling.

    (a) True
    (b) False

56. Electrical equipment rooms or enclosures housing electrical apparatus that are controlled by a lock(s) shall be considered _____ to qualified persons.

    (a) readily accessible
    (b) accessible
    (c) available
    (d) none of these

57. To guard live parts over 50V but less than 600V, equipment is permitted to be _____.

    (a) located in a room accessible only to qualified persons
    (b) located on a balcony accessible only to qualified persons
    (c) elevated 8 ft or more above the floor or other working surface
    (d) any of these

58. Live parts of electrical equipment operating at _____ or more shall be guarded against accidental contact by approved enclosures or by suitable permanent, substantial partitions, or screens arranged so that only qualified persons have access to the space within reach of the live parts.

    (a) 20V
    (b) 30V
    (c) 50V
    (d) 100V

59. In locations where electrical equipment is likely to be exposed to _____, enclosures or guards shall be so arranged and of such strength as to prevent such damage.

    (a) corrosion
    (b) physical damage
    (c) magnetic fields
    (d) weather

60. Entrances to rooms and other guarded locations containing exposed live parts shall be marked with conspicuous _____ forbidding unqualified persons to enter.

    (a) warning signs
    (b) alarms
    (c) a and b
    (d) neither a nor b

61. The term "rainproof" is typically used in conjunction with Enclosure-Type Number _____.

    (a) 3
    (b) 3R
    (c) 3RX
    (d) b and c

CHAPTER 2

WIRING AND PROTECTION

INTRODUCTION TO CHAPTER 2—WIRING AND PROTECTION

Chapter 2 provides general rules for wiring and the protection of conductors. The rules in this chapter apply to all electrical installations covered by the *NEC*—except as modified in Chapters 5, 6, and 7 [90.3].

Communications Systems (Chapter 8 systems) aren't subject to the general requirements of Chapters 1 through 4, or the special requirements of Chapters 5 through 7, unless there's a specific reference in Chapter 8 to a rule in Chapters 1 through 7 [90.3].

As you go through Chapter 2, remember its purpose. Chapter 2 is primarily concerned with correctly sizing and protecting circuits. Every article in Chapter 2 deals with a different aspect of this purpose. This differs from the purpose of Chapter 3, which is to correctly install the conductors that make up those circuits.

Chapter 1 introduced you to the *NEC* and provided a solid foundation for understanding the *Code*. Chapters 2 (Wiring and Protection) and 3 (Wiring Methods and Materials) continue building the foundation for applying the *NEC*. Chapter 4 applies the preceding chapters to general equipment. It's beneficial to learn the first four chapters of the *Code* in a sequential manner because each of the first four chapters builds on the preceding chapter. Once you've mastered the first four chapters, you can learn the next four in any order you wish.

- **Article 200—Use and Identification of Grounded Conductors.** This article contains the requirements for the use and identification of the neutral conductor and its terminals.

Author's Comment: Because the neutral conductor of a solidly grounded system is connected to the earth, it's both a "grounded conductor" and a "neutral conductor." To make it easier for the reader, we'll refer to the "grounded conductor" as the "neutral conductor."

- **Article 210—Branch Circuits.** Article 210 contains the requirements for branch circuits, such as conductor sizing, identification, GFCI protection, as well as receptacle and lighting outlet requirements.

- **Article 215—Feeders.** This article covers the requirements for the installation, minimum size, and ampacity of feeders.

- **Article 220—Branch-Circuit, Feeder, and Service Calculations.** Article 220 provides the requirements for calculating the minimum size for branch circuits, feeders, and services. This article also aids in determining related factors such as the number of receptacles on a circuit in nondwelling installations, and the minimum number of branch circuits required.

- **Article 225—Outside Branch Circuits and Feeders.** This article covers the installation requirements for equipment, including conductors located outside that run on or between buildings, poles, and other structures on the premises.

- **Article 230—Services.** Article 230 covers the installation requirements for service conductors and equipment. It's very important to know where the service begins and ends when applying Article 230.

Author's Comment: Conductors from a battery, uninterruptible power supply, solar photovoltaic system, generator, or transformer aren't considered service conductors; they're feeder conductors.

- **Article 240—Overcurrent Protection.** This article provides the requirements for overcurrent protection and overcurrent devices. Overcurrent protection for conductors and equipment is provided to open the circuit if the current reaches a value that will cause an excessive or dangerous temperature on the conductors or conductor insulation.

- **Article 250—Grounding and Bonding.** Article 250 covers the grounding requirements for providing a low-impedance path to the earth to reduce overvoltage from lightning, and the bonding requirements for a low-impedance fault current path necessary to facilitate the operation of overcurrent devices in the event of a ground fault.

- **Article 285—Surge Protective Devices (SPDs).** This article covers the general requirements, installation requirements, and connection requirements for surge protective devices (SPDs) permanently installed on both the line side and load side of service equipment.

ARTICLE 200

Use and Identification of Grounded Conductors

INTRODUCTION TO ARTICLE 200—USE AND IDENTIFICATION OF GROUNDED CONDUCTORS

This article contains the requirements for the identification of the grounded conductor and its terminals. Article 100 contains definitions for both "Grounded Conductor" and "Neutral Conductor." In some cases, both of these terms apply to the same conductor.

In a system that produces direct-current, such as a photovoltaic system, the "grounded conductor" is not a neutral conductor.

Author's Comment: Throughout this book, we will use the term "neutral" when referring to the grounded conductor when the application is not related to PV systems or corner-grounded delta-connected systems.

Please use the 2011 *Code* book to answer the following questions, which are based on the 2011 *NEC*.

QUESTIONS FOR ARTICLE 200—USE AND IDENTIFICATION OF GROUNDED CONDUCTORS

1. Article 200 contains the requirements for _____.

   (a) identification of terminals
   (b) grounded conductors in premises wiring systems
   (c) identification of grounded conductors
   (d) all of these

2. The continuity of a grounded conductor shall not depend on a connection to a _____.

   (a) metallic enclosure
   (b) raceway
   (c) cable armor
   (d) all of these

3. A single _____ shall not be used for more than one branch circuit, one multiwire branch circuit, or one set of feeder conductors except as allowed elsewhere in the *Code*.

   (a) equipment grounding conductor
   (b) neutral conductor
   (c) grounding electrode conductor
   (d) bonding conductor

4. An insulated grounded conductor of _____ or smaller shall be identified by a continuous white or gray outer finish, or by three continuous white stripes on other than green insulation along its entire length.

   (a) 8 AWG
   (b) 6 AWG
   (c) 4 AWG
   (d) 3 AWG

5. Grounded conductors _____ and larger can be identified by distinctive white or gray markings at their terminations.

   (a) 10 AWG
   (b) 8 AWG
   (c) 6 AWG
   (d) 4 AWG

6. If grounded conductors of different voltage systems are installed in the same raceway, cable, or enclosure, each neutral conductor must be identified to distinguish the systems by _____.

(a) a continuous white or gray outer finish for one system
(b) a neutral conductor with a different continuous white or gray outer finish or white or gray with a stripe for one system
(c) other identification allowed by 200.6(A) or (B) that distinguishes each system from other systems.
(d) a, b, or c

7. If neutral conductors of different voltage systems are installed in the same raceway, cable, or enclosure, the means of identification of the different neutrals shall be documented in a manner that's _____ or be permanently posted where the conductors of different systems originate.

(a) available to the AHJ
(b) available through the engineer
(c) readily available
(d) included in the as-built drawings

8. The white conductor within a cable can be used for a(n) _____ conductor where permanently reidentified to indicate its use as an ungrounded conductor at each location where the conductor is visible and accessible.

(a) grounded
(b) ungrounded
(c) a and b
(d) none of these

9. If used for single-pole, 3-way or 4-way switch loops, the reidentified conductor with white or gray insulation or three continuous white stripes can be used for the supply to the switch but not as a return conductor from the switch to the outlet.

(a) True
(b) False

10. The identification of _____ to which a grounded conductor is to be connected shall be substantially white in color.

(a) wire connectors
(b) circuit breakers
(c) terminals
(d) ground rods

11. Receptacles shall have the terminal intended for connection to the grounded conductor identified by a metal or metal coating that is substantially _____ in color.

(a) green
(b) white
(c) gray
(d) b or c

12. The screw shell of a luminaire or lampholder shall be connected to the _____.

(a) grounded conductor
(b) ungrounded conductor
(c) equipment grounding conductor
(d) forming shell terminal

13. No _____ shall be attached to any terminal or lead so as to reverse designated polarity.

(a) grounded conductor
(b) grounding conductor
(c) ungrounded conductor
(d) grounding connector

Branch Circuits

INTRODUCTION TO ARTICLE 210—BRANCH CIRCUITS

This article contains the requirements for branch circuits, such as conductor sizing and identification, GFCI protection, and receptacle and lighting outlet requirements. It consists of three parts:

- Part I. General Provisions
- Part II. Branch-Circuit Ratings
- Part III. Required Outlets

Table 210.2 of this article identifies specific-purpose branch circuits. The provisions for branch circuits that supply equipment listed in Table 210.2 amend or supplement the provisions given in Article 210 for branch circuits, so it's important to be aware of the contents of this table.

The following sections contain a few key items on which to spend extra time as you study Article 210:

- **210.4—Multiwire Branch Circuits.** The conductors of these circuits must originate from the same panel.

- **210.8—GFCI Protection.** Crawl spaces, unfinished basements, and boathouses are just some of the many locations that require GFCI protection.

- **210.11—Branch Circuits Required.** With three subheadings, 210.11 gives summarized requirements for the number of branch circuits in certain situations, states that a load calculated on a VA per area basis must be evenly proportioned, and covers some minimum branch circuit rules for dwelling units.

- **210.12—Arc-Fault Circuit-Interrupter Protection.** An arc-fault circuit interrupter is a device intended to de-energize a circuit when it detects the current waveform characteristics unique to an arcing fault. The purpose of an AFCI is to protect against a fire hazard, whereas the purpose of a GFCI is to protect people against electrocution.

- **210.19—Conductors—Minimum Ampacity and Size.** This section covers the basic rules for sizing branch-circuit conductors, including continuous and noncontinuous loads.

- **210.21—Outlet Devices.** Outlet devices must have an ampere rating at least as large as the load to be served, as well as following the other rules of this section.

- **210.23—Permissible Loads.** This is intended to prevent a circuit overload from occurring because of improper design and planning of circuitry.

- **210.52—Dwelling Unit Receptacle Outlets.** There are some specific receptacle spacing rules and branch-circuit requirements for dwelling units that don't apply to other occupancies.

Mastering the branch-circuit requirements in Article 210 will give you a jump-start toward completing installations that are free of *Code* violations.

QUESTIONS FOR ARTICLE 210— BRANCH CIRCUITS

1. The rating of a branch circuit shall be determined by the rating of the _____.

   (a) ampacity of the largest device connected to the circuit
   (b) average of the ampacity of all devices
   (c) branch-circuit overcurrent device
   (d) ampacity of the branch-circuit conductors according to Table 310.15(B)(16)

2. A three-phase, 4-wire, _____ power system used to supply power to nonlinear loads may necessitate that the power system design allow for the possibility of high harmonic current on the neutral conductor.

   (a) wye-connected
   (b) delta-connected
   (c) wye/delta-connected
   (d) none of these

3. Each multiwire branch circuit shall be provided with a means that will simultaneously disconnect all _____ conductors at the point where the branch circuit originates.

   (a) circuit
   (b) grounded
   (c) grounding
   (d) ungrounded

4. Multiwire branch circuits shall _____.

   (a) supply only line-to-neutral loads
   (b) not be permitted in dwelling units
   (c) have their conductors originate from different panelboards
   (d) none of these

5. The ungrounded and grounded conductors of each _____ shall be grouped by wire ties or similar means at the panelboard or other point of origination.

   (a) branch circuit
   (b) multiwire branch circuit
   (c) feeder circuit
   (d) service-entrance conductor

6. Where more than one nominal voltage system supplies branch circuits in a building, each _____ conductor of a branch circuit shall be identified by phase and system at all termination, connection, and splice points.

   (a) grounded
   (b) ungrounded
   (c) grounding
   (d) all of these

7. In dwelling units, the voltage between conductors that supply the terminals of _____ shall not exceed 120V, nominal.

   (a) luminaires
   (b) cord-and-plug-connected loads of 1,440 VA or less
   (c) cord-and-plug-connected loads of more than ¼ hp
   (d) a and b

8. Where two or more branch circuits supply devices or equipment on the same yoke, a means to disconnect simultaneously all ungrounded conductors that supply those devices or equipment shall be provided _____.

   (a) at the point where the branch circuit originates
   (b) at the location of the device or equipment
   (c) at the point where the feeder originates
   (d) none of these

9. The GFCI protection required by 210.8(A) and (B) must be _____.

   (a) the circuit breaker type only
   (b) accessible
   (c) readily accessible
   (d) concealed

10. All 15A and 20A, 125V receptacles installed in bathrooms of _____ shall have ground-fault circuit-interrupter (GFCI) protection for personnel.

    (a) guest rooms in hotels/motels
    (b) dwelling units
    (c) office buildings
    (d) all of these

11. GFCI protection shall be provided for all 15A and 20A, 125V receptacles installed in a dwelling unit _____.

    (a) attic
    (b) garage
    (c) laundry room
    (d) all of these

12. GFCI protection shall be provided for all 15A and 20A, 125V receptacles in dwelling unit accessory buildings that have a floor located at or below grade level not intended as _____ and limited to storage areas, work areas, or similar use.

    (a) habitable rooms
    (b) finished space
    (c) a or b
    (d) none of these

13. All 15A and 20A, 125V receptacles located outdoors of dwelling units, including receptacles installed under the eaves of roofs, must be GFCI protected except for a receptacle that's supplied by a branch circuit dedicated to _____ if the receptacle isn't readily accessible and the equipment or receptacle has ground-fault protection of equipment (GFPE) [426.28 or 427.22].

    (a) fixed electric snow-melting or deicing equipment
    (b) pipeline and vessel heating equipment
    (c) holiday decorative lighting
    (d) a or b

14. All 15A and 20A, 125V receptacles installed in crawl spaces at or below grade level of dwelling units shall have GFCI protection.

    (a) True
    (b) False

15. All 15A and 20A, 125V receptacles installed in _____ of dwelling units shall have GFCI protection.

    (a) unfinished attics
    (b) finished attics
    (c) unfinished basements and crawl spaces
    (d) finished basements

16. GFCI protection shall be provided for all 15A and 20A, 125V receptacles _____ in dwelling unit kitchens.

    (a) installed to serve the countertop surfaces
    (b) within 6 ft of the sink
    (c) for all receptacles
    (d) that are readily accessible

17. GFCI protection shall be provided for all 15A and 20A, 125V receptacles installed within 6 ft of all dwelling unit sinks located in areas other than the _____.

    (a) laundry room
    (b) bathroom
    (c) den
    (d) kitchen

18. All 15A and 20A, 125V receptacles installed in dwelling unit boathouses shall have GFCI protection.

    (a) True
    (b) False

19. All 15A and 20A, 125V receptacles _____ of commercial occupancies shall have GFCI protection.

    (a) in bathrooms
    (b) on rooftops
    (c) in kitchens
    (d) all of these

20. In other than dwelling units, GFCI protection shall be provided for all outdoor 15A and 20A, 125V receptacles.

    (a) True
    (b) False

21. All 15A and 20A, 125V receptacles located outdoors or on rooftops in locations other than dwelling units must be GFCI protected except for a receptacle that's supplied by a branch circuit dedicated to _____ if the receptacle isn't readily accessible and the equipment or receptacle has ground-fault protection of equipment (GFPE) [426.28 and 427.22].

(a) fixed electric snow-melting or deicing equipment
(b) pipeline and vessel heating equipment
(c) holiday decorative lighting
(d) a or b

22. In other than dwelling locations, GFCI protection is required in _____.

(a) indoor wet locations
(b) locker rooms adjacent to showering facilities
(c) garages, service bays, and similar areas
(d) all of these

23. All 15A and 20A, 125V receptacles installed within 6 ft of the outside edge of a sink in locations other than dwelling units must be _____.

(a) AFCI protected
(b) GFCI protected
(c) tamperproof
(d) a and b

24. In industrial laboratories, 15A and 20A, 125V receptacles used to supply equipment where removal of power would introduce a greater hazard aren't required to be GFCI protected.

(a) True
(b) False

25. 15A and 20A, 125V receptacles located in patient bed locations of general care or critical care areas of health care facilities aren't required to be GFCI protected.

(a) True
(b) False

26. All 15A and 20A, 125V receptacles installed indoors in wet locations must be GFCI protected.

(a) True
(b) False

27. All 15A and 20A, 125V receptacles installed in locker rooms with associated showering facilities must be GFCI protected.

(a) True
(b) False

28. All 15A and 20A, 125V receptacles installed in garages, service bays, and similar areas where _____ are to be used must be GFCI protected.

(a) electrical diagnostic equipment
(b) electrical hand tools
(c) portable lighting equipment
(d) all of these

29. Ground-fault circuit-interrupter protection shall be provided for outlets not exceeding 240V that supply boat hoists installed in dwelling unit locations.

(a) True
(b) False

30. Two or more _____ small-appliance branch circuits shall be provided to supply power for receptacle outlets in the dwelling unit kitchen, dining room, breakfast room, pantry, or similar dining areas.

(a) 15A
(b) 20A
(c) 30A
(d) either 20A or 30A

31. There shall be a minimum of one _____ branch circuit for the laundry outlet(s) required by 210.52(F).

(a) 15A
(b) 20A
(c) 30A
(d) b and c

32. An individual 20A branch circuit can supply a single dwelling unit bathroom for receptacle outlet(s) and other equipment within the same bathroom.

    (a) True
    (b) False

33. All 15A or 20A, 120V branch circuits that supply outlets in dwelling unit family rooms, dining rooms, living rooms, parlors, libraries, dens, bedrooms, sunrooms, recreation rooms, closets, hallways, or similar rooms or areas shall be AFCI protected by a listed arc-fault circuit interrupter of the combination type.

    (a) True
    (b) False

34. An arc-fault circuit interrupter can be located at the first outlet to provide protection for the remaining portion of the branch circuit if _____.

    (a) the arc-fault circuit interrupter is installed within 8 ft of the branch-circuit overcurrent device
    (b) the circuit conductors up to the arc-fault circuit interrupter are in a metal raceway or steel armored Type AC or Type MC cable with metal outlet and junction boxes
    (c) a and b
    (d) the branch circuit serves only lighting loads

35. Where a listed metal or nonmetallic conduit or tubing is encased in not less than _____ of concrete for the portion of the branch circuit between the branch-circuit overcurrent device and the first outlet, an outlet branch circuit AFCI at the first outlet is permitted to provide protection for the remaining portion of the branch circuit.

    (a) 2 in.
    (b) 4 in.
    (c) 6 in.
    (d) 8 in.

36. AFCI protection can be omitted for an individual branch-circuit to a _____ in accordance with 760.41(B) and 760.121(B), if the circuit conductors are installed in RMC, IMC, EMT, or steel sheath Type AC or MC cable that qualifies as an equipment grounding conductor in accordance with 250.118, with metal outlet and junction boxes.

    (a) smoke alarm
    (b) communication system
    (c) fire alarm system
    (d) sump pump

37. Where branch circuit wiring in a dwelling unit is modified, replaced or extended in any of the areas specified in 210.12(A), the branch circuit must be protected by _____.

    (a) a listed combination AFCI located at the origin of the branch circuit
    (b) a listed outlet branch circuit AFCI located at the first receptacle outlet of the existing branch circuit
    (c) a GFCI circuit breaker or receptacle
    (d) a or b

38. The recommended maximum total voltage drop on branch-circuit conductors is _____ percent.

    (a) 2
    (b) 3
    (c) 4
    (d) 6

39. Where a branch circuit supplies continuous loads, or any combination of continuous and noncontinuous loads, the rating of the overcurrent device shall not be less than the noncontinuous load plus 125 percent of the continuous load.

    (a) True
    (b) False

40. A single receptacle installed on an individual branch circuit shall have an ampere rating not less than that of the branch circuit.

    (a) True
    (b) False

41. When connected to a branch circuit supplying two or more 15A receptacles, each receptacle shall not supply a total cord-and-plug-connected load in excess of _____.

    (a) 12A
    (b) 16A
    (c) 20A
    (d) 24A

42. If a 20A branch circuit supplies multiple receptacles, the receptacles shall have an ampere rating of no less than _____.

    (a) 10A
    (b) 15A
    (c) 20A
    (d) 30A

43. The total rating of utilization equipment fastened in place, shall not exceed _____ percent of the branch-circuit ampere rating where lighting units and cord-and-plug-connected utilization equipment are supplied.

    (a) 50
    (b) 75
    (c) 100
    (d) 125

44. _____ in dwelling units shall supply only loads within that dwelling unit or loads associated only with that dwelling unit.

    (a) Service-entrance conductors
    (b) Ground-fault protection
    (c) Branch circuits
    (d) none of these

45. In multi-occupancy buildings, branch circuits for _____ shall not be supplied from equipment that supplies an individual dwelling unit or tenant space.

    (a) central alarm
    (b) parking lot lighting
    (c) common area purposes
    (d) all of these

46. Receptacle outlets installed for a specific appliance in a dwelling unit, such as laundry equipment, shall be located within _____ of the intended location of the appliance.

    (a) sight
    (b) 3 ft
    (c) 6 ft
    (d) none of these

47. The *Code* provides rules for the minimum number of receptacle outlets required in a dwelling unit. The minimum required receptacle outlets shall be in addition to receptacle outlets that are _____.

    (a) part of a luminaire or appliance
    (b) controlled by a wall switch for use as required illumination
    (c) located more than 5½ ft above the floor
    (d) all of these

48. When applying the general provisions for receptacle spacing to the rooms of a dwelling unit which require receptacles in the wall space, no point along the floor line in any wall space of a dwelling unit may be more than _____ from an outlet.

    (a) 6 ft
    (b) 8 ft
    (c) 10 ft
    (d) 12 ft

49. In a dwelling unit, each wall space _____ or wider requires a receptacle.

    (a) 2 ft
    (b) 3 ft
    (c) 4 ft
    (d) 5 ft

50. In dwelling units, when determining the spacing of receptacle outlets, _____ on exterior walls shall not be considered wall space.

    (a) fixed panels
    (b) fixed glass
    (c) sliding panels
    (d) all of these

51. Receptacle outlets in floors shall not be counted as part of the required number of receptacle outlets for dwelling unit wall spaces, unless they are located within _____ of the wall.

    (a) 6 in.
    (b) 12 in.
    (c) 18 in.
    (d) 24 in.

52. Receptacles installed for countertop surfaces as required by 210.52(C) shall not be used to meet the receptacle requirements for wall space as required by 210.52(A).

    (a) True
    (b) False

53. In dwelling units, outdoor receptacles can be connected to one of the 20A small-appliance branch circuits.

    (a) True
    (b) False

54. A receptacle connected to one of the dwelling unit small-appliance branch circuits can be used to supply an electric clock.

    (a) True
    (b) False

55. A receptacle connected to a dwelling unit small-appliance circuit can supply gas-fired ranges, ovens, or counter-mounted cooking units.

    (a) True
    (b) False

56. Receptacles installed in a dwelling unit kitchen to serve countertop surfaces shall be supplied by not fewer than _____ small-appliance branch circuits.

    (a) one
    (b) two
    (c) three
    (d) four

57. A receptacle outlet shall be installed at each dwelling unit kitchen wall countertop space that is 12 in. or wider and receptacle outlets shall be installed so that no point along the wall line is more than _____, measured horizontally from a receptacle outlet in that space.

    (a) 10 in.
    (b) 12 in.
    (c) 16 in.
    (d) 24 in.

58. A receptacle outlet shall be installed in dwelling units for every kitchen and dining area countertop space _____, and no point along the wall line shall be more than 2 ft, measured horizontally, from a receptacle outlet in that space.

    (a) wider than 10 in.
    (b) wider than 3 ft
    (c) 18 in. or wider
    (d) 12 in. or wider

59. In dwelling units, at least one receptacle outlet shall be installed at each peninsular countertop having a long dimension of _____ in. or greater, and a short dimension of _____ in. or greater.

    (a) 12, 24
    (b) 24, 12
    (c) 24, 48
    (d) 48, 24

60. For the purpose of determining the placement of receptacles in a dwelling unit kitchen, a(n) _____ countertop is measured from the connecting edge.

    (a) island
    (b) usable
    (c) peninsular
    (d) cooking

61. When breaks occur in dwelling unit kitchen countertop spaces for rangetops, refrigerators or sinks, each countertop surface shall be considered a separate counter space for determining receptacle placement.

    (a) True
    (b) False

62. Kitchen and dining room countertop receptacle outlets in dwelling units shall be installed above the countertop surface, and not more than _____ above the countertop.

    (a) 12 in.
    (b) 18 in.
    (c) 20 in.
    (d) 24 in.

63. Receptacle outlets can be installed below the countertop surface in dwelling units when necessary for the physically impaired, or if there is no means available to mount a receptacle above an island or peninsular countertop.

    (a) True
    (b) False

64. In dwelling unit bathrooms, not less than one 15A or 20A, 125V receptacle outlet must be installed within _____ from the outside edge of each bathroom basin.

    (a) 20 in.
    (b) 3 ft
    (c) 4 ft
    (d) 6 ft

65. The receptacle outlet for a dwelling unit bathroom must be located on a _____ adjacent to the basin counter surface, or on the side or face of the basin cabinet not more than 12 in. below the countertop.

    (a) wall
    (b) partition
    (c) light fixture
    (d) a or b

66. Receptacle outlet assemblies listed for the application can be installed in countertops of dwelling unit bathrooms.

    (a) True
    (b) False

67. In dwelling units, the required bathroom receptacle outlet can be installed on the side or face of the basin cabinet if no lower than _____ below the countertop.

    (a) 12 in.
    (b) 18 in.
    (c) 24 in.
    (d) 36 in.

68. There shall be a minimum of _____ receptacle(s) installed outdoors at a one-family or two-family dwelling unit.

    (a) one
    (b) two
    (c) three
    (d) four

69. At least one receptacle outlet not more than _____ above a balcony, deck or porch shall be installed within the perimeter at each balcony, deck or porch of a dwelling unit.

    (a) 3 ft
    (b) 6½ ft
    (c) 8 ft
    (d) 24 in.

70. A laundry receptacle outlet shall not be required in each dwelling unit of a multifamily building, if laundry facilities are provided on the premises for all building occupants.

    (a) True
    (b) False

71. For a one-family dwelling, at least one receptacle outlet shall be required in each _____.

    (a) basement
    (b) attached garage
    (c) detached garage or accessory building with electric power
    (d) all of these

72. Where a portion of the dwelling unit basement is finished into one or more habitable rooms, each separate unfinished portion shall have a receptacle outlet installed.

    (a) True
    (b) False

73. Hallways in dwelling units that are _____ long or longer require a receptacle outlet.

    (a) 6 ft
    (b) 8 ft
    (c) 10 ft
    (d) 12 ft

74. Foyers with an area greater than _____ square feet must have a receptacle located in each wall space as 3 ft or more in width unbroken by doorways, floor-to-ceiling windows, and similar openings.

    (a) 40
    (b) 60
    (c) 80
    (d) 100

75. Guest rooms or guest suites provided with permanent provisions for _____ shall have receptacle outlets installed in accordance with all of the applicable requirements for a dwelling unit as specified in 210.52.

    (a) whirlpool tubs
    (b) bathing
    (c) cooking
    (d) internet access

76. Receptacles installed behind a bed in the guest rooms in hotels and motels shall be located to prevent the bed from contacting an attachment plug, or the receptacle shall be provided with a suitable guard.

    (a) True
    (b) False

77. The number of receptacle outlets for guest rooms in hotels and motels shall not be less than that required for a dwelling unit. These receptacles can be located to be convenient for permanent furniture layout, but at least _____ receptacle outlets shall be readily accessible.

    (a) one
    (b) two
    (c) three
    (d) four

78. At least one receptacle outlet shall be installed within 18 in. of the top of a show window for each _____, or major fraction thereof, of show-window area measured horizontally at its maximum width.

    (a) 10 ft
    (b) 12 ft
    (c) 18 ft
    (d) 24 ft

79. A 15A or 20A, 125V receptacle outlet shall be located within 25 ft of heating, air-conditioning, and refrigeration equipment for _____ occupancies.

    (a) dwelling
    (b) commercial
    (c) industrial
    (d) all of these

80. At least one wall switch-controlled lighting outlet must be installed in every habitable room and bathroom of a dwelling unit.

    (a) True
    (b) False

81. In rooms other than kitchens and bathrooms of dwelling units, one or more receptacles controlled by a wall switch shall be permitted in lieu of _____.

    (a) lighting outlets
    (b) luminaires
    (c) the receptacles required by 210.52(B) and (D)
    (d) all of these

82. In dwelling units, lighting outlets can be controlled by occupancy sensors where equipped with a _____ that will allow the sensor to function as a wall switch.

    (a) manual override
    (b) photo cell
    (c) sensor
    (d) none of these

83. In a dwelling unit, illumination from a lighting outlet shall be provided at the exterior side of each outdoor entrance or exit that has grade-level access.

    (a) True
    (b) False

84. When locating lighting outlets in dwelling units, a vehicle door in a garage shall be considered an outdoor entrance.

    (a) True
    (b) False

85. Where a lighting outlet(s) is installed for interior stairways, there shall be a wall switch at each floor level and each landing level that includes an entryway where the stairway between floor levels has six risers or more unless remote, central, or automatic control is used.

    (a) True
    (b) False

86. In a dwelling unit, illumination for outdoor entrances that have grade-level access can be controlled by _____.

    (a) remote
    (b) central
    (c) automatic control
    (d) any of these

87. In a dwelling unit, at least one lighting outlet _____ shall be located at the point of entry to the attic, underfloor space, utility room, or basement where these spaces are used for storage or contain equipment requiring servicing.

    (a) that is unswitched
    (b) containing a switch
    (c) controlled by a wall switch
    (d) b or c

88. At least one wall switch-controlled lighting outlet shall be installed in every habitable room and bathroom of a guest room or guest suite of hotels, motels, and similar occupancies. A receptacle outlet controlled by a wall switch may be used to meet this requirement in other than _____.

    (a) bathrooms
    (b) kitchens
    (c) sleeping areas
    (d) a and b

89. For attics and underfloor spaces in other than dwelling units that contain heating, air-conditioning, and refrigeration equipment requiring servicing, at least one lighting outlet containing a switch or controlled by a wall switch shall be installed _____.

    (a) at the equipment requiring servicing
    (b) near the equipment requiring servicing
    (c) a or b
    (d) none of these

ARTICLE
215

Feeders

INTRODUCTION TO ARTICLE 215—FEEDERS

Article 215 covers the rules for the installation, minimum size, and ampacity of feeders. The requirements for feeders have some similarities to those for branch circuits, but in some ways, feeders bear a resemblance to service conductors. It's important to understand the distinct differences between these three types of circuits in order to correctly apply the *Code* requirements.

Feeders are the conductors between the service equipment, the separately derived system, or other supply source and the final branch-circuit overcurrent device. Conductors past the final overcurrent device protecting the circuit and the outlet are branch-circuit conductors and fall within the scope of Article 210 [Article 100 Definitions].

Service conductors are the conductors from the service point of the electric utility to the service disconnecting means [Article 100 Definition]. If there's no serving utility, and the electrical power is derived from a generator or other on-site power source, then the conductors from the supply source are defined as feeders and there are no service conductors.

It's easy to be confused between feeder, branch circuit, and service conductors, so it's important to evaluate each installation carefully using the Article 100 Definitions to be sure the correct *Code* rules are followed.

QUESTIONS FOR ARTICLE 215—FEEDERS

1. The minimum feeder conductor ampacity, before the application of any adjustment or correction factors, must be no less than the noncontinuous load plus _____ percent of the continuous load.

    (a) 80
    (b) 100
    (c) 125
    (d) 150

2. Feeder neutral conductors shall be permitted to be sized at _____ percent of the continuous and noncontinuous load.

    (a) 80
    (b) 100
    (c) 125
    (d) 150

3. The feeder conductor ampacity shall not be less than that of the service-entrance conductors where the feeder conductors carry the total load supplied by service conductors with an ampacity of _____ or less.

    (a) 30A
    (b) 55A
    (c) 60A
    (d) 100A

4. Dwelling unit or mobile home feeder conductors need not be larger than the service conductors and can be sized according to 310.15(B)(7).

    (a) True
    (b) False

5. When a feeder supplies _____ in which equipment grounding conductors are required, the feeder shall include or provide an equipment grounding conductor.

(a) an equipment disconnecting means
(b) electrical systems
(c) branch circuits
(d) electric-discharge lighting equipment

6. Ground-fault protection of equipment shall be required for a feeder disconnect if _____.

(a) the disconnect is rated 800A, 208V
(b) the disconnect is rated 800A, 480V
(c) the disconnect is rated 1,000A, 208V
(d) the disconnect is rated 1,000A, 480V

7. Ground-fault protection of equipment shall not be required at a feeder disconnect if ground-fault protection of equipment is provided on the _____ side of the feeder and on the load side of any transformer supplying the feeder.

(a) load
(b) supply
(c) service
(d) none of these

8. Where a premises wiring system contains feeders supplied from more than one nominal voltage system, each ungrounded conductor of a feeder shall be identified by phase and system by _____, or other approved means.

(a) color coding
(b) marking tape
(c) tagging
(d) any of these

Branch-Circuit, Feeder, and Service Calculations

INTRODUCTION TO ARTICLE 220—BRANCH-CIRCUIT, FEEDER, AND SERVICE CALCULATIONS

This five-part article focuses on the requirements for calculating the minimum size of branch circuit, feeder, and service conductors.

Part I describes the layout of Article 220 and provides a table of where other types of load calculations can be found in the *NEC*. Part II provides requirements for branch-circuit calculations and for specific types of branch circuits. Part III covers the requirements for feeder and service calculations, using what's commonly called the standard method of calculation. Part IV provides optional calculations that can be used in place of the standard calculations provided in Parts II and III—if your installation meets certain requirements. Farm Load Calculations are discussed in Part V of the article.

In many cases, either the standard method (Part III) or the optional method (Part IV) can be used; however, these two methods don't yield identical results. In fact, sometimes these two answers may be diverse enough to call for different service sizes. There's nothing to say that either answer is right or wrong. If taking an exam, read the instructions carefully to be sure which method the test wants you to use. As you work through Article 220, be sure to study the illustrations in the textbook to help you fully understand it. Also be sure to review the examples in Annex D of the *NEC* to provide more practice with these calculations.

QUESTIONS FOR ARTICLE 220—BRANCH-CIRCUIT, FEEDER, AND SERVICE CALCULATIONS

1. When calculations in Article 220 result in a fraction of an ampere that is less than _____, such fractions can be dropped.

    (a) 0.49
    (b) 0.50
    (c) 0.51
    (d) 0.80

2. The 3 VA per-square-foot general lighting load for dwelling units does not include _____.

    (a) open porches
    (b) garages
    (c) unused or unfinished spaces not adaptable for future use
    (d) all of these

3. Where fixed multioutlet assemblies are used in other than dwelling units or the guest rooms of hotels or motels, each _____ or fraction thereof of each separate and continuous length shall be considered as 180 VA where appliances are unlikely to be used simultaneously.

    (a) 5 ft
    (b) 5½ ft
    (c) 6 ft
    (d) 6½ ft

4. For other than dwelling occupancies, banks, or office buildings, each receptacle outlet shall be calculated at not less than _____ VA.

    (a) 90
    (b) 180
    (c) 270
    (d) 360

5. A device comprised of _____ or more receptacles shall be calculated at not less than 90 VA per receptacle.

(a) one
(b) two
(c) three
(d) four

6. The 3 VA per-square-foot general lighting load for dwelling units includes general-use receptacles and lighting outlets.

(a) True
(b) False

7. Branch circuits that supply lighting units that have ballasts, autotransformers, or LED drivers shall have the calculated load based on _____ of the units, not to the total wattage of the lamps.

(a) 50 percent of the rating
(b) 80 percent of the rating
(c) the total ampere rating
(d) 150 percent of the rating

8. The minimum feeder load for show-window lighting is _____ per-linear-foot.

(a) 180 VA
(b) 200 VA
(c) 300 VA
(d) 400 VA

9. For other than dwelling units or guest rooms of hotels or motels, the feeder and service calculation for track lighting shall be calculated at 150 VA for every _____ lighting track or fraction thereof unless the track is supplied through a device that limits the current to the track.

(a) 1 ft
(b) 2 ft
(c) 3 ft
(d) 4 ft

10. Feeder and service loads for fixed electric space heating shall be calculated at _____ percent of the total connected load.

(a) 80
(b) 100
(c) 125
(d) 200

11. A dwelling unit containing three 120V small-appliance branch circuits has a calculated load of _____VA for the small appliance circuits.

(a) 1,500
(b) 3,000
(c) 4,500
(d) 6,000

12. A dwelling unit containing two 120V laundry branch circuits has a calculated load of _____VA for the laundry circuits.

(a) 1,500
(b) 3,000
(c) 4,500
(d) 6,000

13. When sizing a feeder for the fixed appliance loads in dwelling units, a demand factor of 75 percent of the total nameplate ratings can be applied if there are _____ or more appliances fastened in place on the same feeder.

(a) two
(b) three
(c) four
(d) five

14. The load for electric clothes dryers in a dwelling unit shall be _____ watts or the nameplate rating, whichever is larger, per dryer.

(a) 1,500
(b) 4,500
(c) 5,000
(d) 8,000

15. Using the standard load calculation method, the feeder demand factor for five household clothes dryers is _____ percent.

    (a) 50
    (b) 70
    (c) 85
    (d) 100

16. To determine the feeder calculated load for ten 3 kW household cooking appliances, use _____ of Table 220.55.

    (a) Column A
    (b) Column B
    (c) Column C
    (d) none of these

17. The feeder/service calculated load for a multifamily dwelling containing nine 12 kW ranges is _____.

    (a) 13,000W
    (b) 14,700W
    (c) 16,000W
    (d) 24,000W

18. Table 220.56 may be applied to determine the load for thermostatically controlled or intermittently used _____ and other kitchen equipment in a commercial kitchen.

    (a) commercial electric cooking equipment
    (b) dishwasher booster heaters
    (c) water heaters
    (d) all of these

19. The demand factors of Table 220.56 apply to space heating, ventilating, or air-conditioning equipment.

    (a) True
    (b) False

20. When applying the demand factors of Table 220.56, the feeder or service demand load shall not be less than the sum of _____.

    (a) the total number of receptacles at 180 VA per receptacle outlet
    (b) the VA rating of all of the small-appliance branch circuits combined
    (c) the largest two kitchen equipment loads
    (d) the kitchen heating and air-conditioning loads

21. Where it is unlikely that two or more noncoincident loads will be in use simultaneously, only the _____ loads used at one time is required to be used in computing the total load to a feeder.

    (a) smaller of the
    (b) largest of the
    (c) difference between the
    (d) none of these

22. The maximum unbalanced feeder load for household electric ranges, wall-mounted ovens, and counter-mounted cooking units shall be considered as _____ percent of the load on the ungrounded conductors.

    (a) 50
    (b) 70
    (c) 85
    (d) 115

23. There shall be no reduction in the size of the neutral or grounded conductor on _____ loads supplied from a 4-wire, wye-connected, three-phase system.

    (a) dwelling unit
    (b) hospital
    (c) nonlinear
    (d) motel

24. Under the optional method for calculating a single-family dwelling service, general loads beyond the initial 10 kVA are assessed at a _____ percent demand factor.

    (a) 40
    (b) 50
    (c) 60
    (d) 75

25. A demand factor of _____ percent applies to a multifamily dwelling with ten units if the optional calculation method is used.

    (a) 43
    (b) 50
    (c) 60
    (d) 75

ARTICLE 225 Outside Branch Circuits and Feeders

INTRODUCTION TO ARTICLE 225—OUTSIDE BRANCH CIRCUITS AND FEEDERS

This article covers the installation requirements for equipment, including conductors, located outdoors on or between buildings, poles, and other structures on the premises. Conductors installed outdoors can serve many purposes such as area lighting, power for outdoor equipment, or providing power to a separate building or structure. It's important to remember that the power supply for buildings or structures aren't always service conductors, but in many cases may be feeders or branch-circuit conductors originating in another building. Be careful not to assume that the conductors supplying power to a building are service conductors until you've identified where the utility service point is and reviewed the Article 100 Definitions for feeders, branch circuits, and service conductors. If they're service conductors, use Article 230. For outside branch circuit and feeder conductors, whatever they feed, use this article.

Section 225.2 provides a listing of other articles that may furnish additional requirements, then Part I of Article 225 goes on to address installation methods intended to provide a secure installation of outside conductors while providing sufficient conductor size, support, attachment means, and maintaining safe clearances.

Part II of the article limits the number of supplies (branch circuits or feeders) permitted to a building or structure and provides rules regarding disconnects for them. These rules include the disconnect rating, construction characteristics, labeling, and where to locate the disconnecting means and the grouping of multiple disconnects.

Outside branch circuits and feeders over 600V are the focus of Part III of Article 225.

QUESTIONS FOR ARTICLE 225—OUTSIDE BRANCH CIRCUITS AND FEEDERS

1. Open individual conductors shall not be smaller than _____ AWG copper for spans up to 50 ft in length and _____ AWG copper for a longer span, unless supported by a messenger wire.

    (a) 10, 8
    (b) 8, 8
    (c) 6, 8
    (d) 6, 6

2. The point of attachment of overhead premises wiring to a building shall in no case be less than _____ above finished grade.

    (a) 8 ft
    (b) 10 ft
    (c) 12 ft
    (d) 15 ft

3. Where mast is used for overhead conductor support, it shall be of adequate strength or be supported by braces or guy wire to withstand safely the strain imposed by the overhead drop.

    (a) True
    (b) False

4. Overhead feeder conductors shall have a minimum _____ vertical clearance over residential property and driveways, as well as those commercial areas not subject to truck traffic, where the voltage is limited to 300 volts-to-ground.

(a) 10 ft
(b) 12 ft
(c) 15 ft
(d) 18 ft

5. The minimum clearance for overhead feeder conductors not exceeding 600V that pass over commercial areas subject to truck traffic is _____.

(a) 10 ft
(b) 12 ft
(c) 15 ft
(d) 18 ft

6. The minimum clearance for overhead feeder conductors that pass over track rails of railroads is _____.

(a) 10 ft
(b) 12 ft
(c) 24.50 ft
(d) 30 ft

7. Overhead feeder conductors installed over roofs shall have a vertical clearance of _____ above the roof surface, unless permitted by an exception.

(a) 3 ft
(b) 8 ft
(c) 12 ft
(d) 15 ft

8. If a set of 120/240V overhead feeder conductors terminates at a through-the-roof raceway or approved support, with less than 6 ft of these conductors passing over the roof overhang, the minimum clearance above the roof for these conductors is _____.

(a) 12 in.
(b) 18 in.
(c) 2 ft
(d) 5 ft

9. The requirement for maintaining a 3 ft vertical clearance from the edge of the roof shall not apply to the final feeder conductor span where the conductors are attached to _____.

(a) a building pole
(b) the side of a building
(c) an antenna
(d) the base of a building

10. Overhead feeder conductors to a building shall have a vertical clearance of final spans above, or within _____ measured horizontally from the platforms, projections, or surfaces from which they might be reached.

(a) 3 ft
(b) 6 ft
(c) 8 ft
(d) 10 ft

11. Outside wiring shall not be installed beneath openings through which materials may be moved, and shall not be installed where they will obstruct entrance to these buildings' openings.

(a) True
(b) False

12. Raceways on exterior surfaces of buildings or other structures shall be arranged to drain, and be suitable for use in _____ locations.

(a) damp
(b) wet
(c) dry
(d) all of these

13. Vegetation such as trees shall not be used for support of _____.

(a) overhead conductor spans
(b) surface wiring methods
(c) luminaires
(d) electric equipment

14. Underground raceways entering a _____ from an underground distribution system shall be sealed or plugged at either or both ends to prevent moisture from contacting energized live parts.

    (a) building
    (b) structure
    (c) highway right-of-way
    (d) a or b

15. A building or structure shall be supplied by a maximum of _____ feeder(s) or branch circuit(s), unless specifically permitted otherwise.

    (a) one
    (b) two
    (c) three
    (d) four

16. The disconnecting means for a building supplied by a feeder shall be installed at a(n) _____ location.

    (a) accessible
    (b) readily accessible
    (c) outdoor
    (d) indoor

17. Where documented safe switching procedures are established and maintained and monitored by _____ individuals, the disconnecting means for a building supplied by a feeder can be located elsewhere on the premises.

    (a) maintenance
    (b) management
    (c) service
    (d) qualified

18. There shall be no more than _____ switches or circuit breakers to serve as the disconnecting means for a building supplied by a feeder.

    (a) two
    (b) four
    (c) six
    (d) eight

19. The two to six disconnects for a disconnecting means for a building supplied by a feeder shall be _____.

    (a) the same size
    (b) grouped
    (c) in the same enclosure
    (d) none of these

20. In a multiple-occupancy building, each occupant shall have access to his or her own _____.

    (a) disconnecting means
    (b) building drops
    (c) building-entrance assembly
    (d) lateral conductors

21. When the disconnecting means for a building supplied by a feeder is a power-operated switch or circuit breaker, it shall be able to be opened by hand in the event of a _____.

    (a) ground fault
    (b) short circuit
    (c) power surge
    (d) power failure

22. The disconnecting means for a building supplied by a feeder shall plainly indicate whether it is in the _____ position.

    (a) open or closed
    (b) correct
    (c) up or down
    (d) none of these

23. A building disconnecting means that supplies only limited loads of a single branch circuit shall have a rating of not less than _____.

    (a) 15A
    (b) 20A
    (c) 25A
    (d) 30A

24. For installations consisting of not more than two 2-wire branch circuits, the building disconnecting means shall have a rating of not less than _____.

(a) 15A
(b) 20A
(c) 25A
(d) 30A

ARTICLE 230

Services

INTRODUCTION TO ARTICLE 230—SERVICES

This article covers the installation requirements for service conductors and service equipment. The requirements for service conductors differ from those for other conductors. For one thing, service conductors for one building/structure can't pass through the interior of another building or structure [230.3], and you apply different rules depending on whether a service conductor is inside or outside a building/structure. When are they "outside" as opposed to "inside?" The answer may seem obvious, but Section 230.6 should be consulted before making this decision.

Let's review the following definitions in Article 100 to understand when the requirements of Article 230 apply:

- Service Point—The point of connection between the serving utility and the premises wiring.
- Service Conductors—The conductors from the service point to the service disconnecting means. Service-entrance conductors can either be overhead or underground.
- Service Equipment—The necessary equipment, usually consisting of circuit breakers or switches and fuses and their accessories, connected to the load end of service conductors at a building or other structure, and intended to constitute the main control and cutoff of the electrical supply. Service equipment doesn't include individual meter socket enclosures [230.66].

After reviewing these definitions, you should understand that service conductors originate at the serving utility (service point) and terminate on the line side of the service disconnecting means. Conductors and equipment on the load side of service equipment are considered feeder conductors or branch circuits, and must be installed in accordance with Articles 210 and 215. They must also comply with Article 225 if they're outside branch circuits and feeders, such as the supply to a building/structure. Feeder conductors include:

- Secondary conductors from customer-owned transformers,
- Conductors from generators, UPS systems, or photovoltaic systems, and
- Conductors to remote buildings or structures

Article 230 consists of seven parts:

- Part I. General
- Part II. Overhead Service Conductors
- Part III. Underground Service Conductors
- Part IV. Service-Entrance Conductors
- Part V. Service Equipment
- Part VI. Disconnecting Means
- Part VIII. Overcurrent Protection

QUESTIONS FOR ARTICLE 230—SERVICES

1. A building or structure shall be supplied by a maximum of _____ service(s), unless specifically permitted otherwise.

   (a) one
   (b) two
   (c) three
   (d) as many as desired

2. Additional services shall be permitted for a single building or other structure sufficiently large to make two or more services necessary if permitted by _____.

   (a) the registered design professional
   (b) special permission
   (c) the engineer of record
   (d) master electricians

3. Additional services shall be permitted for different voltages, frequencies, or phases, or for different uses such as for _____.

   (a) gymnasiums
   (b) different rate schedules
   (c) flea markets
   (d) special entertainment events

4. Where a building or structure is supplied by more than one service, a permanent plaque or directory shall be installed at each service disconnect location denoting all other services supplying that building or structure and the area served by each.

   (a) True
   (b) False

5. Service conductors supplying a building or other structure shall not _____ of another building or other structure.

   (a) be installed on the exterior walls
   (b) pass through the interior
   (c) a and b
   (d) none of these

6. Conductors are considered outside a building when they are installed:

   (a) Under not less than 2 in. of concrete beneath a building or structure.
   (b) Within a building or structure in a raceway encased in not less than a 2 in. thickness of concrete or brick.
   (c) Installed in a vault that meets the construction requirements of Article 450.
   (d) all of these

7. Conductors installed in overhead service masts on the outside surface of the building traveling through the eave of that building are considered to be outside of the building.

   (a) True
   (b) False

8. Conductors other than service conductors shall not be installed in the same _____.

   (a) service raceway
   (b) service cable
   (c) enclosure
   (d) a or b

9. Where a service raceway enters a building or structure from a(n) _____, it shall be sealed in accordance with 300.5(G).

   (a) transformer vault
   (b) underground distribution system
   (c) cable tray
   (d) overhead rack

10. Service conductors installed as unjacketed multiconductor cable shall have a minimum clearance of _____ from windows that are designed to be opened, doors, porches, stairs, fire escapes, or similar locations.

    (a) 3 ft
    (b) 4 ft
    (c) 6 ft
    (d) 10 ft

11. Overhead service conductors to a building shall maintain a vertical clearance of final spans above, or within, _____ measured horizontally from the platforms, projections, or surfaces from which they might be reached.

    (a) 3 ft
    (b) 6 ft
    (c) 8 ft
    (d) 10 ft

12. Service conductors shall not be installed beneath openings through which materials may be moved and shall not be installed where they will obstruct entrance to these buildings' openings.

    (a) True
    (b) False

13. Overhead service conductors can be supported to hardwood trees.

    (a) True
    (b) False

14. Service-drop conductors shall have _____.

    (a) sufficient ampacity to carry the load
    (b) adequate mechanical strength
    (c) a or b
    (d) a and b

15. The minimum size service-drop conductor permitted is _____ AWG copper or _____ AWG aluminum or copper-clad aluminum.

    (a) 8, 8
    (b) 8, 6
    (c) 6, 8
    (d) 6, 6

16. Overhead service conductors installed over roofs shall have a vertical clearance of _____ above the roof surface, unless a lesser distance is permitted by an exception.

    (a) 3 ft
    (b) 8 ft
    (c) 12 ft
    (d) 15 ft

17. If a set of 120/240V overhead service conductors terminate at a through-the-roof raceway or approved support, with less than 6 ft of these conductors passing over the roof overhang, the minimum clearance above the roof for these service conductors shall be _____.

    (a) 12 in.
    (b) 18 in.
    (c) 2 ft
    (d) 5 ft

18. The requirement to maintain a 3 ft vertical clearance from the edge of a roof does not apply to the final conductor span where the service drop is attached to _____.

    (a) a service pole
    (b) the side of a building
    (c) an antenna
    (d) the base of a building

19. If the voltage between overhead service conductors does not exceed 300V and the roof area is guarded or isolated, a reduction in clearance to 3 ft is permitted.

    (a) True
    (b) False

20. Overhead service conductors shall have a minimum of _____ vertical clearance from final grade over residential property and driveways, as well as over commercial areas not subject to truck traffic where the voltage is limited to 300 volts-to-ground.

    (a) 10 ft
    (b) 12 ft
    (c) 15 ft
    (d) 18 ft

21. The minimum clearance for overhead service conductors not exceeding 600V that pass over commercial areas subject to truck traffic is _____.

    (a) 10 ft
    (b) 12 ft
    (c) 15 ft
    (d) 18 ft

22. Overhead service conductors shall have a horizontal clearance of _____ from a pool.

    (a) 8 ft
    (b) 10 ft
    (c) 12 ft
    (d) 14 ft

23. Where communications cables and electric service drop conductors are supported by the same pole, communications cables must have a minimum separation of _____ at any point in the span, including the point of attachment to the building.

    (a) 2 in.
    (b) 6 in.
    (c) 12 in.
    (d) 24 in.

24. The minimum point of attachment of the service-drop conductors to a building shall not be less than _____ above finished grade.

    (a) 8 ft
    (b) 10 ft
    (c) 12 ft
    (d) 15 ft

25. Where raceway-type service masts are used, all raceway fittings shall be _____ for use with service masts.

    (a) identified
    (b) approved
    (c) of a heavy-duty type
    (d) listed

26. Underground service conductors shall have _____.

    (a) adequate mechanical strength
    (b) sufficient ampacity for the loads calculated
    (c) a and b
    (d) none of these

27. Underground copper service conductors supplying more than a single branch circuit shall not be smaller than _____ AWG copper.

    (a) 3
    (b) 4
    (c) 6
    (d) 8

28. Underground service conductors that supply power to limited loads of a single branch circuit shall not be smaller than _____.

    (a) 14 AWG copper
    (b) 14 AWG aluminum
    (c) 12 AWG copper
    (d) 12 AWG aluminum

29. Underground service conductors shall be protected from damage in accordance with _____ including minimum cover requirements.

    (a) 240.6(A)
    (b) 300.5
    (c) 310.15(B)(16)
    (d) 430.52

30. The general requirement for each service drop, set of overhead service conductors, set of underground service conductors, or service lateral is that it shall supply _____ set(s) of service-entrance conductors.

    (a) only one
    (b) only two
    (c) up to six
    (d) an unlimited number of

31. Service conductors can supply _____ service disconnecting means as permitted in 230.71(A).

    (a) only one
    (b) only two
    (c) up to six
    (d) an unlimited number of

32. A single-family dwelling unit and its accessory structure(s) shall be permitted to have one set of service conductors run to each structure from a single service drop, set of overhead service conductors, set of underground service conductors, or service lateral.

    (a) True
    (b) False

33. Two-family dwellings, multifamily dwellings, and multiple occupancy buildings shall be permitted to have one set of service entrance conductors to supply branch circuits for public or common areas.

    (a) True
    (b) False

34. One set of service-entrance conductors connected to the supply side of the normal service disconnecting means shall be permitted to supply standby power systems, fire pump equipment, and fire and sprinkler alarms covered by 230.82(5).

    (a) True
    (b) False

35. Ungrounded service-entrance conductors shall be sized not less than _____ percent of the continuous load, plus 100 percent of the noncontinuous load.

    (a) 100
    (b) 115
    (c) 125
    (d) 150

36. Wiring methods permitted for service-entrance conductors include _____.

    (a) rigid metal conduit
    (b) electrical metallic tubing
    (c) PVC conduit
    (d) all of these

37. Cable trays used to support service-entrance conductors shall contain only service-entrance conductors _____.

    (a) unless a solid fixed barrier separates the service-entrance conductors from other conductors
    (b) under 300V
    (c) in industrial locations
    (d) over 600V

38. Service-entrance conductors can be spliced or tapped by clamped or bolted connections at any time as long as _____.

    (a) the free ends of conductors are covered with an insulation that is equivalent to that of the conductors or with an insulating device identified for the purpose
    (b) wire connectors or other splicing means installed on conductors that are buried in the earth are listed for direct burial
    (c) no splice is made in a raceway
    (d) all of these

39. Underground service-entrance conductors shall be protected against physical damage.

    (a) True
    (b) False

40. Service-entrance cables which are not installed underground, where subject to physical damage, shall be protected by _____.

    (a) rigid metal conduit
    (b) IMC
    (c) Schedule 80 PVC conduit
    (d) any of these

41. Individual open conductors and cables, other than service-entrance cables, shall not be installed within _____ of grade level or where exposed to physical damage.

    (a) 8 ft
    (b) 10 ft
    (c) 12 ft
    (d) 15 ft

42. Service-entrance cables mounted in contact with a building shall be supported at intervals not exceeding _____.

    (a) 24 in.
    (b) 30 in.
    (c) 3 ft
    (d) 4 ft

43. Service raceways for overhead service drops or overhead service conductors shall have a weatherhead listed for _____.

    (a) wet locations
    (b) damp locations
    (c) Class 2 locations
    (d) NEMA 3R

44. Overhead service-entrance cables shall be equipped with a _____.

    (a) raceway
    (b) service head
    (c) cover
    (d) all of these

45. Overhead service-entrance conductors of Type SE cable can be formed in a _____ and taped with self-sealing weather-resistant thermoplastic.

    (a) loop
    (b) circle
    (c) gooseneck
    (d) none of these

46. Service heads shall be located _____, unless impracticable.

    (a) above the point of attachment
    (b) below the point of attachment
    (c) even with the point of attachment
    (d) none of these

47. To prevent moisture from entering service equipment, service-entrance conductors shall _____.

    (a) be connected to service-drop conductors below the level of the service head
    (b) have drip loops formed on the individual service-entrance conductors
    (c) a or b
    (d) a and b

48. Service-entrance and overhead service conductors shall be arranged so that _____ will not enter the service raceway or equipment.

    (a) dust
    (b) vapor
    (c) water
    (d) none of these

49. On a three-phase, 4-wire, delta-connected service where the midpoint of one phase winding is grounded, the service conductor having the higher phase voltage-to-ground shall be durably and permanently marked by an outer finish that is _____ in color, or by other effective means, at each termination or junction point.

    (a) orange
    (b) red
    (c) blue
    (d) any of these

50. The service disconnecting means shall be marked as suitable for use as service equipment and shall be _____.

    (a) weatherproof
    (b) listed
    (c) approved
    (d) acceptable

51. A service disconnecting means shall be installed at a(n) _____ location.

    (a) dry
    (b) readily accessible
    (c) outdoor
    (d) indoor

52. Service disconnecting means shall not be installed in bathrooms.

    (a) True
    (b) False

53. Where a remote-control device actuates the service disconnecting means, the service disconnecting means must still be at a readily accessible location either outside the building or structure, or nearest the point of entry of the service conductors.

    (a) True
    (b) False

54. Each service disconnecting means shall be permanently _____ to identify it as a service disconnect.

    (a) identified
    (b) positioned
    (c) marked
    (d) none of these

55. Each service disconnecting means shall be suitable for _____.

    (a) hazardous (classified) locations
    (b) wet locations
    (c) dry locations
    (d) the prevailing conditions

56. There shall be no more than _____ disconnects installed for each service or for each set of service-entrance conductors as permitted in 230.2 and 230.40.

    (a) two
    (b) four
    (c) six
    (d) eight

57. When the service contains two to six service disconnecting means, they shall be _____.

    (a) the same size
    (b) grouped
    (c) in the same enclosure
    (d) none of these

58. The additional service disconnecting means for fire pumps, emergency systems, legally required standby, or optional standby services, shall be installed remote from the one to six service disconnecting means for normal service to minimize the possibility of _____ interruption of supply.

    (a) intentional
    (b) accidental
    (c) simultaneous
    (d) prolonged

59. In a multiple-occupancy building, each occupant shall have access to the occupant's _____.

    (a) service disconnecting means
    (b) service drops
    (c) distribution transformer
    (d) lateral conductors

60. In a multiple-occupancy building where electric service and electrical maintenance are provided by the building management under continuous building management supervision, the service disconnecting means can be accessible to authorized _____ only.

    (a) inspectors
    (b) tenants
    (c) management personnel
    (d) qualified persons

61. When the service disconnecting means is a power-operated switch or circuit breaker, it shall be able to be opened by hand in the event of a _____.

    (a) ground fault
    (b) short circuit
    (c) power surge
    (d) power supply failure

62. The service disconnecting means shall plainly indicate whether it is in the _____ position.

    (a) open or closed
    (b) tripped
    (c) up or down
    (d) correct

63. For installations that supply only limited loads of a single branch circuit, the service disconnecting means shall have a rating not less than _____.

    (a) 15A
    (b) 20A
    (c) 25A
    (d) 30A

64. For installations consisting of not more than two 2-wire branch circuits, the service disconnecting means shall have a rating of not less than _____.

    (a) 15A
    (b) 20A
    (c) 25A
    (d) 30A

65. The service conductors shall be connected to the service disconnecting means by _____ or other approved means.

    (a) pressure connectors
    (b) clamps
    (c) solder
    (d) a or b

66. A meter disconnect switch located ahead of service equipment must have a short-circuit current rating equal to or greater than the available short-circuit current and be capable of inter-rupting the load served.

    (a) True
    (b) False

67. Electrical equipment shall not be connected to the supply side of the service disconnecting means, except for a few specific exceptions such as _____.

    (a) Type 1 surge protective devices
    (b) taps used to supply legally required optional standby power systems, fire pump equipment, fire and sprinkler alarms, and load (energy) management devices
    (c) Solar photovoltaic systems
    (d) all of these

68. Each _____ service conductor shall have overload protection.

    (a) overhead
    (b) underground
    (c) ungrounded
    (d) none of these

69. Ground-fault protection of equipment shall be provided for solidly grounded wye electrical services of more than 150 volts-to-ground, but not exceeding 600V phase-to-phase for each service disconnecting means rated _____ or more.

    (a) 1,000A
    (b) 1,500A
    (c) 2,000A
    (d) 2,500A

70. As defined by 230.95, the rating of the service disconnect shall be considered to be the rating of the largest _____ that can be installed or the highest continuous current trip setting for which the actual overcurrent device installed in a circuit breaker is rated or can be adjusted.

    (a) fuse
    (b) circuit
    (c) conductor
    (d) all of these

71. The maximum setting for ground-fault protection in a service disconnecting means is _____.

    (a) 800A
    (b) 1,000A
    (c) 1,200A
    (d) 2,000A

72. The ground-fault protection system for service equipment shall be _____ when first installed on-site.

    (a) a Class A device
    (b) identified
    (c) turned on
    (d) performance tested

73. Ground-fault protection that functions to open the service disconnect _____ protect(s) from faults on the line side of the protective element.

    (a) will
    (b) will not
    (c) adequately
    (d) totally

74. When service equipment has ground-fault protection installed, it may be necessary to review the overall wiring system for proper selective overcurrent protection _____.

    (a) rating
    (b) coordination
    (c) devices
    (d) none of these

ARTICLE
240

Overcurrent Protection

INTRODUCTION TO ARTICLE 240—OVERCURRENT PROTECTION

This article provides the requirements for selecting and installing overcurrent devices. Overcurrent exists when current exceeds the rating of equipment or the ampacity of a conductor. This can be due to an overload, short circuit, or ground fault [Article 100].

Overload. An overload is a condition where equipment or conductors carry current exceeding their current rating [Article 100]. A fault, such as a short circuit or ground fault, isn't an overload. An example of an overload is plugging two 12.50A (1,500W) hair dryers into a 20A branch circuit.

Ground Fault. A ground fault is an unintentional, electrically conducting connection between an ungrounded conductor of an electrical circuit and the normally noncurrent-carrying conductors, metallic enclosures, metallic raceways, metallic equipment, or the earth [Article 100]. During the period of a ground fault, dangerous voltages will be present on metal parts until the circuit overcurrent device opens.

Short Circuit. A short circuit is the unintentional electrical connection between any two normally current-carrying conductors of an electrical circuit, either line-to-line or line-to-neutral.

Overcurrent devices protect conductors and equipment. Selecting the proper overcurrent protection for a specific circuit can become more complicated than it sounds. The general rule for overcurrent protection is that conductors must be protected in accordance with their ampacities at the point where they receive their supply [240.4and 240.21]. There are many special cases that deviate from this basic rule, such as the overcurrent protection limitations for small conductors [240.4(D)] and the rules for specific conductor applications found in other articles, as listed in Table 240.4(G). There are also a number of rules allowing tap conductors in specific situations [240.21(B)]. Article 240 even has limits on where overcurrent devices are allowed to be located [240.24].

An overcurrent protection device must be capable of opening a circuit when an overcurrent situation occurs, and must also have an interrupting rating sufficient to avoid damage in fault conditions [110.9]. Carefully study the provisions of this article to be sure you provide sufficient overcurrent protection in the correct location.

QUESTIONS FOR ARTICLE 240—OVERCURRENT PROTECTION

1. Overcurrent protection for conductors and equipment is designed to _____ the circuit if the current reaches a value that will cause an excessive or dangerous temperature in conductors or conductor insulation.

    (a) open
    (b) close
    (c) monitor
    (d) record

2. A device that, when interrupting currents in its current-limiting range, reduces the current flowing in the faulted circuit to a magnitude substantially less than that obtainable in the same circuit if the device were replaced with a solid conductor having comparable impedance, is a(n) _____ protective device.

    (a) short-circuit
    (b) overload
    (c) ground-fault
    (d) current-limiting

3. Conductor overload protection shall not be required where the interruption of the _____ would create a hazard, such as in a material-handling magnet circuit or fire pump circuit. However, short-circuit protection is required.

   (a) circuit
   (b) line
   (c) phase
   (d) system

4. The next higher standard rating overcurrent device above the ampacity of the ungrounded conductors being protected shall be permitted to be used, provided all of the following conditions are met:

   (a) The conductors are not part of a branch circuit supplying more than one receptacle for cord-and-plug-connected portable loads.
   (b) The ampacity of the conductors doesn't correspond with the standard ampere rating of a fuse or circuit breaker.
   (c) The next higher standard rating selected doesn't exceed 800A.
   (d) all of these

5. If the circuit's overcurrent device exceeds _____, the conductor ampacity must have a rating not less than the rating of the overcurrent device.

   (a) 800A
   (b) 1,000A
   (c) 1,200A
   (d) 2,000A

6. Overcurrent protection shall not exceed _____.

   (a) 15A for 14 AWG copper
   (b) 20A for 12 AWG copper
   (c) 30A for 10 AWG copper
   (d) all of these

7. Flexible cords approved for and used with a specific listed appliance or luminaire shall be considered to be protected by the branch-circuit overcurrent device when _____.

   (a) not more than 6 ft in length
   (b) 20 AWG and larger
   (c) applied within the listing requirements
   (d) 16 AWG and larger

8. Flexible cord used in listed extension cord sets shall be considered protected against overcurrent when used _____.

   (a) in indoor installations
   (b) in unclassified locations
   (c) within the extension cord's listing requirements
   (d) within 50 ft of the branch-circuit panelboard

9. Which of the following is not standard size fuses or inverse time circuit breakers?

   (a) 45A
   (b) 70A
   (c) 75A
   (d) 80A

10. The standard ampere ratings for fuses includes _____.

   (a) 1A
   (b) 6A
   (c) 601A
   (d) all of these

11. Supplementary overcurrent protection _____.

   (a) shall not be used in luminaires
   (b) may be used as a substitute for a branch-circuit overcurrent device
   (c) may be used to protect internal circuits of equipment
   (d) shall be readily accessible

12. Supplementary overcurrent devices used in luminaires or appliances are not required to be readily accessible.

   (a) True
   (b) False

13. Ground-fault protection of equipment shall be provided for solidly grounded wye electrical systems of more than 150 volts-to-ground, but not exceeding 600V phase-to-phase for each individual device used as a building or structure main disconnecting means rated _____ or more, unless specifically exempted.

(a) 1,000A
(b) 1,500A
(c) 2,000A
(d) 2,500A

14. A(n) _____ shall be considered equivalent to an overcurrent trip unit for the purpose of providing overcurrent protection of conductors.

(a) current transformer
(b) overcurrent relay
(c) a and b
(d) a or b

15. Circuit breakers shall _____ all ungrounded conductors of the circuit both manually and automatically unless specifically permitted otherwise.

(a) open
(b) close
(c) isolate
(d) inhibit

16. Single-pole breakers with identified handle ties can be used to protect each ungrounded conductor for line-to-line connected loads.

(a) True
(b) False

17. Conductors supplied under the tap rules are allowed to supply another conductor using the tap rules.

(a) True
(b) False

18. Tap conductors not over 25 ft shall be permitted, providing the _____.

(a) ampacity of the tap conductors is not less than one-third the rating of the overcurrent device protecting the feeder conductors being tapped
(b) tap conductors terminate in a single circuit breaker or set of fuses that limit the load to the ampacity of the tap conductors
(c) tap conductors are suitably protected from physical damage
(d) all of these

19. The maximum length of a feeder tap conductor in a high-bay manufacturing building over 35 ft high shall be _____.

(a) 15 ft
(b) 20 ft
(c) 50 ft
(d) 100 ft

20. Outside feeder tap conductors can be of unlimited length without overcurrent protection at the point they receive their supply if:

(a) The tap conductors are suitably protected from physical damage.
(b) The tap conductors terminate at a single circuit breaker or a single set of fuses that limits the load to the ampacity of the conductors.
(c) a and b
(d) none of these

21. Outside secondary conductors can be of unlimited length without overcurrent protection at the point they receive their supply if:

(a) The conductors are suitably protected from physical damage.
(b) The conductors terminate at a single circuit breaker or a single set of fuses that limits the load to the ampacity of the conductors.
(c) a and b
(d) none of these

22. Overcurrent devices shall be _____.

    (a) accessible (as applied to wiring methods)
    (b) accessible (as applied to equipment)
    (c) readily accessible
    (d) inaccessible to unauthorized personnel

23. Overcurrent devices shall be readily accessible and installed so the center of the grip of the operating handle of the switch or circuit breaker, when in its highest position, is not more than _____ above the floor or working platform.

    (a) 2 ft
    (b) 4 ft 6 in.
    (c) 5 ft
    (d) 6 ft 7 in.

24. Overcurrent devices shall not be located _____.

    (a) where exposed to physical damage
    (b) near easily ignitible materials, such as in clothes closets
    (c) in bathrooms of dwelling units
    (d) all of these

25. Overcurrent devices aren't permitted to be located in the bathrooms of _____.

    (a) dwelling units
    (b) dormitories
    (c) guest rooms or guest suites of hotels or motels
    (d) all of these

26. _____ shall not be located over the steps of a stairway.

    (a) Disconnect switches
    (b) Overcurrent devices
    (c) Knife switches
    (d) Transformers

27. Enclosures for overcurrent devices shall be mounted in a _____ position unless impracticable.

    (a) vertical
    (b) horizontal
    (c) vertical or horizontal
    (d) there are no requirements

28. Handles or levers of circuit breakers, and similar parts that may move suddenly in such a way that persons in the vicinity are likely to be injured by being struck by them, shall be _____.

    (a) guarded
    (b) isolated
    (c) a and b
    (d) a or b

29. Plug fuses of 15A or less shall be identified by a(n) _____ configuration of the window, cap, or other prominent part to distinguish them from fuses of higher ampere ratings.

    (a) octagonal
    (b) rectangular
    (c) hexagonal
    (d) triangular

30. Plug fuses of the Edison-base type shall have a maximum rating of _____.

    (a) 20A
    (b) 30A
    (c) 40A
    (d) 50A

31. Plug fuses of the Edison-base type shall be used _____.

    (a) where overfusing is necessary
    (b) as a replacement in existing installations
    (c) as a replacement for Type S fuses
    (d) 50A and above

32. Edison-base fuseholders shall be used only if they are made to accept _____ fuses by the use of adapters.

   (a) Edison-base
   (b) medium-base
   (c) heavy-duty base
   (d) Type S

33. Which of the following statements about Type S fuses are true?

   (a) Adapters shall fit Edison-base fuseholders.
   (b) Adapters are designed to be easily removed.
   (c) Type S fuses shall be classified as not over 125V and 30A.
   (d) a and c

34. Type _____ fuse adapters shall be designed so that once inserted in a fuseholder they cannot be removed.

   (a) A
   (b) E
   (c) S
   (d) P

35. Type S fuses, fuseholders, and adapters shall be designed so that _____ would be difficult.

   (a) installation
   (b) tampering
   (c) shunting
   (d) b or c

36. Dimensions of Type S fuses, fuseholders, and adapters shall be standardized to permit interchangeability regardless of the _____.

   (a) model
   (b) manufacturer
   (c) amperage
   (d) voltage

37. Fuseholders for cartridge fuses shall be so designed that it is difficult to put a fuse of any given class into a fuseholder that is designed for a _____ lower or a _____ higher than that of the class to which the fuse belongs.

   (a) voltage, wattage
   (b) wattage, voltage
   (c) voltage, current
   (d) current, voltage

38. Fuses shall be marked with their _____.

   (a) ampere and voltage rating
   (b) interrupting rating where other than 10,000A
   (c) name or trademark of the manufacturer
   (d) all of these

39. An 800A fuse rated at 600V _____ on a 250V system.

   (a) shall not be used
   (b) shall be used
   (c) can be used
   (d) none of these

40. Cartridge fuses and fuseholders shall be classified according to their _____ ranges.

   (a) voltage
   (b) amperage
   (c) a or b
   (d) a and b

41. Circuit breakers shall be capable of being closed and opened by manual operation. Operation by other means, such as electrical or pneumatic, shall be permitted if means for _____ operation are also provided.

   (a) automated
   (b) timed
   (c) manual
   (d) shunt trip

42. Where the circuit breaker handles are operated vertically, the up position of the handle shall be the _____.

    (a) on position
    (b) off position
    (c) tripped position
    (d) any of these

43. A(n) _____ shall be of such design that any alteration of its trip point (calibration) or the time required for its operation requires dismantling of the device or breaking of a seal for other than intended adjustments.

    (a) Type S fuse
    (b) Edison-base fuse
    (c) circuit breaker
    (d) fuseholder

44. Circuit breakers shall be marked with their ampere rating in a manner that is durable and visible after installation. Such marking can be made visible by removal of a _____.

    (a) trim
    (b) cover
    (c) box
    (d) a or b

45. Circuit breakers rated at _____ amperes or less and _____ volts or less shall have the ampere rating molded, stamped, etched, or similarly marked into their handles or escutcheon areas.

    (a) 100, 600
    (b) 600, 100
    (c) 1,000, 6,000
    (d) 6,000, 1,000

46. A circuit breaker having an interrupting current rating of other than _____ shall have its interrupting rating marked on the circuit breaker.

    (a) 5,000A
    (b) 10,000A
    (c) 22,000A
    (d) 50,000A

47. Circuit breakers used to switch 120V or 277V fluorescent-lighting circuits shall be listed and marked _____.

    (a) UL
    (b) SWD or HID
    (c) Amps
    (d) VA

48. Circuit breakers used to switch high-intensity discharge lighting circuits shall be listed and marked as _____.

    (a) SWD
    (b) HID
    (c) a or b
    (d) a and b

49. A circuit breaker with a _____ voltage rating, such as 240V or 480V, can be used where the nominal voltage between any two conductors does not exceed the circuit breaker's voltage rating.

    (a) straight
    (b) slash
    (c) high
    (d) low

50. A circuit breaker with a _____ rating, such as 120/240V or 277/480V can be used on a solidly grounded circuit where the nominal voltage of any conductor to ground does not exceed the lower of the two values, and the nominal voltage between any two conductors does not exceed the higher value.

    (a) straight
    (b) slash
    (c) high
    (d) low

ARTICLE
250

Grounding and Bonding

INTRODUCTION TO ARTICLE 250—GROUNDING AND BONDING

No other article can match Article 250 for misapplication, violation, and misinterpretation. Terminology used in this article has been a source for much confusion, but that has improved during the last few *NEC* revisions. It's very important to understand the difference between grounding and bonding in order to correctly apply the provisions of Article 250. Pay careful attention to the definitions that apply to grounding and bonding both here and in Article 100 as you begin the study of this important article. Article 250 covers the grounding requirements for providing a path to the earth to reduce overvoltage from lightning, and the bonding requirements for a low-impedance fault current path back to the source of the electrical supply to facilitate the operation of overcurrent devices in the event of a ground fault.

Over the past five *Code* cycles, this article was extensively revised to organize it better and make it easier to understand and implement. It's arranged in a logical manner, so it's a good idea to just read through Article 250 to get a big picture view—after you review the definitions. Next, study the article closely so you understand the details. The illustrations in the textbook will help you understand the key points.

QUESTIONS FOR ARTICLE 250— GROUNDING AND BONDING

Part I. General

1. A conductor on the supply side of a service or within a service equipment enclosure or separately derived system to ensure the electrical conductivity between metal parts required to be electrically connected is know as the _____.

   (a) supply-side bonding jumper
   (b) ungrounded conductor
   (c) the electrical supply source
   (d) grounding electrode conductor

2. An effective ground-fault current path is an intentionally constructed, permanent, low-impedance path designed and intended to carry fault current from the point of a ground fault on a wiring system to _____.

   (a) ground
   (b) earth
   (c) the electrical supply source
   (d) none of these

3. A ground-fault current path is an electrically conductive path from the point of a ground fault through normally noncurrent-carrying conductors, equipment, or the earth to the _____.

   (a) ground
   (b) earth
   (c) electrical supply source
   (d) none of these

4. Examples of ground-fault current paths include any combination of conductive materials including _____.

   (a) equipment grounding conductors
   (b) metallic raceways
   (c) metal water and gas piping
   (d) all of these

5. Grounded electrical systems shall be connected to earth in a manner that will _____.

   (a) limit voltages due to lightning, line surges, or unintentional contact with higher-voltage lines
   (b) stabilize the voltage-to-ground during normal operation
   (c) facilitate overcurrent device operation in case of ground faults
   (d) a and b

6. An important consideration for limiting imposed voltage on electrical systems is to remember that bonding and grounding electrode conductors shouldn't be any longer than necessary and unnecessary bends and loops should be avoided.

   (a) True
   (b) False

7. For grounded systems, normally noncurrent-carrying conductive materials enclosing electrical conductors or equipment shall be connected to earth so as to limit the voltage-to-ground on these materials.

   (a) True
   (b) False

8. For grounded systems, noncurrent-carrying conductive materials enclosing electrical conductors or equipment, or forming part of such equipment, shall be connected together and to the _____ to establish an effective ground-fault current path.

   (a) ground
   (b) earth
   (c) electrical supply source
   (d) none of these

9. In grounded systems, normally noncurrent-carrying electrically conductive materials that are likely to become energized shall be _____ in a manner that establishes an effective ground-fault current path.

   (a) connected together
   (b) connected to the electrical supply source
   (c) connected to the closest grounded conductor
   (d) a and b

10. For grounded systems, electrical equipment and conductive material likely to become energized, shall be installed in a manner that creates a _____ from any point on the wiring system where a ground fault may occur to the electrical supply source.

    (a) circuit facilitating the operation of the overcurrent device
    (b) low-impedance path
    (c) path capable of safely carrying the ground-fault current likely to be imposed on it
    (d) all of these

11. For grounded systems, electrical equipment and electrically conductive material likely to become energized, shall be installed in a manner that creates a low-impedance circuit capable of safely carrying the maximum ground-fault current likely to be imposed on it from where a ground fault may occur to the _____.

    (a) ground
    (b) earth
    (c) electrical supply source
    (d) none of these

12. For grounded systems, the earth is considered an effective ground-fault current path.

    (a) True
    (b) False

13. For ungrounded systems, noncurrent-carrying conductive materials enclosing electrical conductors or equipment shall be connected to the _____ in a manner that will limit the voltage imposed by lightning or unintentional contact with higher-voltage lines.

    (a) ground
    (b) earth
    (c) electrical supply source
    (d) none of these

14. For ungrounded systems, noncurrent-carrying conductive materials enclosing electrical conductors or equipment, or forming part of such equipment, shall be connected together and to the supply system equipment in a manner that creates a low-impedance path for ground-fault current that is capable of carrying _____.

    (a) the maximum branch-circuit current
    (b) at least twice the maximum ground-fault current
    (c) the maximum fault current likely to be imposed on it
    (d) the equivalent to the main service rating

15. Electrically conductive materials that are likely to _____ in ungrounded systems shall be connected together and to the supply system grounded equipment in a manner that creates a low-impedance path for ground-fault current that is capable of carrying the maximum fault current likely to be imposed on it.

    (a) become energized
    (b) require service
    (c) be removed
    (d) be coated with paint or nonconductive materials

16. In ungrounded systems, electrical equipment, wiring, and other electrically conductive material likely to become energized shall be installed in a manner that creates a low-impedance circuit from any point on the wiring system to the electrical supply source to facilitate the operation of overcurrent devices should a(n) _____ fault from a different phase occur on the wiring system.

    (a) isolated ground
    (b) second ground
    (c) arc
    (d) high impedance

17. The grounding of electrical systems, circuit conductors, surge arresters, surge protective devices, and conductive normally noncurrent-carrying metal parts of equipment shall be installed and arranged in a manner that will prevent objectionable current.

    (a) True
    (b) False

18. Temporary currents resulting from abnormal conditions, such as ground faults, are not considered to be objectionable currents.

    (a) True
    (b) False

19. Currents that introduce noise or data errors in electronic equipment are considered objectionable currents in the context of 250.6(D) of the *NEC*.

    (a) True
    (b) False

20. Equipment grounding conductors, grounding electrode conductors, and bonding jumpers shall be connected by _____.

    (a) listed pressure connectors
    (b) terminal bars
    (c) exothermic welding
    (d) any of these

21. Grounding and bonding connection devices shall not depend solely on _____.

    (a) pressure connections
    (b) solder
    (c) lugs
    (d) approved clamps

22. Ground clamps and fittings shall be protected from physical damage by being enclosed in _____ where there may be a possibility of physical damage.

    (a) metal
    (b) wood
    (c) the equivalent of a or b
    (d) none of these

23. _____ on equipment to be grounded shall be removed from contact surfaces to ensure good electrical continuity.

    (a) Paint
    (b) Lacquer
    (c) Enamel
    (d) any of these

Part II. System Grounding

1. Alternating-current circuits of less than 50V shall be grounded if supplied by a transformer whose supply system exceeds 150 volts-to-ground.

    (a) True
    (b) False

2.   Alternating-current systems of 50V to 1,000V that supply premises wiring systems shall be grounded where the system is three-phase, 4-wire, wye connected with the neutral conductor used as a circuit conductor.

(a) True
(b) False

3.   Alternating-current systems of 50V to 1,000V that supply premises wiring systems shall be grounded where supplied by a three-phase, 4-wire, delta-connected system in which the midpoint of one phase winding is used as a circuit conductor.

(a) True
(b) False

4.   _____ alternating-current systems operating at 480V shall have ground detectors installed on the system.

(a) Grounded
(b) Solidly grounded
(c) Effectively grounded
(d) Ungrounded

5.   Alternating-current systems from 50V to less than 1,000V that aren't required to be grounded as per 250.20(B) must have _____.

(a) ground detectors installed
(b) the ground detection sensing equipment connected as close as practicable to where the system receives its supply
(c) a and b
(d) ground fault protection for equipment

6.   Alternating-current systems from 50V to less than 1,000V that are ungrounded systems must be legibly marked Ungrounded System at _____ of the system, with sufficient durability to withstand the environment involved.

(a) the source
(b) the first disconnecting means
(c) every junction box
(d) a or b

7.   The grounding electrode conductor shall be connected to the grounded service conductor at the _____.

(a) load end of the service drop
(b) load end of the service lateral
(c) service disconnecting means
(d) any of these

8.   Where the main bonding jumper is installed from the grounded conductor terminal bar to the equipment grounding terminal bar in service equipment, the _____ conductor is permitted to be connected to the equipment grounding terminal bar.

(a) grounding
(b) grounded
(c) grounding electrode
(d) none of these

9.   For a grounded system, an unspliced _____ shall be used to connect the equipment grounding conductor(s) and the service disconnecting means to the grounded conductor of the system within the enclosure for each service disconnect.

(a) grounding electrode
(b) main bonding jumper
(c) busbar
(d) insulated copper conductor

10.   Where an alternating-current system operating at less than 1,000V is grounded at any point, the _____ conductor(s) shall be routed with the ungrounded conductors to each service disconnecting means and shall be connected to each disconnecting means grounded conductor(s) terminal or bus.

(a) ungrounded
(b) grounded
(c) grounding
(d) none of these

11. The grounded conductor of an alternating-current system operating at less than 1,000V shall be routed with the ungrounded conductors and connected to each disconnecting means grounded conductor terminal or bus, which is then connected to the service disconnecting means enclosure via a(n) _____ that's installed between the service neutral conductor and the service disconnecting means enclosure.

    (a) equipment bonding conductor
    (b) main bonding jumper
    (c) grounding electrode
    (d) intersystem bonding terminal

12. The grounded conductor brought to service equipment shall be routed with the phase conductors and shall not be smaller than specified in Table _____ when the service-entrance conductors are 1,100 kcmil copper and smaller.

    (a) 250.66
    (b) 250.122
    (c) 310.16
    (d) 430.52

13. When service-entrance conductors exceed 1,100 kcmil for copper, the required grounded conductor for the service shall be sized not less than _____ percent of the circular mil area of the largest set of ungrounded service-entrance conductor(s).

    (a) 9
    (b) 11
    (c) 12½
    (d) 15

14. Where service-entrance phase conductors are installed in parallel in two or more raceways, the size of the grounded conductor in each raceway shall be based on the total circular mil area of the parallel ungrounded service-entrance conductor in the raceway, sized per 250.24(C)(1), but not smaller than _____.

    (a) 1/0 AWG
    (b) 2/0 AWG
    (c) 3/0 AWG
    (d) 4/0 AWG

15. A grounding electrode conductor, sized in accordance with 250.66, shall be used to connect the equipment grounding conductors, the service-equipment enclosures, and, where the system is grounded, the grounded service conductor to the grounding electrode(s).

    (a) True
    (b) False

16. A main bonding jumper shall be a _____ or similar suitable conductor.

    (a) wire
    (b) bus
    (c) screw
    (d) any of these

17. Where a main bonding jumper is a screw only, the screw shall be identified by a(n) _____ that shall be visible with the screw installed.

    (a) silver or white finish
    (b) etched ground symbol
    (c) hexagonal head
    (d) green finish

18. Main bonding jumpers and system bonding jumpers shall not be smaller than the sizes shown in _____.

    (a) Table 250.66
    (b) Table 250.122
    (c) Table 310.15(B)(16)
    (d) Chapter 9, Table 8

19. Where the supply conductors are larger than 1,100 kcmil copper or 1,750 kcmil aluminum, the main bonding jumper shall have an area that is _____ the area of the largest phase conductor when of the same material.

    (a) at least equal to
    (b) at least 50 percent of
    (c) not less than 12½ percent of
    (d) not more than 12½ percent of

20. A grounded conductor shall not be connected to normally noncurrent-carrying metal parts of equipment on the _____ side of the system bonding jumper of a separately derived system except as otherwise permitted in Article 250.

    (a) supply
    (b) grounded
    (c) high-voltage
    (d) load

21. An unspliced _____ that is sized based on the derived phase conductors shall be used to connect the grounded conductor and the supply-side bonding jumper, or the equipment grounding conductor, or both, at a separately derived system.

    (a) system bonding jumper
    (b) equipment grounding conductor
    (c) grounded conductor
    (d) grounding electrode conductor

22. The connection of the system bonding jumper for a separately derived system shall be made _____ on the separately derived system from the source to the first system disconnecting means or overcurrent device.

    (a) in at least two locations
    (b) in every location that the grounded conductor is present
    (c) at any single point
    (d) none of these

23. Where an supply side bonding jumper of the wire type is run with the derived phase conductors from the source of a separately derived system to the first disconnecting means, it shall be sized in accordance with 250.102(C), based on _____.

    (a) the size of the primary conductors
    (b) the size of the secondary overcurrent protection
    (c) the size of the derived phase conductors
    (d) one third the size of the primary grounded conductor

24. The grounding electrode for a separately derived system shall be as near as practicable to, and preferably in the same area as, the grounding electrode conductor connection to the system.

    (a) True
    (b) False

25. For a single separately derived system, the grounding electrode conductor connects the grounded conductor of the derived system to the grounding electrode at the same point on the separately derived system where the _____ is connected.

    (a) metering equipment
    (b) transfer switch
    (c) system bonding jumper
    (d) largest circuit breaker

26. The grounding electrode conductor for a single separately derived system is used to connect the grounded conductor of the derived system to the grounding electrode.

    (a) True
    (b) False

27. Grounding electrode conductor taps from a separately derived system to a common grounding electrode conductor are permitted when a building or structure has multiple separately derived systems, provided that the taps terminate at the same point as the system bonding jumper.

    (a) True
    (b) False

28. The common grounding electrode conductor installed for multiple separately derived systems shall not be smaller than _____ copper when using a wire-type conductor.

    (a) 1/0 AWG
    (b) 2/0 AWG
    (c) 3/0 AWG
    (d) 4/0 AWG

29. Each tap conductor to a common grounding electrode conductor for multiple separately derived systems shall be sized in accordance with _____, based on the derived phase conductors of the separately derived system it serves.

    (a) 250.66
    (b) 250.118
    (c) 250.122
    (d) 310.15

30. Tap connections to a common grounding electrode conductor for multiple separately derived systems shall be made at an accessible location by _____.

    (a) a connector listed as grounding and bonding equipment
    (b) listed connections to aluminum or copper busbars
    (c) by the exothermic welding process
    (d) any of these

31. Tap connections to a common grounding electrode conductor for multiple separately derived systems may be made to a copper or aluminum busbar that is _____.

    (a) not over ½ in. x 4 in.
    (b) not over ¼ in. x 2 in.
    (c) at least ¼ in. x 2 in.
    (d) a and c

32. In an area served by a separately derived system, the _____ shall be connected to the grounded conductor of the separately derived system.

    (a) structural steel
    (b) metal piping
    (c) metal building skin
    (d) a and b

33. A grounding electrode shall be required if a building or structure is supplied by a feeder.

    (a) True
    (b) False

34. A grounding electrode at a separate building or structure shall be required where one multiwire branch circuit serves the building or structure.

    (a) True
    (b) False

35. When supplying a grounded system at a separate building or structure, an equipment grounding conductor shall be run with the supply conductors and connected to the building or structure disconnecting means.

    (a) True
    (b) False

36. For a separate building or structure supplied by a feeder or branch circuit, the neutral conductor can serve as the ground-fault return path for the building/structure disconnecting means for existing installations made in compliance with previous editions of the *Code* as long as the installation continues to meet the condition(s) that _____.

    (a) there are no continuous metallic paths between buildings and structures
    (b) ground-fault protection of equipment isn't installed on the supply side of the feeder
    (c) the neutral conductor is sized no smaller than the larger required by 220.61 or 250.122
    (d) all of these

37. For a separate building or structure supplied by a separately derived system when overcurrent protection is provided where the conductors originate, the supply conductors must contain a(n) _____.

    (a) equipment grounding conductor
    (b) copper conductors only
    (c) GFI protection for the feeder
    (d) all of these

38. For a separate building or structure supplied by a separately derived system when overcurrent protection isn't provided for the supply conductors to the building/structure as permitted by 240.21(C)(4), the installation must be _____ in accordance with 250.30(A).

    (a) AFCI protected
    (b) grounded and bonded
    (c) isolated
    (d) all of these

39. The size of the grounding electrode conductor for a building or structure supplied by a feeder shall not be smaller than that identified in _____, based on the largest ungrounded supply conductor.

    (a) 250.66
    (b) 250.122
    (c) Table 310.15(B)(16)
    (d) none of these

40. The frame of a portable generator shall not be required to be connected to a(n) _____ if the generator only supplies equipment mounted on the generator or cord-and-plug connected equipment using receptacles mounted on the generator.

    (a) grounding electrode
    (b) grounded conductor
    (c) ungrounded conductor
    (d) equipment grounding conductor

41. The frame of a vehicle-mounted generator shall not be required to be connected to a(n) _____ if the generator only supplies equipment mounted on the vehicle or cord-and-plug connected equipment, using receptacles mounted on the vehicle.

    (a) grounding electrode
    (b) grounded conductor
    (c) ungrounded conductor
    (d) equipment grounding conductor

42. When a permanently installed generator _____, the requirements of 250.30 apply.

    (a) is a separately derived system
    (b) is not a separately derived system
    (c) supplies only cord and plug connected loads
    (d) none of these

43. High-impedance grounded neutral systems shall be permitted for three-phase ac systems of 480 volts to 1,000 volts where _____.

    (a) the conditions of maintenance ensure that only qualified persons service the installation
    (b) ground detectors are installed on the system
    (c) line-to-neutral loads are not served
    (d) all of these

Part III. Grounding Electrode System and Grounding Electrode Conductor

1. Concrete-encased electrodes of _____ shall not be required to be part of the grounding electrode system where the steel reinforcing bars or rods aren't accessible for use without disturbing the concrete.

    (a) hazardous (classified) locations
    (b) health care facilities
    (c) existing buildings or structures
    (d) agricultural buildings with equipotential planes

2. In order for a metal underground water pipe to be used as a grounding electrode, it shall be in direct contact with the earth for _____.

    (a) 5 ft
    (b) 10 ft or more
    (c) less than 10 ft
    (d) 20 ft or more

3. The metal frame of a building shall be considered a grounding electrode where one of the *NEC*-prescribed methods for connection of the metal frame to earth has been met:

    (a) True
    (b) False

4. A bare 4 AWG copper conductor installed horizontally near the bottom or vertically, and within that portion of a concrete foundation or footing that is in direct contact with the earth can be used as a grounding electrode when the conductor is at least _____ in length.

    (a) 10 ft
    (b) 15 ft
    (c) 20 ft
    (d) 25 ft

5. An electrode encased by at least 2 in. of concrete, located horizontally near the bottom or vertically and within that portion of a concrete foundation or footing that is in direct contact with the earth, shall be permitted as a grounding electrode when it consists of _____.

    (a) at least 20 ft of ½ in. or larger steel reinforcing bars or rods
    (b) at least 20 ft of bare copper conductor of 4 AWG or larger
    (c) a or b
    (d) none of these

6. Reinforcing bars for use as a concrete-encased electrode can be bonded together by the usual steel tie wires or other effective means.

    (a) True
    (b) False

7. Where more than one concrete-encased electrode is present at a building or structure, it shall be permitted to connect to only one of them.

    (a) True
    (b) False

8. A ground ring encircling the building or structure can be used as a grounding electrode when _____.

    (a) the ring is in direct contact with the earth
    (b) the ring consists of at least 20 ft of bare conductor
    (c) the bare copper conductor is not smaller than 2 AWG
    (d) all of these

9. Grounding electrodes that are driven rods require a minimum of _____ in contact with the soil.

    (a) 6 ft
    (b) 8 ft
    (c) 10 ft
    (d) 12 ft

10. Grounding electrodes of the rod type less than _____ in. in diameter shall be listed.

    (a) ½ in.
    (b) 5/8 in.
    (c) ¾ in.
    (d) none of these

11. A buried iron or steel plate used as a grounding electrode shall expose not less than _____ of surface area to exterior soil.

    (a) 2 sq ft
    (b) 4 sq ft
    (c) 9 sq ft
    (d) 10 sq ft

12. Local metal underground systems or structures such as _____ are permitted to serve as grounding electrodes.

    (a) piping systems
    (b) underground tanks
    (c) underground metal well casings
    (d) all of these

13. _____ shall not be used as grounding electrodes.

    (a) Underground gas piping systems
    (b) Aluminum
    (c) Metal well casings
    (d) a and b

14. Where practicable, rod, pipe, and plate electrodes shall be installed _____.

    (a) directly below the electrical meter
    (b) on the north side of the building
    (c) below permanent moisture level
    (d) all of these

15. Where the resistance-to-ground of 25 ohms or less is not achieved for a single rod electrode, _____.

    (a) other means besides electrodes shall be used in order to provide grounding
    (b) the single rod electrode shall be supplemented by one additional electrode
    (c) no additional electrodes are required
    (d) none of these

16. Two or more grounding electrodes bonded together are considered a single grounding electrode system.

    (a) True
    (b) False

17. Where a metal underground water pipe is used as a grounding electrode, the continuity of the grounding path or the bonding connection to interior piping shall not rely on _____ and similar equipment.

    (a) bonding jumpers
    (b) water meters or filtering devices
    (c) grounding clamps
    (d) all of these

18. Where the supplemental electrode is a rod, that portion of the bonding jumper that is the sole connection to the supplemental grounding electrode shall not be required to be larger than _____ AWG copper.

    (a) 8
    (b) 6
    (c) 4
    (d) 1

19. When a ground ring is used as a grounding electrode, it shall be buried at a depth below the earth's surface of not less than _____.

    (a) 18 in.
    (b) 24 in.
    (c) 30 in.
    (d) 8 ft

20. Ground rod electrodes shall be installed so that at least _____ of the length is in contact with the soil.

    (a) 5 ft
    (b) 8 ft
    (c) one-half
    (d) 80 percent

21. The upper end of a ground rod electrode shall be _____ ground level unless the aboveground end and the grounding electrode conductor attachment are protected against physical damage.

    (a) above
    (b) flush with
    (c) below
    (d) b or c

22. Where rock bottom is encountered when driving a ground rod at an angle up to 45 degrees, the electrode can be buried in a trench that is at least _____ deep.

    (a) 18 in.
    (b) 30 in.
    (c) 4 ft
    (d) 8 ft

23. Auxiliary grounding electrodes can be connected to the _____.

    (a) equipment grounding conductor
    (b) grounded conductor
    (c) a and b
    (d) none of these

24. When installing auxiliary electrodes, the earth shall not be used as an effective ground-fault current path.

    (a) True
    (b) False

25. Buildings or structures supplied by multiple services or feeders must use the same _____ to ground enclosures and equipment in or on that building.

    (a) service
    (b) disconnect
    (c) grounding electrode system
    (d) any of these

26. The grounding electrode used for grounding strike termination devices of a lightning protection system can be used as a grounding electrode system for the buildings or structures.

    (a) True
    (b) False

27. Grounding electrode conductors shall be made of _____ wire.

    (a) solid
    (b) stranded
    (c) insulated or bare
    (d) any of these

28. Where used outside, aluminum or copper-clad aluminum grounding electrode conductors shall not be terminated within _____ of the earth.

    (a) 6 in.
    (b) 12 in.
    (c) 15 in.
    (d) 18 in.

29. Bare aluminum or copper-clad aluminum grounding electrode conductors shall not be used where in direct contact with _____ or where subject to corrosive conditions.

    (a) masonry or the earth
    (b) bare copper conductors
    (c) wooden framing members
    (d) all of these

30. Grounding electrode conductors _____ and larger that are not subject to physical damage can be run exposed along the surface of the building construction if it is securely fastened to the construction.

    (a) 10 AWG
    (b) 8 AWG
    (c) 6 AWG
    (d) 4 AWG

31. Grounding electrode conductors smaller than _____ shall be in rigid metal conduit, IMC, PVC conduit, electrical metallic tubing, or cable armor.

    (a) 10 AWG
    (b) 8 AWG
    (c) 6 AWG
    (d) 4 AWG

32. Grounding electrode conductors shall be installed in one continuous length without a splice or joint, unless spliced _____.

    (a) by connecting together sections of a busbar
    (b) by irreversible compression-type connectors listed as grounding and bonding equipment
    (c) by the exothermic welding process
    (d) any of these

33. Where service equipment consists of more than one enclosure, grounding electrode connections shall be permitted to be _____.

    (a) multiple individual grounding electrode conductors
    (b) one grounding electrode conductor at a common location
    (c) common grounding electrode conductor and taps.
    (d) any of these

34. Ferrous metal enclosures for grounding electrode conductors shall be electrically continuous, from the point of attachment to cabinets or equipment, to the grounding electrode.

    (a) True
    (b) False

35. A grounding electrode conductor shall be permitted to be run to any convenient grounding electrode available in the grounding electrode system where the other electrodes, if any, are connected by bonding jumpers per 250.53(C).

(a) True
(b) False

36. A service consisting of 12 AWG service-entrance conductors requires a grounding electrode conductor sized no less than _____.

(a) 10 AWG
(b) 8 AWG
(c) 6 AWG
(d) 4 AWG

37. The largest size grounding electrode conductor required is _____ copper.

(a) 6 AWG
(b) 1/0 AWG
(c) 3/0 AWG
(d) 250 kcmil

38. What size copper grounding electrode conductor is required for a service that has three sets of 600 kcmil copper conductors per phase?

(a) 1 AWG
(b) 1/0 AWG
(c) 2/0 AWG
(d) 3/0 AWG

39. In an ac system, the size of the grounding electrode conductor to a concrete-encased electrode shall not be required to be larger than a(n) _____ copper conductor.

(a) 10 AWG
(b) 8 AWG
(c) 6 AWG
(d) 4 AWG

40. Mechanical elements used to terminate a grounding electrode conductor to a grounding electrode shall be accessible.

(a) True
(b) False

41. An encased or buried connection to a concrete-encased, driven, or buried grounding electrode shall be accessible.

(a) True
(b) False

42. The connection of the grounding electrode conductor to a buried grounding electrode (driven ground rod) shall be made with a listed terminal device that is accessible.

(a) True
(b) False

43. Exothermic or irreversible compression connections, together with the mechanical means used to attach to fireproofed structural metal, shall not be required to be accessible.

(a) True
(b) False

44. When an underground metal water piping system is used as a grounding electrode, bonding shall be provided around insulated joints and around any equipment that is likely to be disconnected for repairs or replacement.

(a) True
(b) False

45. Interior metal water piping located not more than _____ from the point of entrance to the building shall be permitted to be used as a conductor to interconnect electrodes that are part of the grounding electrode system.

(a) 2 ft
(b) 4 ft
(c) 5 ft
(d) 6 ft

46. Where conditions of maintenance and supervision ensure only qualified persons service the installation in _____ buildings, the entire length of the metal water piping system can be used for grounding purposes, provided the entire length, other than short sections passing through walls, floors, or ceilings, is exposed.

    (a) industrial
    (b) institutional
    (c) commercial
    (d) all of these

47. Grounding electrode conductors and grounding electrode bonding jumpers are permitted to terminate to the metal frame of a building/structure that's in direct contact with the earth for 10 ft or more [250.52(A)(2)] or connected to _____.

    (a) a concrete-encased electrode or ground ring
    (b) a ground rod
    (c) other approved earth connection
    (d) any of these

48. The grounding conductor connection to the grounding electrode shall be made by _____.

    (a) listed lugs
    (b) exothermic welding
    (c) listed pressure connectors
    (d) any of these

Part IV. Enclosure, Raceway, and Service Cable Connections

1. Metal enclosures and raceways containing service conductors shall be connected to the grounded system conductor if the electrical system is grounded.

    (a) True
    (b) False

2. Metal enclosures and raceways for other than service conductors shall be connected to the neutral conductor.

    (a) True
    (b) False

3. Short sections of metal enclosures or raceways used to provide support or protection of _____ from physical damage shall not be required to be connected to the equipment grounding conductor.

    (a) conduit
    (b) feeders under 600V
    (c) cable assemblies
    (d) none of these

Part V. Bonding

1. Bonding shall be provided where necessary to ensure _____ and the capacity to conduct safely any fault current likely to be imposed.

    (a) electrical continuity
    (b) fiduciary responsibility
    (c) listing requirements
    (d) electrical demand

2. The noncurrent-carrying metal parts of service equipment, such as _____, shall be bonded together.

    (a) service raceways or service cable armor
    (b) service equipment enclosures containing service conductors, including meter fittings, boxes, or the like, interposed in the service raceway or armor
    (c) service cable trays
    (d) all of these

3. Bonding jumpers for service raceways shall be used around impaired connections such as _____.

    (a) concentric knockouts
    (b) eccentric knockouts
    (c) reducing washers
    (d) any of these

4. Electrical continuity at service equipment, service raceways, and service conductor enclosures shall be ensured by _____.

   (a) bonding equipment to the grounded service conductor
   (b) connections utilizing threaded couplings on enclosures, if made up wrenchtight
   (c) by listed bonding devices, such as bonding-type locknuts, bushings, or bushings with bonding jumpers
   (d) any of these

5. Service raceways threaded into metal service equipment such as bosses (hubs) are considered to be effectively _____ to the service metal enclosure.

   (a) attached
   (b) bonded
   (c) grounded
   (d) none of these

6. Service metal raceways and metal-clad cables are considered effectively bonded when using threadless couplings and connectors that are _____.

   (a) nonmetallic
   (b) made up tight
   (c) sealed
   (d) classified

7. A means external to enclosures for connecting intersystem _____ conductors shall be provided at service equipment or metering equipment enclosure and disconnecting means of buildings or structures supplied by a feeder.

   (a) bonding
   (b) ungrounded
   (c) secondary
   (d) a and b

8. The intersystem bonding termination shall _____.

   (a) be accessible for connection and inspection
   (b) consist of a set of terminals with the capacity for connection of not less than three intersystem bonding conductors
   (c) not interfere with opening the enclosure for a service, building/structure disconnecting means, or metering equipment
   (d) all of these

9. The intersystem bonding termination shall _____.

   (a) be securely mounted and electrically connected to service equipment, the meter enclosure, or exposed nonflexible metallic service raceway, or be mounted at one of these enclosures and be connected to the enclosure or grounding electrode conductor with a minimum 6 AWG copper conductor
   (b) be securely mounted to the building/structure disconnecting means, or be mounted at the disconnecting means and be connected to the metallic enclosure or grounding electrode conductor with a minimum 6 AWG copper conductor
   (c) have terminals that are listed as grounding and bonding equipment
   (d) all of these

10. At existing buildings or structures, an intersystem bonding termination is not required if other acceptable means of bonding exits. An external accessible means for bonding communications systems together can be by the use of _____.

    (a) nonflexible metallic raceway
    (b) an exposed grounding electrode conductor
    (c) a connection to grounded raceway or equipment approved by the authority having jurisdiction
    (d) any of these

11. When bonding enclosures, metal raceways, frames, and fittings, any nonconductive paint, enamel, or similar coating shall be removed at _____.

    (a) contact surfaces
    (b) threads
    (c) contact points
    (d) all of these

12. Where installed to reduce electrical noise for electronic equipment, a metal raceway can terminate to a(n) _____ nonmetallic fitting(s) or spacer on the electronic equipment. The metal raceway shall be supplemented by an internal insulated equipment grounding conductor.

(a) listed
(b) labeled
(c) identified
(d) marked

13. For circuits over 250 volts-to-ground, electrical continuity can be maintained between a box or enclosure where no over-sized, concentric or eccentric knockouts are encountered, and a metal conduit by _____.

(a) threadless fittings for cables with metal sheath
(b) double locknuts on threaded conduit (one inside and one outside the box or enclosure)
(c) fittings that have shoulders that seat firmly against the box with a locknut on the inside or listed fittings
(d) all of these

14. Equipment bonding jumpers shall be of copper or other corrosion-resistant material.

(a) True
(b) False

15. Equipment bonding jumpers on the supply side of the service shall be no smaller than the sizes shown in _____.

(a) Table 250.66
(b) Table 250.122
(c) Table 310.15(B)(16)
(d) Table 310.15(B)(6)

16. The supply side bonding jumper on the supply side of services shall be sized according to the _____.

(a) overcurrent device rating
(b) ungrounded supply conductor size
(c) service-drop size
(d) load to be served

17. What is the minimum size copper supply side bonding jumper for a service raceway containing 4/0 THHN aluminum conductors?

(a) 6 AWG aluminum
(b) 4 AWG aluminum
(c) 4 AWG copper
(d) 3 AWG copper

18. Where ungrounded supply conductors are paralleled in two or more raceways or cables, the bonding jumper for each raceway or cable shall be based on the size of the _____ in each raceway or cable.

(a) overcurrent protection for conductors
(b) grounded conductors
(c) ungrounded supply conductors
(d) sum of all conductors

19. A service is supplied by three metal raceways, each containing 600 kcmil ungrounded conductors. Determine the copper supply side bonding jumper size for each service raceway.

(a) 1/0 AWG
(b) 3/0 AWG
(c) 250 kcmil
(d) 500 kcmil

20. What is the minimum size copper equipment bonding jumper for a 40A rated circuit?

(a) 14 AWG
(b) 12 AWG
(c) 10 AWG
(d) 8 AWG

21. An equipment bonding jumper can be installed on the outside of a raceway, providing the length of the equipment bonding jumper is not more than _____ and the equipment bonding jumper is routed with the raceway.

(a) 12 in.
(b) 24 in.
(c) 36 in.
(d) 72 in.

22. Metal water piping system(s) shall be bonded to the _____.

    (a) grounded conductor at the service
    (b) service equipment enclosure
    (c) equipment grounding bar or bus at any panelboard within a single occupancy building
    (d) a or b

23. The bonding jumper used to bond the metal water piping system shall be sized in accordance with _____.

    (a) Table 250.66
    (b) Table 250.122
    (c) Table 310.15(B)(16)
    (d) Table 310.15(B)(6)

24. Where isolated metal water piping systems are installed in a multiple-occupancy building, the water pipes can be bonded with bonding jumpers sized according to Table 250.122, based on the size of the _____.

    (a) service-entrance conductors
    (b) feeder conductors
    (c) rating of the service equipment overcurrent device
    (d) rating of the overcurrent device supplying the occupancy

25. A building or structure that is supplied by a feeder shall have the interior metal water piping system bonded with a conductor sized in accordance with _____.

    (a) Table 250.66
    (b) Table 250.122
    (c) Table 310.15(B)(16)
    (d) none of these

26. Metal gas piping shall be considered bonded by the equipment grounding conductor of the circuit that is likely to energize the piping.

    (a) True
    (b) False

27. Exposed structural metal interconnected to form a metal building frame that is not intentionally grounded and is likely to become energized, shall be bonded to the _____.

    (a) service equipment enclosure or building disconnecting means
    (b) grounded conductor at the service
    (c) grounding electrode conductor where of sufficient size
    (d) any of these

28. Lightning protection system ground terminals _____ be bonded to the building grounding electrode system.

    (a) shall
    (b) shall not
    (c) shall be permitted to
    (d) none of these

Part VI. Equipment Grounding and Equipment Grounding Conductors

1. Exposed noncurrent-carrying metal parts of fixed equipment likely to become energized shall be connected to the equipment conductor where located _____.

    (a) within 8 ft vertically or 5 ft horizontally of ground or grounded metal objects and subject to contact by persons
    (b) in wet or damp locations and not isolated
    (c) in electrical contact with metal
    (d) any of these

2. Electrical equipment permanently mounted on skids, and the skids themselves, shall be connected to the equipment grounding conductor sized as required by _____.

    (a) 250.50
    (b) 250.66
    (c) 250.122
    (d) 310.15

3.   Which of the following appliances installed in residential occupancies need not be connected to an equipment grounding conductor?

(a) toaster
(b) aquarium
(c) dishwasher
(d) refrigerator

4.   Listed FMC can be used as the equipment grounding conductor if the length in any ground return path does not exceed 6 ft and the circuit conductors contained in the conduit are protected by overcurrent devices rated at _____ or less.

(a) 15A
(b) 20A
(c) 30A
(d) 60A

5.   Listed FMC and LFMC shall contain an equipment grounding conductor if the raceway is installed for the reason of _____.

(a) physical protection
(b) flexibility after installation
(c) minimizing transmission of vibration from equipment
(d) b or c

6.   The *Code* requires the installation of an equipment grounding conductor of the wire type in _____.

(a) Rigid metal conduit (RMC).
(b) Intermediate metal conduit (IMC).
(c) Electrical metallic tubing (EMT).
(d) Listed flexible metal conduit over 6 ft in length

7.   Listed liquidtight flexible metal conduit (LFMC) is acceptable as an equipment grounding conductor when it terminates in listed fittings and is protected by an overcurrent device rated 60A or less for sizes ⅜ in. through ½ in.

(a) True
(b) False

8.   The armor of Type AC cable containing an aluminum bonding strip is recognized by the *NEC* as an equipment grounding conductor.

(a) True
(b) False

9.   Type MC cable provides an effective ground-fault current path and is recognized by the *NEC* as an equipment grounding conductor when _____.

(a) It contains an insulated or uninsulated equipment grounding conductor in compliance with 250.118(1)
(b) the combined metallic sheath and uninsulated equipment grounding/bonding conductor of interlocked metal tape–type MC cable is listed and identified as an equipment grounding conductor
(c) a or b
(d) only when it is hospital grade Type MC cable

10. An equipment grounding conductor shall be identified by _____.

(a) a continuous outer finish that is green
(b) being bare
(c) a continuous outer finish that is green with one or more yellow stripes
(d) any of these

11. Conductors with the color _____ insulation shall not be used for ungrounded or grounded conductors.

(a) green
(b) green with one or more yellow stripes
(c) a or b
(d) white

12. An equipment grounding conductor is permitted to be used as a grounding electrode conductor.

(a) True
(b) False

13. The equipment grounding conductor shall not be required to be larger than the circuit conductors.

    (a) True
    (b) False

14. When ungrounded circuit conductors are increased in size, the equipment grounding conductor must be proportionately increased in size according to the _____ of the ungrounded conductors.

    (a) ampacity
    (b) circular mil area
    (c) diameter
    (d) none of these

15. When a single equipment grounding conductor is used for multiple circuits in the same raceway, cable or cable tray, the single equipment grounding conductor shall be sized according to _____.

    (a) combined rating of all the overcurrent devices
    (b) largest overcurrent device of the multiple circuits
    (c) combined rating of all the loads
    (d) any of these

16. Equipment grounding conductors for motor branch circuits shall be sized in accordance with Table 250.122, based on the rating of the _____ device.

    (a) motor overload
    (b) motor over-temperature
    (c) branch circuit short-circuit and ground-fault protective
    (d) feeder overcurrent protection

17. Where conductors are run in parallel in multiple raceways or cables and include an EGC of the wire type, the equipment grounding conductor must be installed in parallel in each raceway or cable, sized in compliance with 250.122.

    (a) True
    (b) False

18. Equipment grounding conductors for feeder taps are not required to be larger than the tap conductors.

    (a) True
    (b) False

19. The terminal of a wiring device for the connection of the equipment grounding conductor shall be identified by a green-colored, _____.

    (a) not readily removable terminal screw with a hexagonal head
    (b) hexagonal, not readily removable terminal nut
    (c) pressure wire connector
    (d) any of these

Part VII. Methods of Equipment Grounding

1. The structural metal frame of a building can be used as the required equipment grounding conductor for ac equipment.

    (a) True
    (b) False

2. Metal parts of cord-and-plug-connected equipment shall be connected to an equipment grounding conductor that terminates to a grounding-type attachment plug.

    (a) True
    (b) False

3. A grounded circuit conductor is permitted to ground noncurrent-carrying metal parts of equipment, raceways, and other enclosures on the supply side or within the enclosure of the ac service-disconnecting means.

    (a) True
    (b) False

4. It shall be permissible to ground meter enclosures located near the service disconnecting means to the _____ circuit conductor on the load side of the service disconnect, if service ground-fault protection is not provided.

    (a) grounding
    (b) bonding
    (c) grounded
    (d) phase

5. A(n) _____ shall be used to connect the grounding terminal of a grounding-type receptacle to a grounded box.

    (a) equipment bonding jumper
    (b) grounded conductor jumper
    (c) a or b
    (d) a and b

6. Where the box is mounted on the surface, direct metal-to-metal contact between the device yoke and the box shall be permitted to ground the receptacle to the box if at least _____ of the insulating washers of the receptacle is (are) removed.

    (a) one
    (b) two
    (c) three
    (d) none of these

7. A listed exposed work cover can be the grounding and bonding means when the device is attached to the cover with at least _____ permanent fastener(s) and the cover mounting holes are located on a non-raised portion of the cover.

    (a) one
    (b) two
    (c) three
    (d) none of these

8. Receptacle yokes designed and _____ as self-grounding can establish the grounding circuit between the device yoke and a grounded outlet box.

    (a) approved
    (b) advertised
    (c) listed
    (d) installed

9. The receptacle grounding terminal of an isolated ground receptacle shall be connected to a(n) _____ equipment grounding conductor run with the circuit conductors.

    (a) insulated
    (b) covered
    (c) bare
    (d) solid

10. Where circuit conductors are spliced or terminated on equipment within a box, any equipment grounding conductors associated with those circuit conductors shall be connected to the box with devices suitable for the use.

    (a) True
    (b) False

11. The arrangement of grounding connections shall be such that the disconnection or the removal of a receptacle, luminaire, or other device does not interrupt the grounding continuity.

    (a) True
    (b) False

12. A connection between equipment grounding conductors and a metal box shall be by _____.

    (a) a grounding screw used for no other purpose
    (b) equipment listed for grounding
    (c) a listed grounding device
    (d) any of these

ARTICLE 285

Surge Protective Devices (SPDs)

INTRODUCTION TO ARTICLE 285—SURGE PROTECTIVE DEVICES (SPDS)

This article covers the general requirements, installation requirements, and connection requirements for surge protective devices (arresters and TVSSs) rated 1kV or less that are permanently installed on premises wiring systems. The *NEC* doesn't require surge protective devices to be installed, but if they are, they must comply with this article.

Surge protective devices are designed to reduce transient voltages present on premises power distribution wiring and load-side equipment, particularly electronic equipment such as computers, telecommunications equipment, security systems, and electronic appliances.

These transient voltages can originate from a number of sources, including anything from lightning to a laser printers. The best line of defense for all types of electronic equipment may be the installation of surge protective devices at the electrical service, source of power, as well as at the location of the utilization equipment.

The intent of a surge protection device is to limit transient voltages by diverting or limiting surge current and preventing continued flow of current while remaining capable of repeating these functions [Article 100].

QUESTIONS FOR ARTICLE 285— SURGE PROTECTIVE DEVICES

1. Article 285 covers surge protective devices rated over 1 kV.

   (a) True
   (b) False

2. Transient voltage surge suppressors (TVSSs) are also known as Type 2 and Type 3 surge protective devices (SPDs).

   (a) True
   (b) False

3. Where used, the surge protective device shall be connected to the grounded conductor of the circuit.

   (a) True
   (b) False

4. Surge protective devices shall be listed.

   (a) True
   (b) False

5. Surge protective devices shall be marked with a short-circuit current rating and shall not be installed where the available fault current is in excess of that rating.

   (a) True
   (b) False

6. Surge protective devices shall only be located outdoors.

   (a) True
   (b) False

7. The conductors used to connect the surge protective device to ground shall not be any longer than _____ and shall avoid unnecessary bends.

    (a) 6 in.
    (b) 12 in.
    (c) 18 in.
    (d) necessary

8. A Type 2 surge protective device is permitted to be connected on either the line or load side of the service equipment.

    (a) True
    (b) False

9. Type 3 surge protective devices can be installed on the load side of a branch-circuit overcurrent device up to the equipment served. If _____, the Type 3 SPD connection must be a minimum 30 ft of conductor distance from the service or separately derived system disconnect.

    (a) voltage drop is excessive
    (b) installed in a metal raceway or cable
    (c) included in the manufacturer's instructions
    (d) b and c

CHAPTER 3

WIRING METHODS AND MATERIALS

INTRODUCTION TO CHAPTER 3—WIRING METHODS AND MATERIALS

Chapter 3 covers wiring methods and materials, and provides some very specific installation requirements for conductors, cables, boxes, raceways, and fittings. This chapter includes detailed information about the installation and restrictions involved with wiring methods.

It may be because of that detail that many people incorrectly apply the rules from this chapter. Be sure to pay careful attention to the details, and be sure that you make your installation in compliance with the rules in the *Code*, not just in the manner that you may have been taught or because "it's always been done that way." This is especially true when it comes to applying the Tables.

Violations of the rules for wiring methods found in Chapter 3 can result in problems with power quality and can lead to fire, shock, and other hazards.

The type of wiring method you'll use depends on several factors: Job specifications, *Code* requirements, the environment, need, and cost are among them.

Chapter 3 begins with rules that are common to most wiring methods [Article 300], it then covers conductors [Article 310], and enclosures [Articles 312 and 314]. The articles that follow become more specific and deal more in-depth with individual wiring methods such as specific types of cables [Articles 320 through 340] and various raceways [Articles 342 through 390]. The chapter winds up with Article 392, a support system, and the final articles [Articles 394 through 398] for open wiring.

Notice as you read through the various wiring methods that the *Code* attempts to use similar subsection numbering for similar topics from one article to the next, using the same digits after the decimal point in the section number for the same topic. This makes it easier to locate specific requirements in a particular article. For example, the rules for securing and supporting can be found in the section that ends with .30 of each article. In addition to this, you'll find a "uses permitted" and "uses not permitted" section in nearly every article.

Wiring Method Articles

- **Article 300—Wiring Methods.** Article 300 contains the general requirements for all wiring methods included in the *NEC*, except for signaling and communications systems, which are covered in Chapters 7 and 8.

- **Article 310—Conductors for General Wiring.** This article contains the general requirements for conductors, such as insulation markings, ampacity ratings, and conductor use. Article 310 doesn't apply to conductors that are part of flexible cords, fixture wires, or conductors that are an integral part of equipment [90.6 and 300.1(B)].

- **Article 312—Cabinets, Cutout Boxes, and Meter Socket Enclosures.** Article 312 covers the installation and construction specifications for cabinets, cutout boxes, and meter socket enclosures.

- **Article 314—Outlet, Device, Pull and Junction Boxes, Conduit Bodies, Fittings, and Handhole Enclosures.** Installation requirements for outlet boxes, pull and junction boxes, as well as conduit bodies, and handhole enclosures are contained in this article.

Cable Articles

Articles 320 through 340 address specific types of cables. If you take the time to become familiar with the various types of cables, you'll:

- Understand what's available for doing the work.
- Recognize cable types that have special *NEC* requirements.
- Avoid buying cable that you can't install due to *Code* requirements you can't meet with that particular wiring method.

Here's a brief overview of each one:

- **Article 320—Armored Cable (Type AC).** Armored cable is an assembly of insulated conductors, 14 AWG through 1 AWG, individually wrapped with waxed paper. The conductors are contained within a flexible spiral metal (steel or aluminum) sheath that interlocks at the edges. Armored cable looks like flexible metal conduit. Many electricians call this metal cable "BX®."

- **Article 330—Metal-Clad Cable (Type MC).** Metal-clad cable encloses insulated conductors in a metal sheath of either corrugated or smooth copper or aluminum tubing, or spiral interlocked steel or aluminum. The physical characteristics of Type MC cable make it a versatile wiring method permitted in almost any location and for almost any application. The most commonly used Type MC cable is the interlocking kind, which looks similar to armored cable or flexible metal conduit.

- **Article 334—Nonmetallic-Sheathed Cable (Type NM).** Nonmetallic-sheathed cable encloses two, three, or four insulated conductors, 14 AWG through 2 AWG, within a nonmetallic outer jacket. Because this cable is nonmetallic, it contains a separate equipment grounding conductor. Nonmetallic-sheathed cable is a common wiring method used for residential and commercial branch circuits. Many electricians call this plastic-sheathed cable "Romex®."

- **Article 336—Power and Control Tray Cable (Type TC).** Power and control tray cable is a factory assembly of two or more insulated conductors under a nonmetallic sheath for installation in cable trays, in raceways, or supported by a messenger wire.

- **Article 338—Service-Entrance Cable (Types SE and USE).** Service-entrance cable can be a single-conductor or a multiconductor assembly within an overall nonmetallic covering. This cable is used primarily for services not over 600V, but is also permitted for feeders and branch circuits.

- **Article 340—Underground Feeder and Branch-Circuit Cable (Type UF).** Underground feeder cable is a moisture-, fungus-, and corrosion-resistant cable suitable for direct burial in the earth, and it comes in sizes 14 AWG through 4/0 AWG [340.104]. Multiconductor UF cable is covered in molded plastic that surrounds the insulated conductors.

Raceway Articles

Articles 342 through 390 address specific types of raceways. Refer to Article 100 for the definition of a raceway. If you take the time to become familiar with the various types of raceways, you'll:

- Understand what's available for doing the work.
- Recognize raceway types that have special *Code* requirements.
- Avoid buying a raceway that you can't install due to *NEC* requirements you can't meet with that particular wiring method.

Here's a brief overview of each one:

- **Article 342—Intermediate Metal Conduit (Type IMC).** Intermediate metal conduit is a circular metal raceway with the same outside diameter as rigid metal conduit. The wall thickness of intermediate metal conduit is less than that of rigid metal conduit, so it's a greater interior cross-sectional area for holding conductors. Intermediate metal conduit is lighter and less expensive than rigid metal conduit, but it's permitted in all the same locations as rigid metal conduit. Intermediate metal conduit also uses a different steel alloy, which makes it stronger than rigid metal conduit, even though the walls are thinner.

- **Article 344—Rigid Metal Conduit (Type RMC).** Rigid metal conduit is similar to intermediate metal conduit, except the wall thickness is greater, so it's a smaller interior cross-sectional area. Rigid metal conduit is heavier than intermediate metal conduit and it's permitted to be installed in any location, just like intermediate metal conduit.

- **Article 348—Flexible Metal Conduit (Type FMC).** Flexible metal conduit is a raceway of circular cross section made of a helically wound, interlocked metal strip of either steel or aluminum. It's commonly called "Greenfield" or "Flex."

- **Article 350—Liquidtight Flexible Metal Conduit (Type LFMC).** Liquidtight flexible metal conduit is a raceway of circular cross section with an outer liquidtight, nonmetallic, sunlight-resistant jacket over an inner flexible metal core, with associated couplings, connectors, and fittings. It's listed for the installation of electric conductors. Liquidtight flexible metal conduit is commonly called "Sealtite®" or simply "liquidtight." Liquidtight flexible metal conduit is of similar construction to flexible metal conduit, but it has an outer thermoplastic covering.

- **Article 352—Rigid Polyvinyl Chloride Conduit (Type PVC).** Rigid polyvinyl chloride conduit is a nonmetallic raceway of circular cross section with integral or associated couplings, connectors, and fittings. It's listed for the installation of electrical conductors.

- **Article 356—Liquidtight Flexible Nonmetallic Conduit (Type LFNC).** Liquidtight flexible nonmetallic conduit is a raceway of circular cross section with an outer liquidtight, nonmetallic, sunlight-resistant jacket over an inner flexible core, with associated couplings, connectors, and fittings. It's listed for the installation of electrical conductors. LFNC is available in three types:
  - Type LFNC-A (orange). A smooth seamless inner core and cover bonded together with reinforcement layers inserted between the core and covers.
  - Type LFNC-B (gray). A smooth inner surface with integral reinforcement within the conduit wall.
  - Type LFNC-C (black). A corrugated internal and external surface without integral reinforcement within the conduit wall.

- **Article 358—Electrical Metallic Tubing (EMT).** Electrical metallic tubing is a nonthreaded thinwall raceway of circular cross section designed for the physical protection and routing of conductors and cables. Compared to rigid metal conduit and intermediate metal conduit, electrical metallic tubing is relatively easy to bend, cut, and ream. EMT isn't threaded, so all connectors and couplings are of the threadless type. Today, It's available in a range of colors, such as red and blue.

- **Article 362—Electrical Nonmetallic Tubing (ENT).** Electrical nonmetallic tubing is a pliable, corrugated, circular raceway made of PVC. It's often called "Smurf Pipe" or "Smurf Tube," because it was available only in blue when it came out and at the time the children's cartoon characters "The Smurfs," were popular. It's now available in multiple colors such as red and yellow as well as blue.

- **Article 376—Metal Wireways.** A metal wireway is a sheet metal trough with hinged or removable covers for housing and protecting electrical conductors and cable, in which conductors are placed after the wireway has been installed as a complete system.

- **Article 380—Multioutlet Assemblies.** A multioutlet assembly is a surface, flush, or freestanding raceway designed to hold conductors and receptacles. It's assembled in the field or at the factory.

- **Article 386—Surface Metal Raceways.** A surface metal raceway is a metallic raceway intended to be mounted to the surface with associated accessories, in which conductors are placed after the raceway has been installed as a complete system.

- **Article 388—Surface Nonmetallic Raceways.** A surface nonmetallic raceway is intended to be surface mounted with associated accessories. Conductors are placed inside after the raceway has been installed as a complete system.

Cable Tray

- **Article 392—Cable Trays.** A cable tray system is a unit or assembly of units or sections with associated fittings that form a structural system used to securely fasten or support cables and raceways. A cable tray isn't a raceway; it's a support system for raceways, cables, and enclosures.

Notes

ARTICLE 300
Wiring Methods

QUESTIONS FOR INTRODUCTION TO ARTICLE 300—WIRING METHODS

Article 300 contains the general requirements for all wiring methods included in the *NEC*. However, the article doesn't apply to communications systems, which are covered in Chapter 8, except when Article 300 is specifically referenced in Chapter 8.

This article is primarily concerned with how to install, route, splice, protect, and secure conductors and raceways. How well you conform to the requirements of Article 300 will generally be evident in the finished work, because many of the requirements tend to determine the appearance of the installation.

Because of this, it's often easy to spot Article 300 problems if you're looking for *Code* violations. For example, you can easily see when someone runs an equipment grounding conductor outside a raceway instead of grouping all conductors of a circuit together, as required by 300.3(B).

A good understanding of Article 300 will start you on the path to correctly installing the wiring methods included in Chapter 3. Be sure to carefully consider the accompanying illustrations, in the accompanying textbook and refer to the definitions in Article 100 as needed.

 Please use the 2011 *Code* book to answer the following questions, which are based on the 2011 *NEC*.

QUESTIONS FOR ARTICLE 300—WIRING METHODS

1. Conductors shall be installed within a raceway, cable, or enclosure.

    (a) True
    (b) False

2. All conductors of a circuit, including the grounded and equipment grounding conductors, shall be contained within the same _____, unless otherwise permitted elsewhere in the *Code*.

    (a) raceway
    (b) cable
    (c) trench
    (d) all of these

3. Conductors of ac and dc circuits, rated 600V or less, shall be permitted to occupy the same _____ provided that all conductors have an insulation rating equal to the maximum voltage applied to any conductor.

    (a) enclosure
    (b) cable
    (c) raceway
    (d) all of these

4. Where cables or nonmetallic raceways are installed through bored holes in joists, rafters, or wood members, holes shall be bored so that the edge of the hole is _____ the nearest edge of the wood member.

    (a) not less than 1¼ in. from
    (b) immediately adjacent to
    (c) not less than ¹⁄₁₆ in. from
    (d) 90° away from

5. Cables laid in wood notches require protection against nails or screws by using a steel plate at least _____ thick, installed before the building finish is applied.

   (a) ¹⁄₁₆ in.
   (b) ⅛ in.
   (c) ¼ in.
   (d) ½ in.

6. Where Type NM cable passes through factory or field openings in metal members, it shall be protected by _____ bushings or _____ grommets that cover metal edges.

   (a) approved
   (b) identified
   (c) listed
   (d) none of these

7. Where Type NM cables pass through cut or drilled slots or holes in metal members, the cable shall be protected by _____ which are installed in the opening prior to the installation of the cable and which securely cover all metal edges.

   (a) listed bushings
   (b) listed grommets
   (c) plates
   (d) a or b

8. Where nails or screws are likely to penetrate nonmetallic-sheathed cable or ENT installed through metal framing members, a steel sleeve, steel plate, or steel clip not less than _____ in thickness shall be used to protect the cable or tubing.

   (a) ¹⁄₁₆ in.
   (b) ⅛ in.
   (c) ½ in.
   (d) ¾ in.

9. Wiring methods installed behind panels that allow access shall be _____ according to their applicable articles.

   (a) supported
   (b) painted
   (c) in a metal raceway
   (d) all of these

10. Where cables and nonmetallic raceways are installed parallel to framing members, the nearest outside surface of the cable or raceway shall be _____ the nearest edge of the framing member where nails or screws are likely to penetrate.

    (a) not less than 1¼ in. from
    (b) immediately adjacent to
    (c) not less than ¹⁄₁₆ in. from
    (d) 90° away from

11. A cable, raceway, or box installed under metal-corrugated sheet roof decking shall be supported so the top of the cable, raceway, or box is not less than _____ from the lowest surface of the roof decking to the top of the cable, raceway, or box.

    (a) ½ in.
    (b) 1 in.
    (c) 1½ in.
    (d) 2 in.

12. When installed under metal-corrugated sheet roof decking, cables, raceways, and enclosures are permitted in concealed locations of metal-corrugated sheet decking type roofing if they are at least 2 in. away from a structural support member.

    (a) True
    (b) False

13. When installed under metal-corrugated sheet roof decking, the rules for spacing from roof decking apply equally to rigid metal conduit and intermediate metal conduit.

    (a) True
    (b) False

14. Where raceways contain insulated circuit conductors _____ AWG and larger, the conductors shall be protected from abrasion during and after installation by a fitting that provides a smooth, rounded insulating surface.

    (a) 8
    (b) 6
    (c) 4
    (d) 2

15. A listed expansion/deflection fitting or other approved means must be used where a raceway crosses a _____ intended for expansion, contraction or deflection used in buildings, bridges, parking garages, or other structures.

    (a) junction box
    (b) structural joint
    (c) cable tray
    (d) unistrut hanger

16. What is the minimum cover requirement for direct burial Type UF cable installed outdoors that supplies a 120V, 30A circuit?

    (a) 6 in.
    (b) 12 in.
    (c) 18 in.
    (d) 24 in.

17. Rigid metal conduit that is directly buried outdoors shall have at least _____ of cover.

    (a) 6 in.
    (b) 12 in.
    (c) 18 in.
    (d) 24 in.

18. When installing PVC conduit underground without concrete cover, there shall be a minimum of _____ of cover.

    (a) 6 in.
    (b) 12 in.
    (c) 18 in.
    (d) 22 in.

19. What is the minimum cover requirement for Type UF cable supplying power to a 120V, 15A GFCI-protected circuit outdoors under a driveway of a one-family dwelling?

    (a) 6 in.
    (b) 12 in.
    (c) 16 in.
    (d) 24 in.

20. Type UF cable used with a 24V landscape lighting system can have a minimum cover of _____.

    (a) 6 in.
    (b) 12 in.
    (c) 18 in.
    (d) 24 in.

21. _____ is defined as the area between the top of direct-burial cable and the top surface of the finished grade.

    (a) Notch
    (b) Cover
    (c) Gap
    (d) none of these

22. The interior of underground raceways shall be considered a _____ location.

    (a) wet
    (b) dry
    (c) damp
    (d) corrosive

23. Type MC Cable listed for _____ is permitted to be installed underground under a building without installation in a raceway.

    (a) direct burial
    (b) damp and wet locations
    (c) rough service
    (d) b and c

24. Where direct-buried conductors and cables emerge from grade, they shall be protected by enclosures or raceways to a point at least _____ above finished grade.

    (a) 3 ft
    (b) 6 ft
    (c) 8 ft
    (d) 10 ft

25. Direct-buried service conductors that are not encased in concrete and that are buried 18 in. or more below grade shall have their location identified by a warning ribbon placed in the trench at least _____ above the underground installation.

    (a) 6 in.
    (b) 10 in.
    (c) 12 in.
    (d) 18 in.

26. Direct-buried conductors or cables can be spliced or tapped without the use of splice boxes when the splice or tap is made in accordance with 110.14(B).

    (a) True
    (b) False

27. Backfill used for underground wiring shall not _____.

    (a) damage the wiring method
    (b) prevent compaction of the fill
    (c) contribute to the corrosion of the raceway
    (d) all of these

28. Conduits or raceways through which moisture may contact live parts shall be _____ at either or both ends.

    (a) sealed
    (b) plugged
    (c) bushed
    (d) a or b

29. When installing direct-buried cables, a _____ shall be used at the end of a conduit that terminates underground.

    (a) splice kit
    (b) terminal fitting
    (c) bushing
    (d) b or c

30. All conductors of the same circuit shall be _____, unless otherwise specifically permitted in the *Code*.

    (a) in the same raceway or cable
    (b) in close proximity in the same trench
    (c) the same size
    (d) a or b

31. Each direct-buried single conductor cable must be located _____ in the trench to the other single conductor cables in the same parallel set of conductors, including equipment grounding conductors.

    (a) perpendicular
    (b) bundled together
    (c) in close proximity
    (d) spaced apart

32. Direct-buried conductors, cables, or raceways, which are subject to movement by settlement or frost, shall be arranged to prevent damage to the _____ or to equipment connected to the raceways.

    (a) siding of the building mounted on
    (b) landscaping around the cable or raceway
    (c) the enclosed conductors
    (d) expansion fitting

33. Cables or raceways installed using directional boring equipment shall be _____ for this purpose.

    (a) marked
    (b) listed
    (c) labeled
    (d) approved

34. Raceways, cable trays, cablebus, auxiliary gutters, cable armor, boxes, cable sheathing, cabinets, elbows, couplings, fittings, supports, and support hardware shall be of materials suitable for _____.

    (a) corrosive locations
    (b) wet locations
    (c) the environment in which they are to be installed
    (d) none of these

35. Where corrosion protection is necessary for ferrous metal equipment and the conduit is threaded in the field, the threads shall be coated with a(n) _____, electrically conductive, corrosion-resistant compound.

    (a) marked
    (b) listed
    (c) labeled
    (d) approved

36. Which of the following metal parts shall be protected from corrosion?

    (a) Ferrous metal raceways.
    (b) Ferrous metal elbows.
    (c) Ferrous boxes.
    (d) all of these

37. Ferrous metal raceways, boxes, fittings, supports, and support hardware can be installed in concrete or in direct contact with the earth or other areas subject to severe corrosive influences, where _____ approved for the conditions.

    (a) the soil is
    (b) made of material
    (c) the qualified installer is
    (d) none of these

38. Aluminum raceways, cable trays, cablebus, auxiliary gutters, cable armor, boxes, cable sheathing, cabinets, elbows, couplings, nipples, fittings, supports, and support hardware _____ shall be provided with supplementary corrosion protection.

    (a) embedded or encased in concrete
    (b) in direct contact with the earth
    (c) likely to become energized
    (d) a or b

39. Where exposed to sunlight, nonmetallic raceways, cable trays, boxes, cables with a nonmetallic outer jacket, fittings, and support hardware shall be _____.

    (a) listed as sunlight resistant
    (b) identified as sunlight resistant
    (c) a and b
    (d) a or b

40. Where nonmetallic wiring methods are subject to exposure to chemical solvents or vapors, they shall be inherently resistant to chemicals based upon their being _____.

    (a) listed for the chemical
    (b) identified for the chemical
    (c) a and b
    (d) a or b

41. An exposed wiring system for indoor wet locations where walls are frequently washed shall be mounted so that there is at least a _____ between the mounting surface and the electrical equipment.

    (a) ¼ in. airspace
    (b) separation by insulated bushings
    (c) separation by noncombustible tubing
    (d) none of these

42. In general, areas where acids and alkali chemicals are handled and stored may present corrosive conditions, particularly when wet or damp.

    (a) True
    (b) False

43. Where portions of a cable raceway or sleeve are subjected to different temperatures and condensation is known to be a problem, the _____ shall be filled with an approved material to prevent the circulation of warm air to a colder section of the raceway or sleeve.

    (a) raceway
    (b) sleeve
    (c) a or b
    (d) none of these

44. Raceways shall be provided with expansion fittings where necessary to compensate for thermal expansion and contraction.

    (a) True
    (b) False

45. Raceways or cable trays containing electric conductors shall not contain any pipe or tube for steam, water, air, gas, drainage, or any service other than _____.

(a) as permitted by the authority having jurisdiction
(b) electrical
(c) pneumatic
(d) as designed by the engineer

46. Where raceways are installed in wet locations above grade, the interior of these raceways shall be considered a _____ location.

(a) wet
(b) dry
(c) damp
(d) corrosive

47. Metal raceways, cable armors, and other metal enclosures shall be _____ joined together into a continuous electric conductor so as to provide effective electrical continuity.

(a) electrically
(b) permanently
(c) metallically
(d) none of these

48. Raceways, cable assemblies, boxes, cabinets, and fittings shall be securely fastened in place.

(a) True
(b) False

49. Where independent support wires of a ceiling assembly are used to support raceways, cable assemblies, or boxes above a ceiling, they shall be secured at _____ ends.

(a) one
(b) both
(c) a or b
(d) none of these

50. Electrical wiring within the cavity of a fire-rated floor-ceiling or roof-ceiling assembly shall not be supported by the ceiling assembly or ceiling support wires.

(a) True
(b) False

51. The independent support wires for supporting electrical wiring methods in a fire-rated ceiling assembly shall be distinguishable from fire-rated suspended-ceiling framing support wires by _____.

(a) color
(b) tagging
(c) other effective means
(d) any of these

52. Ceiling-support wires used for the support of electrical raceways and cables within nonfire-rated assemblies shall be distinguishable from the suspended-ceiling framing support wires.

(a) True
(b) False

53. Raceways can be used as a means of support of Class 2 circuit conductors or cables that connect to the same equipment.

(a) True
(b) False

54. Cable wiring methods shall not be used as a means of support for _____.

(a) other cables
(b) raceways
(c) nonelectrical equipment
(d) all of these

55. Metal or nonmetallic raceways, cable armors, and cable sheaths _____ between cabinets, boxes, fittings or other enclosures or outlets.

    (a) can be attached with electrical tape
    (b) are allowed gaps for expansion
    (c) shall be continuous
    (d) none of these

56. Raceways and cables installed into the _____ of open-bottom equipment shall not be required to be mechanically secured to the equipment.

    (a) bottom
    (b) sides
    (c) top
    (d) any of these

57. Conductors in raceways shall be _____ between outlets, boxes, devices, and so forth.

    (a) continuous
    (b) installed
    (c) copper
    (d) in conduit

58. In multiwire branch circuits, the continuity of the _____ conductor shall not be dependent upon the device connections.

    (a) ungrounded
    (b) grounded
    (c) grounding electrode
    (d) a and b

59. When the opening to an outlet, junction, or switch point is less than 8 in. in any dimension, each conductor shall be long enough to extend at least _____ outside the opening of the enclosure.

    (a) 0 in.
    (b) 3 in.
    (c) 6 in.
    (d) 12 in.

60. Fittings and connectors shall be used only with the specific wiring methods for which they are designed and listed.

    (a) True
    (b) False

61. A box or conduit body shall not be required where cables enter or exit from conduit or tubing that is used to provide cable support or protection against physical damage.

    (a) True
    (b) False

62. A box or conduit body shall not be required for splices and taps in direct-buried conductors and cables as long as the splice is made with a splicing device that is identified for the purpose.

    (a) True
    (b) False

63. A box or conduit body shall not be required for conductors in handhole enclosures, except where connected to electrical equipment.

    (a) True
    (b) False

64. A bushing shall be permitted in lieu of a box or terminal where the conductors emerge from a raceway and enter or terminate at equipment such as open switchboards, unenclosed control equipment, or similar equipment.

    (a) True
    (b) False

65. The number and size of conductors permitted in a raceway is limited to _____.

    (a) permit heat to dissipate
    (b) prevent damage to insulation during installation
    (c) prevent damage to insulation during removal of conductors
    (d) all of these

66. Raceways shall be _____ between outlet, junction, or splicing points prior to the installation of conductors.

    (a) installed complete
    (b) tested for ground faults
    (c) a minimum of 80 percent complete
    (d) none of these

67. Prewired raceway assemblies shall be used only where specifically permitted in the *NEC* for the applicable wiring method.

    (a) True
    (b) False

68. Short sections of raceways used for _____ shall not be required to be installed complete between outlet, junction, or splicing points.

    (a) meter to service enclosure connection
    (b) protection of cables from physical damage
    (c) nipples
    (d) separately derived systems

69. Metal raceways shall not be _____ by welding to the raceway.

    (a) supported
    (b) terminated
    (c) connected
    (d) all of these

70. A vertical run of 4/0 AWG copper shall be supported at intervals not exceeding _____.

    (a) 40 ft
    (b) 80 ft
    (c) 100 ft
    (d) 120 ft

71. Conductors in ferrous metal raceways and enclosures shall be arranged so as to avoid heating the surrounding ferrous metal by alternating-current induction. To accomplish this, the _____ conductor(s) shall be grouped together.

    (a) phase
    (b) grounded
    (c) equipment grounding
    (d) all of these

72. _____ is a nonferrous, nonmagnetic metal that has no heating due to hysteresis heating.

    (a) Steel
    (b) Iron
    (c) Aluminum
    (d) all of these

73. Electrical installations in hollow spaces, vertical shafts, and ventilation or air-handling ducts shall be made so that the possible spread of fire or products of combustion is not _____.

    (a) substantially increased
    (b) allowed
    (c) inherent
    (d) possible

74. Openings around electrical penetrations into or through fire-resistant-rated walls, partitions, floors, or ceilings shall _____ to maintain the fire-resistance rating.

    (a) be documented
    (b) not be permitted
    (c) be firestopped using approved methods
    (d) be enlarged

75. No wiring of any type shall be installed in ducts used to transport _____.

    (a) dust
    (b) flammable vapors
    (c) loose stock
    (d) all of these

76. Equipment and devices shall only be permitted within ducts or plenum chambers specifically fabricated to transport environmental air if necessary for their direct action upon, or sensing of, the _____.

   (a) contained air
   (b) air quality
   (c) air temperature
   (d) none of these

77. The space above a hung ceiling used for environmental air-handling purposes is an example of _____, and the wiring limitations of _____ apply.

   (a) a specifically fabricated duct used for environmental air, 300.22(B)
   (b) other space used for environmental air (plenum), 300.22(C)
   (c) a supply duct used for environmental air, 300.22(B)
   (d) none of these

78. Wiring methods permitted in the ceiling areas used for environmental air include _____.

   (a) electrical metallic tubing
   (b) FMC of any length
   (c) RMC without an overall nonmetallic covering
   (d) all of these

79. _____ shall be permitted to support the wiring methods and equipment permitted to be used in other spaces used for environmental air (plenum).

   (a) Metal cable tray system
   (b) Nonmetallic wireways
   (c) PVC conduit
   (d) Surface nonmetallic raceways

80. Electrical equipment with _____ and having adequate fire-resistant and low-smoke-producing characteristics can be installed within an air-handling space (plenum).

   (a) a metal enclosure
   (b) a nonmetallic enclosures listed for use within an air-handling (plenum) space
   (c) any type of enclosure
   (d) a or b

81. Wiring methods and equipment installed behind suspended-ceiling panels shall be arranged and secured to allow access to the electrical equipment.

   (a) True
   (b) False

ARTICLE 310

Conductors for General Wiring

INTRODUCTION TO ARTICLE 310—CONDUCTORS FOR GENERAL WIRING

This article contains the general requirements for conductors, such as insulation markings, ampacity ratings, and conditions of use. Article 310 doesn't apply to conductors that are part of flexible cords, fixture wires, or to conductors that are an integral part of equipment [90.7 and 300.1(B)].

People often make errors in applying the ampacity tables contained in Article 310. If you study the explanations carefully, you'll avoid common errors such as applying Table 310.15(B)(17) when you should be applying Table 310.15(B)(16).

Why so many tables? Why does Table 310.15(B)(17) list the ampacity of 6 THHN as 105 amperes, yet Table 310.15(B)(16) lists the same conductor as having an ampacity of only 75 amperes? To answer that, go back to Article 100 and review the definition of ampacity. Notice the phrase "conditions of use." These tables set a maximum current value at which premature failure of the conductor insulation shouldn't occur during normal use, under the conditions described in the tables.

The designations THHN, THHW, RHH, and so on, are insulation types. Every type of insulation has a limit to how much heat it can withstand. When current flows through a conductor, it creates heat. How well the insulation around a conductor can dissipate that heat depends on factors such as whether that conductor is in free air or not. Think about what happens when you put on a sweater, a jacket, and then a coat—all at the same time. You heat up. Your skin can't dissipate heat with all that clothing on nearly as well as it dissipates heat in free air. The same principal applies to conductors.

Conductor insulation also fails with age. That's why we conduct cable testing and take other measures to predict failure and replace certain conductors (for example, feeders or critical equipment conductors) while they're still within design specifications. But conductor insulation failure takes decades under normal use—and it's a maintenance issue. However, if a conductor is forced to exceed the ampacity listed in the appropriate table, and as a result its design temperature is exceeded, insulation failure happens much more rapidly—often catastrophically. Consequently, exceeding the allowable ampacity of a conductor is a serious safety issue.

QUESTIONS FOR ARTICLE 310— CONDUCTORS FOR GENERAL WIRING

1. Conductors shall be permitted for use in any of the wiring methods recognized in Chapter 3 and as permitted in the *NEC*.

   (a) True
   (b) False

2. Insulated conductors used in wet locations shall be _____.

   (a) moisture-impervious metal sheathed
   (b) MTW, RHW, RHW-2, TW, THW, THW-2, THHW, THWN, THWN-2, XHHW, XHHW-2, ZW
   (c) listed for wet locations
   (d) any of these

3. In general, the minimum size conductor permitted for use in parallel installations is _____ AWG.

   (a) 10
   (b) 4
   (c) 1
   (d) 1/0

4. Conductors smaller than 1/0 AWG can be connected in parallel to supply control power, provided _____.

   (a) they are all contained within the same raceway or cable
   (b) each parallel conductor has an ampacity sufficient to carry the entire load
   (c) the circuit overcurrent device rating does not exceed the ampacity of any individual parallel conductor
   (d) all of these

5. Parallel conductors shall have the same _____.

   (a) length
   (b) material
   (c) size in circular mil area
   (d) all of these

6. Where conductors in parallel are run in separate raceways, the raceways shall have the same electrical characteristics.

   (a) True
   (b) False

7. No conductor shall be used where its operating temperature exceeds that designated for the type of insulated conductor involved.

   (a) True
   (b) False

8. The _____ rating of a conductor is the maximum temperature, at any location along its length, which the conductor can withstand over a prolonged period of time without serious degradation.

   (a) ambient
   (b) temperature
   (c) maximum withstand
   (d) short-circuit

9. There are four principal determinants of conductor operating temperature, one of which is _____ generated internally in the conductor as the result of load current flow, including fundamental and harmonic currents.

   (a) friction
   (b) magnetism
   (c) heat
   (d) none of these

10. The ampacities listed in the Tables of Article 310.15(B)(6) do not take _____ into consideration.

    (a) continuous loads
    (b) voltage drop
    (c) insulation
    (d) wet locations

11. The ampacity of a conductor can be different along the length of the conductor. The higher ampacity can be used beyond the point of transition for a distance of no more than _____ ft, or no more than _____ percent of the circuit length figured at the higher ampacity, whichever is less.

    (a) 10, 10
    (b) 10, 20
    (c) 15, 15
    (d) 20, 10

12. Each current-carrying conductor of a paralleled set of conductors shall be counted as a current-carrying conductor for the purpose of applying the adjustment factors of 310.15(B)(3)(a).

    (a) True
    (b) False

13. Where six current-carrying conductors are run in the same conduit or cable, the ampacity of each conductor shall be adjusted by a factor of _____ percent.

    (a) 40
    (b) 60
    (c) 80
    (d) 90

14. Conductor adjustment factors shall not apply to conductors in raceways having a length not exceeding _____.

    (a) 12 in.
    (b) 24 in.
    (c) 36 in.
    (d) 48 in.

15. The ampacity adjustment factors of Table 310.15(B)(3)(a) does not apply to Type AC or Type MC cable without an overall outer jacket, if which of the following conditions are met?

    (a) Each cable has not more than three current-carrying conductors.
    (b) The conductors are 12 AWG copper.
    (c) No more than 20 current-carrying conductors are installed without maintaining spacing.
    (d) all of these

16. Where conductors or cables are installed in circular conduits exposed to direct sunlight on or above rooftops, the ambient temperature shall be increased by _____ where the conduits are less than ½ in. from the rooftop.

    (a) 30°F
    (b) 40°F
    (c) 50°F
    (d) 60°F

17. When bare conductors are installed with insulated conductors, their ampacities shall be limited to _____.

    (a) 60°C
    (b) 75°C
    (c) 90°C
    (d) the lowest temperature rating for any of the insulated conductors

18. A _____ conductor that carries only the unbalanced current from other conductors of the same circuit shall not be required to be counted when applying the provisions of 310.15(B)(3)(a).

    (a) neutral
    (b) ungrounded
    (c) grounding
    (d) none of these

19. On a three-phase, 4-wire, wye circuit, where the major portion of the load consists of nonlinear loads, the neutral conductor shall be counted when applying 310.15(B)(3)(a) adjustment factors.

    (a) True
    (b) False

20. When determining the number of current-carrying conductors, a grounding or bonding conductor shall not be counted when applying the provisions of 310.15(B)(3)(a) _____.

    (a) True
    (b) False

21. For individual dwelling units of _____ dwellings, Table 310.15(B)(7) can be used to size 3-wire, single-phase, 120/240V service or feeder conductors that serve as the main power feeder.

    (a) one-family
    (b) two-family
    (c) multifamily
    (d) any of these

22. THWN insulated conductors are rated _____.

    (a) 75°C
    (b) for wet locations
    (c) a and b
    (d) not enough information

23. THW insulation has a _____ rating when installed within electric-discharge lighting equipment, such as through fluorescent luminaires.

    (a) 60°C
    (b) 75°C
    (c) 90°C
    (d) 105°C

24. Which conductor type has an insulation temperature rating of 90°C?

    (a) THWN
    (b) RHW
    (c) THHN
    (d) TW

25. The minimum size conductor permitted for branch circuits under 600V is _____ AWG.

    (a) 14
    (b) 12
    (c) 10
    (d) 8

26. Where installed in raceways, conductors _____ AWG and larger shall be stranded.

    (a) 10
    (b) 8
    (c) 6
    (d) 4

27. Letters used to designate the number of conductors within a cable are _____.

    (a) D - Two insulated conductors laid parallel
    (b) M - Two or more insulated conductors twisted spirally
    (c) T - Two or more insulated conductors twisted in parallel
    (d) a and b

ARTICLE 312

Cabinets, Cutout Boxes, and Meter Socket Enclosures

INTRODUCTION TO ARTICLE 312—CABINETS, CUTOUT BOXES, AND METER SOCKET ENCLOSURES

This article addresses the installation and construction specifications for the items mentioned in its title. In Article 310, we observed that the conditions of use have an effect on the ampacity of a conductor. Likewise, the conditions of use have an effect on the selection and application of cabinets, cutout boxes, and meter socket enclosures. For example, you can't use just any enclosure in a wet location or in a hazardous location. The conditions of use impose special requirements for these situations.

For all such enclosures, certain requirements apply—regardless of the use. For example, you must cover any openings, protect conductors from abrasion, and allow sufficient bending room for conductors.

Notice that Article 408 covers switchboards and panelboards, with primary emphasis on the interior, or "guts" while the cabinet that would be used to enclose a panelboard is covered here in Article 312. Therefore you'll find that some important considerations such as wire-bending space at terminals of panelboards are included in this article.

Article 312 covers the installation and construction specifications for cabinets, cutout boxes, and meter socket enclosures. [312.1].

Author's Comment: A cabinet is an enclosure for either surface mounting or flush mounting and provided with a frame in which a door may be hung. A cutout box is designed for surface mounting with a swinging door [Article 100]. The industry name for a meter socket enclosure is "meter can."

QUESTIONS FOR ARTICLE 312— CABINETS, CUTOUT BOXES, AND METER SOCKET ENCLOSURES

1. Surface-type cabinets, cutout boxes, and meter socket enclosures in damp or wet locations shall be mounted so there is at least _____ airspace between the enclosure and the wall or supporting surface.

    (a) ¹⁄₁₆ in.
    (b) ¼ in.
    (c) 1¼ in.
    (d) 6 in.

2. Cabinets, cutout boxes, and meter socket enclosures installed in wet locations shall be _____.

    (a) waterproof
    (b) raintight
    (c) weatherproof
    (d) watertight

3. Where raceways or cables enter above the level of uninsulated live parts of cabinets, cutout boxes, and meter socket enclosures in a wet location, a(n) _____ shall be used.

    (a) fitting listed for wet locations
    (b) explosionproof seal
    (c) fitting listed for damp locations
    (d) insulated fitting

4. In walls constructed of wood or other _____ material, electrical cabinets shall be flush with the finished surface or project there from.

   (a) nonconductive
   (b) porous
   (c) fibrous
   (d) combustible

5. Noncombustible surfaces that are broken or incomplete shall be repaired so there will be no gaps or open spaces greater than _____ at the edge of a cabinet or cutout box employing a flush-type cover.

   (a) $\frac{1}{32}$ in.
   (b) $\frac{1}{16}$ in.
   (c) $\frac{1}{8}$ in.
   (d) $\frac{1}{4}$ in.

6. Openings in cabinets, cutout boxes, and meter socket enclosures through which conductors enter shall be _____.

   (a) adequately closed
   (b) made using concentric knockouts only
   (c) centered in the cabinet wall
   (d) identified

7. Each cable entering a cutout box _____.

   (a) shall be secured to the cutout box
   (b) can be sleeved through a chase
   (c) shall have a maximum of two cables per connector
   (d) all of these

8. Nonmetallic cables can enter the top of surface-mounted cabinets, cutout boxes, and meter socket enclosures through nonflexible raceways not less than 18 in. or more than _____ in length if all of the required conditions are met.

   (a) 3 ft
   (b) 10 ft
   (c) 25 ft
   (d) 100 ft

9. Enclosures for switches or overcurrent devices are allowed to have conductors feeding through where the wiring space at any cross section is not filled to more than _____ percent of the cross-sectional area of the space.

   (a) 20
   (b) 30
   (c) 40
   (d) 60

10. Cabinets, cutout boxes, and meter socket enclosures can be used for conductors feeding through, spliced, or tapping off to other enclosures, switches, or overcurrent devices where _____.

   (a) the total area of the conductors at any cross section doesn't exceed 40 percent of the cross-sectional area of the space
   (b) the total area of conductors, splices, and taps installed at any cross section doesn't exceed 75 percent of the cross-sectional area of that space
   (c) a warning label on the enclosure identifies the disconnecting means for feed-through conductors
   (d) all of these

Outlet, Device, Pull and Junction Boxes; Conduit Bodies; and Handhole Enclosures

INTRODUCTION TO ARTICLE 314—OUTLET, DEVICE, PULL AND JUNCTION BOXES; CONDUIT BODIES; AND HANDHOLE ENCLOSURES

Article 314 contains installation requirements for outlet boxes, pull and junction boxes, conduit bodies, and handhole enclosures. As with Article 312, the conditions of use have a bearing on the type of material and equipment selected for a particular installation. If a raceway is installed in a wet location, for example, the correct fittings and the proper installation methods must be used.

Article 314 provides guidance for selecting and installing outlet and device boxes, pull and junction boxes, conduit bodies, and handhole enclosures. Information in this article will help you size an outlet box using the proper cubic-inch capacity as well as calculating the minimum dimensions for larger pull boxes. There are limits on the amount of weight that can be supported by an outlet box and rules on how to support a device or outlet box to various surfaces. This article will help you understand these type of rules so that your installation will be compliant with the *NEC*. As always, the clear illustrations in the accompanying textbook will help you visualize the finished installation.

QUESTIONS FOR ARTICLE 314—OUTLET, DEVICE, PULL AND JUNCTION BOXES; CONDUIT BODIES; AND HANDHOLE ENCLOSURES

1. Nonmetallic boxes can be used with _____.

    (a) nonmetallic cables
    (b) nonmetallic raceways
    (c) flexible cords
    (d) all of these

2. Metal boxes shall be _____ in accordance with Article 250.

    (a) grounded
    (b) bonded
    (c) a and b
    (d) none of these

3. Boxes, conduit bodies, and fittings installed in wet locations shall be required to be listed for use in wet locations.

    (a) True
    (b) False

4. The total volume occupied by two internal cable clamps, six 12 AWG conductors, and a single-pole switch is _____.

    (a) 2.00 cu in.
    (b) 4.50 cu in.
    (c) 14.50 cu in.
    (d) 20.25 cu in.

5. According to the *NEC*, the volume of a 3 x 2 x 2 in. device box is _____.

    (a) 8 cu in.
    (b) 10 cu in.
    (c) 12 cu in.
    (d) 14 cu in.

6. When counting the number of conductors in a box, a conductor running through the box with an unbroken loop or coil not less than twice the minimum length required for free conductors shall be counted as _____ conductor(s).

    (a) one
    (b) two
    (c) three
    (d) four

7. Equipment grounding conductor(s), and not more than _____ fixture wires smaller than 14 AWG can be omitted from the calculations where they enter the box from a domed luminaire or similar canopy and terminate within that box.

   (a) one
   (b) two
   (c) three
   (d) four

8. Where one or more internal cable clamps are present in the box, a single volume allowance in accordance with Table 314.16(B) shall be made, based on the largest conductor present in the box.

   (a) True
   (b) False

9. Where a luminaire stud or hickey is present in the box, a _____ volume allowance in accordance with Table 314.16(B) shall be made for each type of fitting, based on the largest conductor present in the box.

   (a) single
   (b) double
   (c) single allowance for each gang
   (d) none of these

10. For the purposes of determining box fill, each device or utilization equipment in the box which is wider than a single device box counts as two conductors for each _____ required for the mounting.

    (a) inch
    (b) kilometer
    (c) gang
    (d) box

11. Each strap containing one or more devices shall count as a _____ volume allowance in accordance with Table 314.16(B), based on the largest conductor connected to a device(s) or equipment supported by the strap.

    (a) single
    (b) double
    (c) triple
    (d) none of these

12. A device or utilization equipment wider than a single 2 in. device box shall have _____ volume allowances provided for each gang required for mounting.

    (a) single
    (b) double
    (c) triple
    (d) none of these

13. Where one or more equipment grounding conductors enter a box, a _____ volume allowance in accordance with Table 314.16(B) shall be made, based on the largest equipment grounding conductor.

    (a) single
    (b) double
    (c) triple
    (d) none of these

14. Conduit bodies containing conductors larger than 6 AWG shall have a cross-sectional area at least twice that of the largest conduit to which they can be attached.

    (a) True
    (b) False

15. Conduit bodies that are durably and legibly marked by the manufacturer with their volume can contain splices, taps, or devices.

    (a) True
    (b) False

16. Short-radius conduit bodies such as capped elbows, and service-entrance elbows that enclose conductors 6 AWG and smaller shall not contain _____.

(a) splices
(b) taps
(c) devices
(d) any of these

17. When Type NM cable is used with nonmetallic boxes not larger than 2¼ in. x 4 in., securing the cable to the box shall not be required if the cable is fastened within _____ of that box.

(a) 6 in.
(b) 8 in.
(c) 10 in.
(d) 12 in.

18. In noncombustible walls or ceilings, the front edge of a box, plaster ring, extension ring, or listed extender employing a flush-type cover, shall be set back not more than _____ from the finished surface.

(a) ⅛ in.
(b) ¼ in.
(c) ⅜ in.
(d) ½ in.

19. In walls or ceilings constructed of wood or other combustible surface material, boxes, plaster rings, extension rings, or listed extenders shall _____.

(a) be flush with the surface
(b) project from the surface
(c) a or b
(d) be set back no more than ¼ in.

20. Noncombustible surfaces that are broken or incomplete around boxes employing a flush-type cover or faceplate shall be repaired so there will be no gaps or open spaces larger than _____ at the edge of the box.

(a) ¹⁄₁₆ in.
(b) ⅛ in.
(c) ¼ in.
(d) ½ in.

21. Surface extensions shall be made by mounting and mechanically securing an extension ring over the box, unless otherwise permitted.

(a) True
(b) False

22. A surface extension can be made from the cover of a box where the cover is designed so it is unlikely to fall off or be removed if its securing means becomes loose. The wiring method shall be _____ for a length sufficient to permit removal of the cover and provide access to the box interior, and arranged so that any grounding continuity is independent of the connection between the box and cover.

(a) solid
(b) flexible
(c) rigid
(d) cord

23. Surface-mounted outlet boxes shall be _____.

(a) rigidly and securely fastened in place
(b) supported by cables that protrude from the box
(c) supported by cable entries from the top and permitted to rest against the supporting surface
(d) none of these

24. _____ can be used to fasten boxes to structural members of a building using brackets on the outside of the enclosure.

(a) Nails
(b) Screws
(c) Bolts
(d) a and b

25. A wood brace used for supporting a box for structural mounting shall have a cross-section not less than nominal _____.

(a) 1 in. x 2 in.
(b) 2 in. x 2 in.
(c) 2 in. x 3 in.
(d) 2 in. x 4 in.

26. When mounting an enclosure in a finished surface, the enclosure shall be _____ secured to the surface by clamps, anchors, or fittings identified for the application.

    (a) temporarily
    (b) partially
    (c) never
    (d) rigidly

27. Outlet boxes can be secured to suspended-ceiling framing members by mechanical means such as _____, or by other means identified for the suspended-ceiling framing member(s).

    (a) bolts
    (b) screws
    (c) rivets
    (d) all of these

28. Enclosures not over 100 cu in. having threaded entries and not containing a device shall be considered to be adequately supported where _____ or more conduits are threaded wrenchtight into the enclosure and each conduit is secured within 3 ft of the enclosure.

    (a) one
    (b) two
    (c) three
    (d) none of these

29. Two intermediate metal or rigid metal conduits threaded wrenchtight into the enclosure can be used to support an outlet box containing devices or luminaires, if each raceway is supported within _____ of the box.

    (a) 12 in.
    (b) 18 in.
    (c) 24 in.
    (d) 36 in.

30. In completed installations, each outlet box shall have a _____.

    (a) cover
    (b) faceplate
    (c) canopy
    (d) any of these

31. A wall-mounted luminaire weighing not more than _____ can be supported to a device box or plaster ring with no fewer than two No. 6 or larger screws.

    (a) 4 lb
    (b) 6 lb
    (c) 8 lb
    (d) 10 lb

32. Boxes used at luminaire or lampholder outlets in a ceiling shall be designed so that a luminaire or lampholder can be attached and shall be required to support a luminaire weighing a minimum of _____.

    (a) 20 lb
    (b) 30 lb
    (c) 40 lb
    (d) 50 lb

33. A luminaire that weighs more than _____ can be supported by an outlet box that is listed and marked for the weight of the luminaire.

    (a) 20 lb
    (b) 30 lb
    (c) 40 lb
    (d) 50 lb

34. Floor boxes _____ specifically for the application shall be used for receptacles located in the floor.

    (a) identified
    (b) listed
    (c) approved
    (d) none of these

35. Listed outlet boxes to support ceiling-suspended fans that weigh more than _____ lb shall have the maximum allowable weight marked on the box.

    (a) 35 lb
    (b) 50 lb
    (c) 60 lb
    (d) 70 lb

36. Utilization equipment weighing less than 6 lb can be supported to any box or plaster ring secured to a box, provided the equipment is secured with at least two _____ or larger screws.

    (a) No. 6
    (b) No. 8
    (c) No. 10
    (d) self tapping

37. In straight pulls, the length of the box or conduit body shall not be less than _____ times the trade size of the largest raceway.

    (a) six
    (b) eight
    (c) twelve
    (d) none of these

38. Where angle or U pulls are made, the distance between each raceway entry inside the box or conduit body and the opposite wall of the box or conduit body shall not be less than _____ times the trade size of the largest raceway in a row plus the sum of the trade sizes of the remaining raceways in the same wall and row.

    (a) six
    (b) eight
    (c) twelve
    (d) none of these

39. Pull boxes or junction boxes with any dimension over _____ shall have all conductors cabled or racked in an approved manner.

    (a) 3 ft
    (b) 6 ft
    (c) 9 ft
    (d) 12 ft

40. Power distribution blocks shall be permitted in pull and junction boxes over 100 cubic inches when they comply with the provisions of 314.28(E).

    (a) True
    (b) False

41. Power distribution blocks shall be permitted in pull and junction boxes over 100 cubic inches when _____.

    (a) they are listed as a power distribution block.
    (b) they are installed in a box not smaller than required by the installation instructions of the power distribution block.
    (c) the junction box is sized so that the wire-bending space requirements of 312.6 can be met.
    (d) all of these

42. Exposed live parts on the power distribution block are allowed when the junction box cover is removed.

    (a) True
    (b) False

43. Where the junction box contains a power distribution block, and it has conductors that don't terminate on the power distribution block(s), the through conductors must be arranged so the power distribution block terminals are _____ following installation.

    (a) unobstructed
    (b) above the through conductors
    (c) visible
    (d) labeled

44. _____ shall be installed so that the wiring contained can be rendered accessible without removing any part of the building or, in underground circuits, without excavating sidewalks, paving, or earth.

    (a) Boxes
    (b) Conduit bodies
    (c) Handhole enclosures
    (d) all of these

45. Listed boxes and handhole enclosures designed for underground installation can be directly buried when covered by _____, if their location is effectively identified and accessible.

    (a) concrete
    (b) gravel
    (c) noncohesive granulated soil
    (d) b or c

46. Handhole enclosures shall be designed and installed to withstand _____.

    (a) 600 lb
    (b) 3,000 lb
    (c) 6,000 lb
    (d) all loads likely to be imposed

47. Underground raceways and cable assemblies entering a handhole enclosure shall extend into the enclosure, but they are not required to be _____.

    (a) bonded
    (b) insulated
    (c) mechanically connected to the handhole enclosure
    (d) below minimum cover requirements after leaving the handhole

48. Conductors, splices or terminations in a handhole enclosure shall be listed as _____.

    (a) suitable for wet locations
    (b) suitable for damp locations
    (c) suitable for direct burial in the earth
    (d) none of these

49. Handhole enclosure covers shall have an identifying _____ that prominently identifies the function of the enclosure, such as electric.

    (a) mark
    (b) logo
    (c) a or b
    (d) manual

50. Handhole enclosure covers shall require the use of tools to open, or they shall weigh over _____.

    (a) 45 lb
    (b) 70 lb
    (c) 100 lb
    (d) 200 lb

51. Boxes and conduit bodies, covers, extension rings, plaster rings, and the like shall be durably and legibly marked with the manufacturer's name or trademark.

    (a) True
    (b) False

ARTICLE
320

Armored Cable (Type AC)

INTRODUCTION TO ARTICLE 320—ARMORED CABLE (TYPE AC)

Armored cable is an assembly of insulated conductors, 14 AWG through 1 AWG, individually wrapped within waxed paper and contained within a flexible spiral metal sheath. The outside appearance of armored cable looks like flexible metal conduit as well as metal-clad cable to the casual observer. This cable has been referred to as "BX®" cable over the years and used in residential wiring in some areas of the country.

QUESTIONS FOR ARTICLE 320— ARMORED CABLE (TYPE AC)

1. Type _____ cable is a fabricated assembly of insulated conductors in a flexible interlocked metallic armor.

    (a) AC
    (b) MC
    (c) NM
    (d) b and c

2. Type AC cable is permitted in _____ installations.

    (a) wet
    (b) cable tray
    (c) exposed
    (d) b and c

3. Armored cable shall not be installed _____.

    (a) in damp or wet locations
    (b) where subject to physical damage
    (c) where exposed to corrosive conditions
    (d) all of these

4. Exposed runs of Type AC cable can be installed on the underside of joists where supported at each joist and located so they are not subject to physical damage.

    (a) True
    (b) False

5. Type AC cable installed through, or parallel to, framing members shall be protected against physical damage from penetration by screws or nails.

    (a) True
    (b) False

6. When Type AC cable is run across the top of a floor joist in an attic without permanent ladders or stairs, substantial guard strips within _____ of the scuttle hole, or attic entrance, shall protect the cable.

    (a) 3 ft
    (b) 4 ft
    (c) 5 ft
    (d) 6 ft

7. When armored cable is run parallel to the sides of rafters, studs, or floor joists in an accessible attic, the cable shall be protected with running boards.

    (a) True
    (b) False

8. The radius of the curve of the inner edge of any bend shall not be less than _____ for Type AC cable.

   (a) five times the largest conductor within the cable
   (b) three times the diameter of the cable
   (c) five times the diameter of the cable
   (d) six times the outside diameter of the conductors

9. Type AC cable can be supported and secured by _____.

   (a) staples
   (b) cable ties
   (c) straps
   (d) all of these

10. Type AC cable shall be secured at intervals not exceeding 4½ ft and within _____ of every outlet box, cabinet, conduit body, or fitting.

    (a) 6 in.
    (b) 8 in.
    (c) 10 in.
    (d) 12 in.

11. Type AC cable installed horizontally through wooden or metal framing members is considered supported where support doesn't exceed _____.

    (a) 2 ft
    (b) 3 ft
    (c) 4½ ft
    (d) 6 ft

12. Armored cable used to connect recessed luminaires or equipment within an accessible ceiling can be unsecured for lengths up to _____.

    (a) 2 ft
    (b) 3 ft
    (c) 4½ ft
    (d) 6 ft

13. At Type AC cable terminations, a(n) _____ shall be provided.

    (a) fitting (or box design) that protects the conductors from abrasion
    (b) insulating bushing between the conductors and the cable armor
    (c) a and b
    (d) none of these

14. Type AC cable installed in thermal insulation shall have conductors that are rated at 90°C. The ampacity of the cable in this application shall be based on _____.

    (a) that of 60°C conductors
    (b) that of 75°C conductors
    (c) that of 90°C conductors
    (d) none of these

ARTICLE
330

Metal-Clad Cable (Type MC)

INTRODUCTION TO ARTICLE 330—METAL-CLAD CABLE (TYPE MC)

Metal-clad cable encloses insulated conductors in a metal sheath of either corrugated or smooth copper or aluminum tubing, or spiral inter-locked steel or aluminum. The physical characteristics of Type MC cable make it a versatile wiring method that you can use in almost any location, and for almost any application. The most commonly used Type MC cable is the interlocking kind, which looks similar to armored cable or flexible metal conduit. Traditional interlocked Type MC cable isn't permitted to serve as an equipment grounding conductor, there-fore this cable must contain an insulated equipment grounding conductor in accordance with 250.118(1). There is a fairly new product called interlocked Type MC^AP cable containing an aluminum grounding/bonding conductor running just below the metal armor, which allows the sheath to serve as an equipment grounding conductor [250.118(10)(b)].

QUESTIONS FOR ARTICLE 330—
METAL-CLAD CABLE (TYPE MC)

1. Type _____ is a factory assembly of insulated circuit conduc-tors within an armor of interlocking metal tape, or a smooth or corrugated metallic sheath.

    (a) AC
    (b) MC
    (c) NM
    (d) b and c

2. Type MC cable shall not be _____ unless the metallic sheath or armor is resistant to the conditions, or is protected by mate-rial resistant to the conditions.

    (a) used for direct burial in the earth
    (b) embedded in concrete
    (c) exposed to cinder fill
    (d) all of these

3. Type MC cable installed through, or parallel to, framing members shall be protected against physical damage from penetration by screws or nails by 1¼ in. separation or protected by a suitable metal plate.

    (a) True
    (b) False

4. Smooth-sheath Type MC cable with an external diameter not greater than ¾ in. shall have a bending radius not more than _____ times the cable external diameter.

    (a) five
    (b) 10
    (c) 12
    (d) 13

5. Bends made in interlocked or corrugated sheath Type MC cable shall have a radius of at least _____ times the external diam-eter of the metallic sheath.

    (a) 5
    (b) 7
    (c) 10
    (d) 12

6. Type MC cable containing four or fewer conductors, sized no larger than 10 AWG, shall be secured within _____ of every box, cabinet, fitting, or other cable termination.

    (a) 8 in.
    (b) 12 in.
    (c) 18 in.
    (d) 24 in.

7. Type MC cable shall be secured at intervals not exceeding _____.

(a) 3 ft
(b) 4 ft
(c) 6 ft
(d) 8 ft

8. Type MC cable installed horizontally through wooden or metal framing members are considered secured and supported where such support doesn't exceed _____ intervals.

(a) 3 ft
(b) 4 ft
(c) 6 ft
(d) 8 ft

9. Type MC cable can be unsupported where _____.

(a) fished between concealed access points in finished buildings or structures and support is impracticable
(b) not more than 2 ft in length at terminals where flexibility is necessary
(c) not more than 6 ft from the last point of support within an accessible ceiling for the connection of luminaires or other electrical equipment
(d) a or c

10. Fittings used for connecting Type MC cable to boxes, cabinets, or other equipment shall _____.

(a) be nonmetallic only
(b) be listed and identified for such use
(c) be listed and identified as weatherproof
(d) include anti-shorting bushings

11. The minimum size copper conductor permitted for Type MC cable is _____.

(a) 18 AWG
(b) 16 AWG
(c) 14 AWG
(d) 12 AWG

12. The metallic sheath of metal-clad cable shall be continuous and _____.

(a) flame-retardant
(b) weatherproof
(c) close fitting
(d) all of these

ARTICLE 334

Nonmetallic-Sheathed Cable (Types NM and NMC)

INTRODUCTION TO ARTICLE 334—NONMETALLIC-SHEATHED CABLE (TYPES NM AND NMC)

Nonmetallic-sheathed cable is flexible, inexpensive, and easily installed. It provides very limited physical protection for the conductors, so the installation restrictions are strict. Its low cost and relative ease of installation make it a common wiring method for residential and commercial branch circuits. In the field, Type NM cable is typically referred to as "Romex®."

QUESTIONS FOR ARTICLE 334—NONMETALLIC-SHEATHED CABLE (TYPES NM AND NMC)

1. Type _____ cable is a wiring method that encloses two or more insulated conductors within a nonmetallic jacket.

   (a) AC
   (b) MC
   (c) NM
   (d) b and c

2. Type NM cable shall be _____.

   (a) marked
   (b) approved
   (c) identified
   (d) listed

3. Type NM cables shall not be used in one- and two-family dwellings exceeding three floors above grade.

   (a) True
   (b) False

4. Type NM and Type NMC cables shall be permitted in _____.

   (a) in one- and two-family dwellings and their attached/ detached garages or storage buildings
   (b) multifamily dwellings permitted to be of Types III, IV, and V construction
   (c) other structures permitted to be of Types III, IV, and V construction, except as prohibited in 334.12.
   (d) any of these

5. Type NM cable can be installed as open runs in dropped or suspended ceilings in other than one- and two-family and multifamily dwellings.

   (a) True
   (b) False

6. Type NM cable shall not be used _____.

   (a) in other than dwelling units
   (b) in the air void of masonry block not subject to excessive moisture
   (c) for exposed work
   (d) embedded in poured cement, concrete, or aggregate

7. Type NM cable shall closely follow the surface of the building finish or running boards when run exposed.

   (a) True
   (b) False

8. Type NM cable shall be protected from physical damage by _____.

   (a) EMT
   (b) Schedule 80 PVC conduit
   (c) RMC
   (d) any of these

9. Type NM cable on a wall of an unfinished basement installed in a listed raceway shall have a(n) _____ installed at the point where the cable enters the raceway.

    (a) insulating bushing or adapter
    (b) sealing fitting
    (c) bonding bushing
    (d) junction box

10. Where Type NM cable is run at angles with joists in unfinished basements and crawl spaces, it is permissible to secure cables not smaller than _____ conductors directly to the lower edges of the joist.

    (a) two, 6 AWG
    (b) three, 8 AWG
    (c) three, 10 AWG
    (d) a or b

11. Grommets or bushings for the protection of Type NM cable shall be _____ for the purpose.

    (a) marked
    (b) approved
    (c) identified
    (d) listed

12. Type NM cable can be supported and secured by _____.

    (a) staples
    (b) cable ties
    (c) straps
    (d) all of these

13. Type NM cable protected from physical damage by a raceway shall not be required to be _____ within the raceway.

    (a) covered
    (b) insulated
    (c) secured
    (d) unspliced

14. Flat Type NM cables shall not be stapled on edge.

    (a) True
    (b) False

15. Where more than two Type NM cables are installed through the same opening in wood framing that is to be sealed with thermal insulation, caulk, or sealing foam, the allowable ampacity of each conductor shall be _____.

    (a) no more than 20A
    (b) adjusted in accordance with Table 310.15(B)(3)(a)
    (c) limited to 30A
    (d) calculated by an engineer

16. For Type NM and NMC cable, the conductor ampacity used for ambient temperature correction [310.15(B)(2)(a)], conductor bundling adjustment [310.15(B)(3)(a)], or both, is based on the 90ºC conductor insulation rating [310.15(B)(2)], provided the adjusted or corrected ampacity doesn't exceed that for a _____ rated conductor.

    (a) 60°C
    (b) 75°C
    (c) 90°C
    (d) 120°C

17. The insulation temperature rating of conductors in Type NM cable shall be _____.

    (a) 60°C
    (b) 75°C
    (c) 90°C
    (d) 105°C

18. The difference in construction between Type NM cable and Type NMC cable is that Type NMC cable is _____, which Type NM is not.

    (a) corrosion resistant
    (b) flame-retardant
    (c) fungus-resistant
    (d) a and c

ARTICLE 338

Service-Entrance Cable (Types SE and USE)

INTRODUCTION TO ARTICLE 338—SERVICE-ENTRANCE CABLE (TYPES SE AND USE)

Service-entrance cable is a single conductor or multiconductor assembly with or without an overall moisture-resistant covering. This cable is used primarily for services not over 600V, but can also be used for feeders and branch circuits when the limitations of this article are observed.

QUESTIONS FOR ARTICLE 338—SERVICE-ENTRANCE CABLE (TYPES SE AND USE)

1. Type _____ cable is an assembly primarily for services.

   (a) NM
   (b) TC
   (c) SE
   (d) none of these

2. Type _____ is a multiconductor cable identified for use as underground service-entrance cable.

   (a) SE
   (b) NM
   (c) UF
   (d) USE

3. Type SE cable shall be permitted to be used as _____ in wiring systems where all of the circuit conductors of the cable are of the thermoset or thermoplastic type.

   (a) branch circuits
   (b) feeders
   (c) a or b
   (d) neither a or b

4. Type SE cables shall be permitted to be used for branch circuits or feeders where the insulated conductors are used for circuit wiring and the uninsulated conductor is used only for _____ purposes.

   (a) grounded connection
   (b) equipment grounding
   (c) remote control and signaling
   (d) none of these

5. Type SE cable can be used for interior wiring as long as it complies with the installation requirements of Part II of Article 334, excluding 334.80.

   (a) True
   (b) False

6. Type USE cable is not permitted for _____ wiring.

   (a) underground
   (b) interior
   (c) a or b
   (d) a and b

7. Type USE cable used for service laterals shall be permitted to emerge from the ground if terminated in an enclosure at an outside location and protected in accordance with 300.5(D).

   (a) True
   (b) False

8. The radius of the curve of the inner edge of any bend, during or after installation, shall not be less than _____ times the diameter of Type USE or SE cable.

    (a) five
    (b) seven
    (c) 10
    (d) 12

ARTICLE 340

Underground Feeder and Branch-Circuit Cable (Type UF)

INTRODUCTION TO ARTICLE 340—UNDERGROUND FEEDER AND BRANCH-CIRCUIT CABLE (TYPE UF)

UF cable is a moisture-, fungus-, and corrosion-resistant cable suitable for direct burial in the earth.

QUESTIONS FOR ARTICLE 340— UNDERGROUND FEEDER AND BRANCH-CIRCUIT CABLE (TYPE UF)

1. Type _____ cable is a factory assembly of conductors with an overall covering of nonmetallic material suitable for direct burial in the earth.

   (a) NM
   (b) UF
   (c) SE
   (d) TC

2. Type UF cable is permitted to be used for inside wiring.

   (a) True
   (b) False

3. Type UF cable can be used for service conductors.

   (a) True
   (b) False

4. Type UF cable can be used in commercial garages.

   (a) True
   (b) False

5. Type UF cable shall not be used in _____.

   (a) motion picture studios
   (b) storage battery rooms
   (c) hoistways
   (d) all of these

6. Type UF cable shall not be used _____.

   (a) in any hazardous (classified) location except as otherwise permitted in this *Code*
   (b) embedded in poured cement, concrete, or aggregate
   (c) where exposed to direct rays of the sun, unless identified as sunlight resistant
   (d) all of these

7. Type UF cable shall not be used where subject to physical damage.

   (a) True
   (b) False

8. The ampacity of Type UF cable shall be that of _____ in accordance with 310.15.

   (a) 60°C conductors
   (b) 75°C conductors
   (c) 90°C conductors
   (d) 105°C

9. The maximum size of conductors in Type UF cable shall be _____ AWG.

(a) 14

(b) 10

(c) 1/0

(d) 4/0

10. The overall covering of Type UF cable is _____.

(a) flame retardant

(b) moisture, fungus, and corrosion resistant

(c) suitable for direct burial in the earth

(d) all of these

ARTICLE 342

Intermediate Metal Conduit (Type IMC)

INTRODUCTION TO ARTICLE 342—INTERMEDIATE METAL CONDUIT (TYPE IMC)

Intermediate metal conduit (IMC) is a circular metal raceway with an outside diameter equal to that of rigid metal conduit. The wall thickness of intermediate metal conduit is less than that of rigid metal conduit (RMC), so it's a greater interior cross-sectional area for containing conductors. Intermediate metal conduit is lighter and less expensive than rigid metal conduit, but it can be used in all of the same locations as rigid metal conduit. Intermediate metal conduit also uses a different steel alloy that makes it stronger than rigid metal conduit, even though the walls are thinner. Intermediate metal conduit is manufactured in both galvanized steel and aluminum; the steel type is much more common.

QUESTIONS FOR ARTICLE 342—INTERMEDIATE METAL CONDUIT (TYPE IMC)

1. IMC can be installed in or under cinder fill subject to permanent moisture _____.

   (a) where the conduit is not less than 18 in. under the fill
   (b) when protected on all sides by 2 in. of noncinder concrete
   (c) where protected by corrosion protection judged suitable for the condition
   (d) any of these

2. Materials such as straps, bolts, screws, and so forth, which are associated with the installation of IMC in wet locations shall be _____.

   (a) weatherproof
   (b) weathertight
   (c) corrosion resistant
   (d) none of these

3. Where practicable, contact of dissimilar metals shall be avoided in an IMC raceway installation to prevent _____.

   (a) corrosion
   (b) galvanic action
   (c) shorts
   (d) none of these

4. A run of IMC shall not contain more than the equivalent of _____ quarter bends between pull points such as conduit bodies and boxes.

   (a) one
   (b) two
   (c) three
   (d) four

5. When IMC is cut in the field, reaming is required to remove the burrs and rough edges.

   (a) True
   (b) False

6. IMC must be secured _____.

   (a) by fastening within 3 ft of each outlet box, junction box, device box, cabinet, conduit body, or other conduit termination
   (b) within 5 ft of a box or termination fitting when structural members don't permit the raceway to be secured within 3 ft of the termination
   (c) except when the IMC is within 3 ft of the service head for an above-the-roof termination of a mast
   (d) a, b, or c

7. Trade size 1 IMC shall be supported at intervals not exceeding
    _____.

    (a) 8 ft
    (b) 10 ft
    (c) 12 ft
    (d) 14 ft

8. Horizontal runs of IMC supported by openings through framing
    members at intervals not exceeding 10 ft and securely fastened
    within 3 ft of terminations shall be permitted.

    (a) True
    (b) False

9. Threadless couplings and connectors used on threaded IMC
    ends shall be listed for the purpose.

    (a) True
    (b) False

10. Threadless couplings approved for use with IMC in wet loca-
    tions shall be _____.

    (a) rainproof
    (b) listed for wet locations
    (c) moistureproof
    (d) concrete-tight

11. Running threads shall not be used on IMC for connection at
    couplings.

    (a) True
    (b) False

12. Where IMC enters a box, fitting, or other enclosure, _____
    shall be provided to protect the wire from abrasion, unless
    the design of the box, fitting, or enclosure affords equivalent
    protection.

    (a) a bushing
    (b) duct seal
    (c) electrical tape
    (d) seal fittings

ARTICLE 344

Rigid Metal Conduit (Type RMC)

INTRODUCTION TO ARTICLE 344—RIGID METAL CONDUIT (TYPE RMC)

Rigid metal conduit, commonly called "rigid," has long been the standard raceway for providing protection from physical impact and from difficult environments. The outside diameter of rigid metal conduit is the same as intermediate metal conduit. However, the wall thickness of rigid metal conduit is greater than intermediate metal conduit; therefore it's a smaller interior cross-sectional area. Rigid metal conduit is heavier and more expensive than intermediate metal conduit, and it can be used in any location. Rigid metal conduit is manufactured in both galvanized steel and aluminum; the steel type is much more common.

QUESTIONS FOR ARTICLE 344— RIGID METAL CONDUIT (TYPE RMC)

1. Galvanized steel, stainless steel and red brass RMC can be installed in concrete, in direct contact with the earth, or in areas subject to severe corrosive influences when protected by _____ and judged suitable for the condition.

   (a) ceramic
   (b) corrosion protection
   (c) backfill
   (d) a natural barrier

2. Galvanized steel, stainless steel, and red brass RMC shall be permitted in or under cinder fill subject to permanent moisture, when protected on all sides by a layer of noncinder concrete not less than _____ thick.

   (a) 2 in.
   (b) 4 in.
   (c) 6 in.
   (d) 18 in.

3. Materials such as straps, bolts, and so forth., associated with the installation of RMC in wet locations shall be _____.

   (a) weatherproof
   (b) weathertight
   (c) corrosion resistant
   (d) none of these

4. Aluminum fittings and enclosures can be used with _____ conduit where not subject to severe corrosive influences.

   (a) steel rigid metal
   (b) aluminum rigid metal
   (c) PVC-coated rigid conduit only
   (d) a and b

5. The minimum radius of a field bend on trade size 1¼ RMC is _____.

   (a) 7 in.
   (b) 8 in.
   (c) 10 in.
   (d) 14 in.

6. A run of RMC shall not contain more than the equivalent of _____ quarter bends between pull points such as conduit bodies and boxes.

   (a) one
   (b) two
   (c) three
   (d) four

7. Cut ends of RMC shall be _____ or otherwise finished to remove rough edges.

   (a) threaded
   (b) reamed
   (c) painted
   (d) galvanized

8. Horizontal runs of RMC supported by openings through _____ at intervals not exceeding 10 ft and securely fastened within 3 ft of termination points shall be permitted.

   (a) walls
   (b) trusses
   (c) rafters
   (d) framing members

9. Threadless couplings and connectors used with RMC in wet locations shall be _____.

   (a) listed for wet locations
   (b) listed for damp locations
   (c) nonabsorbent
   (d) weatherproof

10. Threadless couplings and connectors used with RMC buried in masonry or concrete shall be the _____ type.

    (a) raintight
    (b) wet and damp location
    (c) nonabsorbent
    (d) concrete-tight

11. Running threads shall not be used on RMC for connection at _____.

    (a) boxes
    (b) cabinets
    (c) couplings
    (d) meter sockets

12. Where RMC enters a box, fitting, or other enclosure, _____ shall be provided to protect the wire from abrasion, unless the design of the box, fitting, or enclosure affords equivalent protection.

    (a) a bushing
    (b) duct seal
    (c) electrical tape
    (d) seal fittings

13. Each length of RMC shall be clearly and durably identified in every _____.

    (a) 3 ft
    (b) 5 ft
    (c) 10 ft
    (d) 20 ft

14. The standard length of RMC shall _____.

    (a) be 10 ft
    (b) include a coupling on each length
    (c) be threaded on each end
    (d) all of these

ARTICLE 348

Flexible Metal Conduit (Type FMC)

INTRODUCTION TO ARTICLE 348—FLEXIBLE METAL CONDUIT (TYPE FMC)

Flexible metal conduit (FMC), commonly called "Greenfield" or "flex," is a raceway of an interlocked metal strip of either steel or aluminum. It's primarily used for the final 6 ft or less of raceways between a more rigid raceway system and equipment that moves, shakes, or vibrates. Examples of such equipment include pump motors and industrial machinery.

QUESTIONS FOR ARTICLE 348— FLEXIBLE METAL CONDUIT (TYPE FMC)

1. _____ is a raceway of circular cross section made of a helically wound, formed, interlocked metal strip.

    (a) Type MC cable
    (b) Type AC Cable
    (c) LFMC
    (d) FMC

2. FMC shall not be installed _____.

    (a) in wet locations
    (b) embedded in poured concrete
    (c) where subject to physical damage
    (d) all of these

3. FMC can be installed exposed or concealed where not subject to physical damage.

    (a) True
    (b) False

4. Bends in FMC shall be made so that the conduit is not damaged and the internal diameter of the conduit is _____.

    (a) larger than ⅜ in.
    (b) not effectively reduced
    (c) increased
    (d) larger than 1 in.

5. Bends in FMC _____ between pull points.

    (a) shall not be made
    (b) need not be limited (in degrees)
    (c) shall not exceed 360 degrees
    (d) shall not exceed 180 degrees

6. Cut ends of FMC shall be trimmed or otherwise finished to remove rough edges, except where fittings _____.

    (a) are the crimp-on type
    (b) thread into the convolutions
    (c) contain insulated throats
    (d) are listed for grounding

7. FMC shall be supported and secured _____.

    (a) at intervals not exceeding 4½ ft
    (b) within 8 in. on each side of a box where fished
    (c) where fished
    (d) at intervals not exceeding 6 ft

8. Flexible metal conduit must be securely fastened by a means approved by the authority having jurisdiction within _____ of termination.

    (a) 6 in.
    (b) 10 in.
    (c) 1 ft
    (d) 10 ft

9. Flexible metal conduit shall not be required to be _____ where fished between access points through concealed spaces in finished buildings or structures and supporting is impracticable.

   (a) secured
   (b) supported
   (c) complete
   (d) a and b

10. For flexible metal conduit, if flexibility is necessary after installation, unsecured lengths from the last point the raceway is securely fastened must not exceed _____.

    (a) 3 ft for trade sizes ½ through 1 ¼
    (b) 4 ft for trade sizes 1 ½ through 2
    (c) 5 ft for trade sizes 2 ½ and larger
    (d) all of these

11. FMC to a luminaire or electrical equipment within an accessible ceiling is permitted to be unsupported for not more than 6 ft from the last point where the raceway is securely fastened.

    (a) True
    (b) False

12. In an FMC installation, _____ connectors shall not be concealed.

    (a) straight
    (b) angle
    (c) grounding-type
    (d) none of these

13. When FMC is used where flexibility is necessary to minimize the transmission of vibration from equipment or to provide flexibility for equipment that requires movement after installation, _____ shall be installed.

    (a) an equipment grounding conductor
    (b) an expansion fitting
    (c) flexible nonmetallic connectors
    (d) none of these

ARTICLE 350

Liquidtight Flexible Metal Conduit (Type LFMC)

INTRODUCTION TO ARTICLE 350—LIQUIDTIGHT FLEXIBLE METAL CONDUIT (TYPE LFMC)

Liquidtight flexible metal conduit (LFMC), with its associated connectors and fittings, is a flexible raceway commonly used for connections to equipment that vibrate or are required to move occasionally. Liquidtight flexible metal conduit is commonly called "Sealtight®" or "liquidtight." Liquidtight flexible metal conduit is of similar construction to flexible metal conduit, but it also has an outer liquidtight thermoplastic covering. It has the same primary purpose as flexible metal conduit, but it also provides protection from moisture and some corrosive effects.

QUESTIONS FOR ARTICLE 350—LIQUIDTIGHT FLEXIBLE METAL CONDUIT (TYPE LFMC)

1. _____ is a raceway of circular cross section having an outer liquidtight, nonmetallic, sunlight-resistant jacket over an inner flexible metal core.

   (a) FMC
   (b) LFNMC
   (c) LFMC
   (d) none of these

2. The use of LFMC shall be permitted for _____.

   (a) direct burial where listed and marked for the purpose
   (b) exposed work
   (c) concealed work
   (d) all of these

3. Liquidtight flexible metal conduit must be securely fastened by a means approved by the authority having jurisdiction within _____ of termination.

   (a) 6 in.
   (b) 10 in.
   (c) 1 ft
   (d) 10 ft

4. LFMC shall be supported and secured _____.

   (a) at intervals not exceeding 4½ ft
   (b) within 8 in. on each side of a box where fished
   (c) where fished
   (d) at intervals not exceeding 6 ft

5. LFMC shall not be required to be secured or supported where fished between access points through _____ spaces in finished buildings or structures and supporting is impractical.

   (a) concealed
   (b) exposed
   (c) hazardous
   (d) completed

6. For liquidtight flexible metal conduit, if flexibility is necessary after installation, unsecured lengths from the last point the raceway is securely fastened must not exceed _____.

   (a) 3 ft for trade sizes ½ through 1 ¼
   (b) 4 ft for trade sizes 1 ½ through 2
   (c) 5 ft for trade sizes 2 ½ and larger
   (d) all of these

7. _____ connectors shall not be concealed when used in installations of LFMC.

(a) Straight
(b) Angle
(c) Grounding-type
(d) none of these

8. When LFMC is used to connect equipment where flexibility is necessary to minimize the transmission of vibration from equipment of for equipment requiring movement after installation, a(n) _____ conductor shall be installed.

(a) main bonding
(b) grounded
(c) equipment grounding
(d) none of these

9. Where flexibility _____, liquidtight flexible metal conduit shall be permitted to be used as an equipment grounding conductor when installed in accordance with 250.118(6).

(a) is required after installation
(b) is not required after installation
(c) either a or d
(d) is optional

INTRODUCTION TO ARTICLE 352—RIGID POLYVINYL CHLORIDE CONDUIT (TYPE PVC)

Rigid polyvinyl chloride conduit (PVC) is a rigid nonmetallic conduit that provides many of the advantages of rigid metal conduit, while allowing installation in areas that are wet or corrosive. It's an inexpensive raceway, and easily installed. It's lightweight, easily cut, glued together, and relatively strong. However, conduits manufactured from polyvinyl chloride (PVC) are brittle when cold, and they sag when hot. This type of conduit is commonly used as an underground raceway because of its low cost, ease of installation, and resistance to corrosion and decay.

QUESTIONS FOR ARTICLE 352—RIGID POLYVINYL CHLORIDE CONDUIT (TYPE PVC)

1. Extreme _____ may cause PVC conduit to become brittle, and therefore more susceptible to damage from physical contact.

   (a) sunlight
   (b) corrosive conditions
   (c) heat
   (d) cold

2. PVC conduit shall be permitted for exposed work where subject to physical damage if identified for such use.

   (a) True
   (b) False

3. PVC conduit can support nonmetallic conduit bodies not larger than the largest entering raceway, but the conduit bodies shall not contain devices, luminaires, or other equipment.

   (a) True
   (b) False

4. Conductors rated at a temperature _____ than the listed temperature rating of PVC conduit shall not be installed in PVC conduit, unless the conductors are not operated at a temperature above the raceways listed temperature rating of the PVC conduit.

   (a) lower
   (b) the same as
   (c) higher
   (d) a or b

5. PVC conduit shall not be used _____, unless specifically permitted.

   (a) in hazardous (classified) locations
   (b) for the support of luminaires or other equipment
   (c) where subject to physical damage unless identified for such use
   (d) all of these

6. The number of conductors permitted in PVC conduit shall not exceed the percentage fill specified in _____.

   (a) Chapter 9, Table 1
   (b) Table 250.66
   (c) Table 310.15(B)(16)
   (d) 240.6

7. Bends in PVC conduit shall be made only _____.

(a) by hand forming the bend
(b) with bending equipment identified for the purpose
(c) with a truck exhaust pipe
(d) by use of an open flame torch

8. Bends in PVC conduit shall _____ between pull points.

(a) not be made
(b) not be limited in degrees
(c) be limited to 360 degrees
(d) be limited to 180 degrees

9. The cut ends of PVC conduit must be trimmed to remove the burrs and rough edges.

(a) True
(b) False

10. PVC conduit shall be securely fastened within _____ of each box.

(a) 6 in.
(b) 12 in.
(c) 24 in.
(d) 36 in.

11. Where PVC conduit enters a box, fitting, or other enclosure, a bushing or adapter shall be provided to protect the conductor from abrasion unless the design of the box, fitting, or enclosure affords equivalent protection.

(a) True
(b) False

12. Joints between PVC conduit, couplings, fittings, and boxes shall be made by _____.

(a) the authority having jurisdiction
(b) set screw fittings
(c) an approved method
(d) expansion fittings

13. PVC conduit and fittings for use above ground shall have the following characteristics _____.

(a) flame retardant
(b) resistance to low temperatures and sunlight
(c) resistance to distortion from heat
(d) all of these

Liquidtight Flexible Nonmetallic Conduit (Type LFNC)

INTRODUCTION TO ARTICLE 356—LIQUIDTIGHT FLEXIBLE NONMETALLIC CONDUIT (TYPE LFNC)

Liquidtight flexible nonmetallic conduit (LFNC) is a listed raceway of circular cross section having an outer liquidtight, nonmetallic, sunlight-resistant jacket over an inner flexible core with associated couplings, connectors, and fittings.

QUESTIONS FOR ARTICLE 356—LIQUIDTIGHT FLEXIBLE NONMETALLIC CONDUIT (TYPE LFNC)

1. LFNC shall be permitted for _____.

   (a) direct burial where listed and marked for the purpose
   (b) exposed work
   (c) outdoors where listed and marked for this purpose
   (d) all of these

2. The number of conductors permitted in LFNC shall not exceed the percentage fill specified in _____.

   (a) Chapter 9, Table 1
   (b) Table 250.66
   (c) Table 310.15(B)(16)
   (d) 240.6

3. Bends in LFNC shall be made so that the conduit will not be damaged and the internal diameter of the conduit will not be effectively reduced. Bends can be made _____.

   (a) manually without auxiliary equipment
   (b) with bending equipment identified for the purpose
   (c) with any kind of conduit bending tool that will work
   (d) by the use of an open flame torch

4. Bends in LFNC shall _____ between pull points.

   (a) not be made
   (b) not be limited in degrees
   (c) be limited to 360 degrees
   (d) be limited to 180 degrees

5. When LFNC is used to connect equipment requiring flexibility after installation, a separate _____ shall be installed.

   (a) equipment grounding conductor
   (b) expansion fitting
   (c) flexible nonmetallic connector
   (d) none of these

INTRODUCTION TO ARTICLE 358—ELECTRICAL METALLIC TUBING (TYPE EMT)

Electrical metallic tubing (EMT) is a lightweight raceway that's relatively easy to bend, cut, and ream. Because it isn't threaded, all connectors and couplings are of the threadless type and provide quick, easy, and inexpensive installation when compared to other metallic conduit systems, which makes it very popular. Electrical metallic tubing is manufactured in both galvanized steel and aluminum; the steel type is the most common type used.

QUESTIONS FOR ARTICLE 358—ELECTRICAL METALLIC TUBING (TYPE EMT)

1. _____ is a listed thin-wall, metallic tubing of circular cross section used for the installation and physical protection of electrical conductors when joined together with listed fittings.

    (a) LFNC
    (b) EMT
    (c) NUCC
    (d) RTRC

2. EMT, elbows, couplings, and fittings can be installed in concrete, in direct contact with the earth, or in areas subject to severe corrosive influences if _____.

    (a) protected by corrosion protection
    (b) approved as suitable for the condition
    (c) a and b
    (d) list for wet locations

3. When EMT is installed in wet locations, all supports, bolts, straps, and screws shall be _____.

    (a) of corrosion-resistant materials
    (b) protected against corrosion
    (c) a or b
    (d) of nonmetallic materials only

4. EMT shall not be used where _____.

    (a) subject to severe physical damage
    (b) protected from corrosion only by enamel
    (c) used for the support of luminaires
    (d) any of these

5. EMT shall not be threaded.

    (a) True
    (b) False

6. EMT couplings and connectors shall be made up _____.

    (a) of metal
    (b) in accordance with industry standards
    (c) tight
    (d) none of these

ARTICLE 362

Electrical Nonmetallic Tubing (Type ENT)

INTRODUCTION TO ARTICLE 362—ELECTRICAL NONMETALLIC TUBING (TYPE ENT)

Electrical nonmetallic tubing (ENT) is a pliable, corrugated, circular raceway made of polyvinyl chloride. In some parts of the country, the field name for electrical nonmetallic tubing is "Smurf Pipe" or "Smurf Tube," because it was only available in blue when it originally came out at the time the children's cartoon characters "The Smurfs" were most popular. Today, the raceway is available in a rainbow of colors such as white, yellow, red, green, and orange, and is sold in both fixed lengths and on reels.

QUESTIONS FOR ARTICLE 362—ELECTRICAL NONMETALLIC TUBING (TYPE ENT)

1. ENT is composed of a material resistant to moisture and chemical atmospheres, and is _____.

   (a) flexible
   (b) flame retardant
   (c) fireproof
   (d) flammable

2. When a building is supplied with a(n) _____ fire sprinkler system, ENT shall be permitted to be used within walls, floors, and ceilings, exposed or concealed, in buildings exceeding three floors above grade.

   (a) listed
   (b) identified
   (c) NFPA 13-2010
   (d) none of these

3. When a building is supplied with a fire sprinkler system, ENT can be installed above any suspended ceiling.

   (a) True
   (b) False

4. ENT and fittings can be_____, provided fittings identified for this purpose are used.

   (a) encased in poured concrete
   (b) embedded in a concrete slab on grade where the tubing is placed on sand or approved screenings
   (c) a or b
   (d) none of these

5. ENT is not permitted in hazardous (classified) locations, unless permitted in other articles of the *Code*.

   (a) True
   (b) False

6. ENT shall be permitted for direct earth burial when used with fittings listed for this purpose.

   (a) True
   (b) False

7. ENT shall not be used where exposed to the direct rays of the sun, unless identified as _____.

   (a) high-temperature rated
   (b) sunlight resistant
   (c) Schedule 80
   (d) never can be

8. The number of conductors permitted in ENT shall not exceed the percentage fill specified in _____.

    (a) Chapter 9, Table 1
    (b) Table 250.66
    (c) Table 310.15(B)(16)
    (d) 240.6

9. Cut ends of ENT shall be trimmed inside and _____ to remove rough edges.

    (a) outside
    (b) tapered
    (c) filed
    (d) beveled

10. Unbroken lengths of electric nonmetallic tubing shall not be required to be secured where fished between access points for _____ work in finished buildings or structures and supporting is impractical.

    (a) concealed
    (b) exposed
    (c) hazardous
    (d) completed

11. Bushings or adapters shall be provided at ENT terminations to protect the conductors from abrasion, unless the box, fitting, or enclosure design provides equivalent protection.

    (a) True
    (b) False

12. Joints between lengths of ENT, couplings, fittings, and boxes shall be made by _____.

    (a) a qualified person
    (b) set screw fittings
    (c) an approved method
    (d) exothermic welding

13. The _____ of conductors used in prewired ENT manufactured assemblies shall be identified by means of a printed tag or label attached to each end of the manufactured assembly.

    (a) type
    (b) size
    (c) quantity
    (d) all of these

ARTICLE
376

Metal Wireways

INTRODUCTION TO ARTICLE 376—METAL WIREWAYS

Metal wireways are commonly used where access to the conductors within the raceway is required to make terminations, splices, or taps to several devices at a single location. High cost precludes their use for other than short distances, except in some commercial or industrial occupancies where the wiring is frequently revised.

Author's Comment: Both metal wireways and nonmetallic wireways are often called "troughs" or "gutters" in the field.

QUESTIONS FOR ARTICLE 376— METAL WIREWAYS

1. Metal wireways are sheet metal troughs with _____ for housing and protecting electric conductors and cable.

    (a) removable covers
    (b) hinged covers
    (c) a or b
    (d) none of these

2. Wireways shall be permitted for _____.

    (a) exposed work
    (b) totally concealed work
    (c) wet locations if listed for the purpose
    (d) a and c

3. Wireways can pass transversely through a wall _____.

    (a) if the length passing through the wall is unbroken
    (b) if the wall is of fire-rated construction
    (c) in hazardous (classified) locations
    (d) if the wall is not of fire-rated construction

4. Conductors larger than that for which the wireway is designed can be installed in any wireway.

    (a) True
    (b) False

5. The sum of the cross-sectional areas of all contained conductors at any cross-section of a metal wireway shall not exceed _____.

    (a) 50 percent
    (b) 20 percent
    (c) 25 percent
    (d) 80 percent

6. The ampacity adjustment factors in 310.15(B)(3)(a) shall be applied to a metal wireway only where the number of current-carrying conductors in the wireway exceeds _____.

    (a) 30
    (b) 40
    (c) 50
    (d) 60

7. Where insulated conductors are deflected within a metal wireway, the wireway shall be sized to meet the bending requirements corresponding to _____ wire per terminal in Table 312.6(A).

   (a) one
   (b) two
   (c) three
   (d) four

8. Power distribution blocks installed in metal wireways shall be listed.

   (a) True
   (b) False

9. Power distribution blocks installed in metal wireways shall _____.

   (a) allow for sufficient wire-bending space at terminals
   (b) not have uninsulated exposed live parts
   (c) a or b
   (d) a and b

ARTICLE
380

Multioutlet Assemblies

INTRODUCTION TO ARTICLE 380—MULTIOUTLET ASSEMBLIES

A multioutlet assembly is a surface, flush, or freestanding raceway designed to hold conductors and receptacles, and is assembled in the field or at the factory [Article 100]. It's not limited to systems commonly referred to by the trade names "Plugtrak®" or "Plugmold®."

QUESTIONS FOR ARTICLE 380—MULTIOUTLET ASSEMBLIES

1. A multioutlet assembly can be installed in _____.

   (a) dry locations
   (b) wet locations
   (c) a and b
   (d) damp locations

2. A multioutlet assembly shall not be installed _____.

   (a) in hoistways
   (b) where subject to severe physical damage
   (c) where subject to corrosive vapors
   (d) all of these

3. Metal multioutlet assemblies can pass through a dry partition, provided no receptacle is concealed in the partition and the cover of the exposed portion of the system can be removed.

   (a) True
   (b) False

ARTICLE 386 Surface Metal Raceways

INTRODUCTION TO ARTICLE 386—SURFACE METAL RACEWAYS

A surface metal raceway is a common method of adding a raceway when exposed traditional raceway systems aren't acceptable, and concealing the raceway isn't economically feasible. It comes in several colors, and is now available with colored or real wood inserts designed to make it look like molding rather than a raceway. Surface metal raceway is commonly known as "Wiremold®" in the field.

QUESTIONS FOR ARTICLE 386—SURFACE METAL RACEWAYS

1. Surface metal raceway is a metallic raceway that is intended to be mounted to the surface of a structure, with associated couplings, connectors, boxes, and fittings for the installation of electrical conductors.

    (a) True
    (b) False

2. Unbroken lengths of surface metal raceways can be run through dry _____.

    (a) walls
    (b) partitions
    (c) floors
    (d) all of these

3. Surface metal raceways shall not be used _____.

    (a) where subject to severe physical damage
    (b) where subject to corrosive vapors
    (c) in hoistways
    (d) all of these

4. The voltage between conductors in a surface metal raceway shall not exceed _____ unless the metal has a thickness of not less than 0.040 in. nominal.

    (a) 150V
    (b) 300V
    (c) 600V
    (d) 1,000V

5. The maximum size conductors permitted in a metal surface raceway shall not be larger than that for which the wireway is designed.

    (a) True
    (b) False

6. The maximum number of conductors permitted in any surface raceway shall be _____.

    (a) no more than 30 percent of the inside diameter
    (b) no greater than the number for which it was designed
    (c) no more than 75 percent of the cross-sectional area
    (d) that which is permitted in Table 312.6(A)

7. The ampacity adjustment factors of 310.15(B)(3)(a) shall not apply to conductors installed in surface metal raceways where _____.

   (a) the cross-sectional area exceeds 4 sq in.
   (b) the current-carrying conductors do not exceed 30 in number
   (c) the total cross-sectional area of all conductors does not exceed 20 percent of the interior cross-sectional area of the raceway
   (d) all of these

8. Surface metal raceways shall be secured and supported at intervals _____.

   (a) in accordance with the manufacturer's installation instructions
   (b) appropriate for the building design
   (c) not exceeding 4 ft
   (d) not exceeding 8 ft

9. The conductors, including splices and taps, in a metal surface raceway having a removable cover shall not fill the raceway to more than _____ percent of its cross-sectional area at that point.

   (a) 38
   (b) 40
   (c) 53
   (d) 75

10. Surface metal raceway enclosures providing a transition from other wiring methods shall have a means for connecting a(n) _____.

    (a) grounded conductor
    (b) ungrounded conductor
    (c) equipment grounding conductor
    (d) all of these

11. Where combination surface metal raceways are used for both signaling conductors and lighting and power circuits, the different systems shall be run in separate compartments identified by _____ of the interior finish.

    (a) stamping
    (b) imprinting
    (c) color coding
    (d) any of these

ARTICLE 392

Cable Trays

INTRODUCTION TO ARTICLE 392—CABLE TRAYS

A cable tray system is a unit or an assembly of units or sections with associated fittings that forms a structural system used to securely fasten or support cables and raceways. Cable tray systems include ladder, ventilated trough, ventilated channel, solid bottom, and other similar structures. Cable trays are manufactured in many forms, from a simple hanger or wire mesh to a substantial, rigid, steel support system. Cable trays are designed and manufactured to support specific wiring methods, as identified in 392.10(A).

QUESTIONS FOR ARTICLE 392—CABLE TRAYS

1. A cable tray is a unit or assembly of units or sections and associated fittings forming a _____ system used to securely fasten or support cables and raceways.

    (a) structural
    (b) flexible
    (c) movable
    (d) secure

2. Cable trays can be used as a support system for _____.

    (a) service conductors, feeders, and branch circuits
    (b) communications circuits
    (c) control and signaling circuits
    (d) all of these

3. Where exposed to the direct rays of the sun, insulated conductors and jacketed cables installed in cable trays shall be _____ as being sunlight resistant.

    (a) listed
    (b) approved
    (c) identified
    (d) none of these

4. Cable trays and their associated fittings shall be _____ for the intended use.

    (a) listed
    (b) approved
    (c) identified
    (d) none of these

5. Any of the following wiring methods can be installed in a cable tray:

    (a) Metal raceways.
    (b) Nonmetallic raceways.
    (c) Cables.
    (d) all of these

6. Cable tray systems shall not be used _____.

    (a) in hoistways
    (b) where subject to severe physical damage
    (c) in hazardous (classified) locations
    (d) a or b

7. Each run of cable tray shall be _____ before the installation of cables.

    (a) tested for 25 ohms resistance
    (b) insulated
    (c) completed
    (d) all of these

8. Cable trays shall be _____ except as permitted by 392.10(D).

   (a) exposed
   (b) accessible
   (c) concealed
   (d) a and b

9. In industrial facilities where conditions of maintenance and supervision ensure that only qualified persons will service the installation, cable tray systems can be used to support _____.

   (a) raceways
   (b) cables
   (c) boxes and conduit bodies
   (d) all of these

10. For raceways terminating at a cable tray, a(n) _____ cable tray clamp or adapter shall be used to securely fasten the raceway to the cable tray system.

    (a) listed
    (b) approved
    (c) identified
    (d) none of these

11. Where single conductor cables comprising each phase, neutral, or grounded conductor of a circuit are connected in parallel in a cable tray, the conductors shall be installed _____, to prevent current unbalance in the paralleled conductors due to inductive reactance.

    (a) in groups consisting of not more than three conductors per phase or neutral
    (b) in groups consisting of not more than one conductor per phase or neutral
    (c) as individual conductors securely bound to the cable tray
    (d) in separate groups

12. Cable trays shall be supported at intervals in accordance with the installation instructions.

    (a) True
    (b) False

13. A box shall not be required where cables or conductors from cable trays are installed in bushed conduit and tubing used as support or for protection against _____.

    (a) abuse
    (b) unauthorized access
    (c) physical damage
    (d) tampering

14. Cable _____ made and insulated by approved methods can be located within a cable tray provided they are accessible, and do not project above the side rails where the splices are subject to physical damage.

    (a) connections
    (b) jumpers
    (c) splices
    (d) conductors

15. Metal cable trays containing only non-power conductors such as communication, data, signal, conductors and cables must be electrically continuous, through listed connections or the use of an insulated stranded bonding jumper not smaller than _____.

    (a) 12 AWG
    (b) 10 AWG
    (c) 6 AWG
    (d) 4 AWG

16. Steel or aluminum cable tray systems shall be permitted to be used as an equipment grounding conductor, provided the cable tray sections and fittings are identified as _____, among other requirements.

    (a) an equipment grounding conductor
    (b) special
    (c) industrial
    (d) all of these

17. The conductor ampacity adjustment factors only apply to the number of current-carrying conductors in the cable and not to the number of conductors in the cable tray.

    (a) True
    (b) False

18. Cable trays shall _____.

    (a) include fittings or other suitable means for changes in direction and elevation

    (b) have side rails or equivalent structural members

    (c) be made of corrosion-resistant material or protected from corrosion as required by 300.6

    (d) all of these

19. Nonmetallic cable trays shall be made of _____ material.

    (a) fire-resistant

    (b) waterproof

    (c) corrosive

    (d) flame-retardant

Notes

CHAPTER 4

EQUIPMENT FOR GENERAL USE

INTRODUCTION TO CHAPTER 4—EQUIPMENT FOR GENERAL USE

With the first three chapters behind you, the final chapter in the *NEC* for building a solid foundation in general work is Chapter 4. This chapter helps you apply the first three chapters to installations involving general equipment. These first four chapters follow a natural sequential progression. Each of the next four *NEC* Chapters—5, 6, 7, and 8—build upon the first four, but in no particular order. You need to understand all of the first four chapters to properly apply any of the next four.

As in the preceding chapters, Chapter 4 is also arranged logically. Here are the groupings:

- Flexible cords and cables, fixture wires, switches, and receptacles.
- Switchboards and panelboards.
- Lamps, luminaires, appliances, and space heaters.
- Motors, refrigeration equipment, generators, and transformers.
- Capacitors and other components.

These groupings make sense. For example, motors, refrigeration equipment, generators, and transformers are all inductive equipment.

This logical arrangement of the *NEC* is something to keep in mind when you're searching for a particular item. You know, for example, that transformers are general equipment. So you'll find the *Code* requirements for them in Chapter 4. You know they're wound devices, so you'll find transformer requirements located somewhere near motor requirements.

- **Article 400—Flexible Cords and Flexible Cables.** Article 400 covers the general requirements, applications, and construction specifications for flexible cords and flexible cables.

- **Article 402—Fixture Wires.** This article covers the general requirements and construction specifications for fixture wires.

- **Article 404—Switches.** The requirements of Article 404 apply to switches of all types. These include snap (toggle) switches, dimmer switches, fan switches, knife switches, circuit breakers used as switches, and automatic switches such as time clocks, timers, and switches and circuit breakers used for disconnecting means.

- **Article 406—Receptacles, Cord Connectors, and Attachment Plugs (Caps).** This article covers the rating, type, and installation of receptacles, cord connectors, and attachment plugs (cord caps). It also covers flanged surface inlets.

- **Article 408—Switchboards and Panelboards.** Article 408 covers specific requirements for switchboards, panelboards, and distribution boards that supply lighting and power circuits.

- **Article 410—Luminaires, Lampholders, and Lamps.** This article contains the requirements for luminaires, lampholders, and lamps. Because of the many types and applications of luminaires, manufacturer's instructions are very important and helpful for proper installation. Underwriters Laboratories produces a pamphlet called the *Luminaire Marking Guide*, which provides information for properly installing common types of incandescent, fluorescent, and high-intensity discharge (HID) luminaires.

- **Article 411—Lighting Systems Operating at 30V or Less.** Article 411 covers lighting systems, and their associated components, that operate at 30V or less.

- **Article 422—Appliances.** This article covers electric appliances used in any occupancy.

- **Article 424—Fixed Electric Space-Heating Equipment.** Article 424 covers fixed electric equipment used for space heating. For the purpose of this article, heating equipment includes heating cable, unit heaters, boilers, central systems, and other fixed electric space-heating equipment. Article 424 doesn't apply to process heating and room air-conditioning.

- **Article 430—Motors, Motor Circuits, and Controllers.** This article contains the specific requirements for conductor sizing, overcurrent protection, control circuit conductors, motor controllers, and disconnecting means. The installation requirements for motor control centers are covered in Article 430, Part VIII.

- **Article 440—Air-Conditioning and Refrigeration Equipment.** Article 440 applies to electrically driven air-conditioning and refrigeration equipment with a motorized hermetic refrigerant compressor. The requirements in this article are in addition to, or amend, the requirements in Article 430 and other articles.

- **Article 445—Generators.** Article 445 contains the electrical installation requirements for generators and other requirements, such as where they can be installed, nameplate markings, conductor ampacity, and disconnecting means.

- **Article 450—Transformers.** This article covers the installation of transformers.

- **Article 480—Batteries.** Article 480 covers stationary installations of storage batteries.

ARTICLE 400

Flexible Cords and Flexible Cables

INTRODUCTION TO ARTICLE 400—FLEXIBLE CORDS AND FLEXIBLE CABLES

This article covers the general requirements, applications, and construction specifications for flexible cords and flexible cables. The *NEC* doesn't consider flexible cords to be wiring methods like those defined in Chapter 3.

Always use a cord (and fittings) identified for the application. Table 400.4 will help you in that regard. For example, use cords listed for a wet location if you're using them outdoors. The jacket material of any cord is tested to maintain its insulation properties and other characteristics in the environments for which its been listed. Tables 400.5(A)(1) and 400.5(A)(2) are also important tables to turn to when looking for the ampacity of flexible cords and cables.

 Please use the 2011 *Code* book to answer the following questions, which are based on the 2011 *NEC.*

QUESTIONS FOR ARTICLE 400—FLEXIBLE CORDS AND FLEXIBLE CABLES

1. HPD cord shall be permitted for _____.

    (a) not hard usage
    (b) hard usage
    (c) extra-hard usage
    (d) all of these

2. TPT and TST cords shall be permitted in lengths not exceeding _____ when attached directly to a portable appliance rated 50W or less.

    (a) 8 ft
    (b) 10 ft
    (c) 15 ft
    (d) 20 ft

3. The allowable ampacity of flexible cords and cables is found in _____.

    (a) Table 310.15(B)(16)
    (b) Tables 400.5(A)(1) and (2)
    (c) Chapter 9, Table 1
    (d) Table 430.52

4. Where flexible cords are used in ambient temperatures other than _____ the temperature correction factors from Table 310.15(B)(2)(a) shall be applied to the ampacity from Table 400.5(A)(2).

    (a) 30°C
    (b) 60°C
    (c) 75°C
    (d) 90°C

5. A 3-conductor SJE cable (one conductor is used for grounding) has a maximum ampacity of _____ for each 16 AWG conductor.

    (a) 9A
    (b) 11A
    (c) 13A
    (d) 15A

6. Conductors within flexible cords and cables shall not be associated together in such a way that the _____ temperature of the conductors is exceeded.

   (a) operating
   (b) governing
   (c) ambient
   (d) limiting

7. Flexible cords and cables can be used for _____.

   (a) wiring of luminaires
   (b) connection of portable luminaires or appliances
   (c) connection of utilization equipment to facilitate frequent interchange
   (d) all of these

8. Flexible cords shall not be used as a substitute for _____ wiring.

   (a) temporary
   (b) fixed
   (c) overhead
   (d) none of these

9. Flexible cords and cables shall not be used where _____.

   (a) run through holes in walls, ceilings, or floors
   (b) run through doorways, windows, or similar openings
   (c) attached to building surfaces, unless permitted by 368.56(B)
   (d) all of these

10. Flexible cords and cables shall not be concealed behind building _____, or run through doorways, windows, or similar openings.

    (a) structural ceilings
    (b) suspended or dropped ceilings
    (c) floors or walls
    (d) all of these

11. Flexible cords and cables shall be connected to fittings so that tension will not be transmitted to joints or terminal screws by _____.

    (a) knotting the cord
    (b) winding the cord with tape
    (c) fittings designed for the purpose
    (d) any of these

12. Flexible cords and cables shall be protected by _____ where passing through holes in covers, outlet boxes, or similar enclosures.

    (a) bushings
    (b) fittings
    (c) a or b
    (d) none of these

13. In industrial establishments where conditions of maintenance and supervision ensure that only qualified persons service the installation, flexible cords and cables can be installed in aboveground raceways that are no longer than _____, to protect the flexible cord or cable from physical damage.

    (a) 25 ft
    (b) 50 ft
    (c) 100 ft
    (d) no limit

14. One conductor of flexible cords intended to be used as a(n) _____ conductor shall have a continuous marker readily distinguishing it from the other conductors. One means of identification is a braid finished to show a white or gray color on one conductor.

    (a) grounded circuit
    (b) equipment grounding
    (c) ungrounded
    (d) all of these

15. A flexible cord conductor intended to be used as a(n) _____ conductor shall have a continuous identifying marker readily distinguishing it from the other conductor or conductors. One means of identification is a braid finished to show a continuous green color or a green color with one or more yellow stripes on one conductor.

    (a) ungrounded
    (b) equipment grounding
    (c) service
    (d) high-leg

ARTICLE
402

Fixture Wires

INTRODUCTION TO ARTICLE 402—FIXTURE WIRES

This article covers the general requirements and construction specifications for fixture wires. One such requirement is that no fixture wire can be smaller than 18 AWG. Another requirement is that fixture wires must be of a type listed in Table 402.3. That table makes up the bulk of Article 402. Table 402.5 lists the allowable ampacity for fixture wires.

QUESTIONS FOR ARTICLE 402—FIXTURE WIRES

1. The ampacity of 18 TFFN is _____.

   (a) 6A
   (b) 8A
   (c) 10A
   (d) 14A

2. The smallest size fixture wire permitted by the *NEC* is _____ AWG.

   (a) 22
   (b) 20
   (c) 18
   (d) 16

3. The number of fixture wires in a single conduit or tubing shall not exceed the percentage fill specified in _____.

   (a) Chapter 9, Table 1
   (b) Table 250.66
   (c) Table 310.15(B)(16)
   (d) 240.6

4. Fixture wires are used to connect luminaires to the _____ conductors supplying the luminaires.

   (a) service
   (b) branch-circuit
   (c) feeder
   (d) none of these

5. Fixture wires shall not be used for branch-circuit wiring, except as permitted in other articles of the *Code*.

   (a) True
   (b) False

Switches

INTRODUCTION TO ARTICLE 404—SWITCHES

The requirements of Article 404 apply to switches of all types, including snap (toggle) switches, dimmer switches, fan switches, knife switches, circuit breakers used as switches, and automatic switches, such as time clocks and timers.

QUESTIONS FOR ARTICLE 404—SWITCHES

1. Three-way and four-way switches shall be wired so that all switching is done only in the _____ circuit conductor.

   (a) ungrounded
   (b) grounded
   (c) equipment ground
   (d) neutral

2. When grouping conductors of switch loops in the same raceway, it is not required to include a grounded conductor in every switch loop.

   (a) True
   (b) False

3. Switches or circuit breakers shall not disconnect the grounded conductor of a circuit unless the switch or circuit breaker _____.

   (a) can be opened and closed by hand levers only
   (b) simultaneously disconnects all conductors of the circuit
   (c) opens the grounded conductor before it disconnects the ungrounded conductors
   (d) none of these

4. As a general rule, switches controlling line-to-neutral lighting loads must have a neutral provided at the switch location.

   (a) True
   (b) False

5. Switches controlling line-to-neutral lighting loads must have a neutral provided at the switch location unless _____.

   (a) the conductors for switches enter the device box through a raceway that has sufficient cross-sectional area to accommodate a neutral conductor
   (b) cable assemblies for switches enter the box through a framing cavity that's open at the top or bottom on the same floor level, or through a wall, floor, or ceiling that's unfinished on one side
   (c) the lighting consists of all fluorescent fixtures with integral disconnects for the ballasts
   (d) a or b

6. Surface-mounted switches or circuit breakers in a damp or wet location shall be enclosed in a _____ enclosure or cabinet that complies with 312.2.

   (a) weatherproof
   (b) rainproof
   (c) watertight
   (d) raintight

7. Switches shall not be installed within wet locations in tub or shower spaces unless installed as part of a listed tub or shower assembly.

   (a) True
   (b) False

8. Single-throw knife switches shall be installed so that gravity will tend to close the switch.

(a) True
(b) False

9. Which of the following switches must indicate whether they are in the open (off) or closed (on) position?

(a) General-use switches.
(b) Motor-circuit switches.
(c) Circuit breakers.
(d) all of these

10. Switches and circuit breakers used as switches shall be installed so that they may be operated from a readily accessible place.

(a) True
(b) False

11. Switches and circuit breakers used as switches can be mounted _____ if they are installed adjacent to motors, appliances, or other equipment that they supply and are accessible by portable means.

(a) not higher than 6 ft 7 in.
(b) higher than 6 ft 7 in.
(c) in the mechanical equipment room
(d) up to 8 ft high

12. Snap switches shall not be grouped or ganged in enclosures unless the voltage between adjacent devices does not exceed _____.

(a) 100V
(b) 200V
(c) 300V
(d) 400V

13. A multipole, general-use snap switch shall not be fed from more than a single circuit unless it is listed and marked as a 2-circuit or 3-circuit switch, or unless its voltage rating is not less than the nominal _____ voltage of the system supplying the circuits.

(a) line-to-ground
(b) line-to-neutral
(c) line-to-line
(d) phase-to-phase

14. Snap switches, including dimmer and similar control switches, shall be connected to an equipment grounding conductor and shall provide a means to connect metal faceplates to the equipment grounding conductor, whether or not a metal faceplate is installed.

(a) True
(b) False

15. Snap switches are considered to be part of the effective ground-fault current path when _____.

(a) the switch is connected to the intersystem bonding termination
(b) the switch is mounted with metal screws to a metal box or a metal cover that's connected to an equipment grounding conductor of a type recognized in 250.118
(c) an equipment grounding conductor or equipment bonding jumper is connected to the grounding terminal of the metal mounting yoke
(d) b or c

16. A snap switch that does not have means for connection to an equipment grounding conductor shall be permitted for replacement purposes only where the wiring method does not include an equipment grounding conductor and the switch is _____.

(a) provided with a faceplate of nonconducting, noncombustible material with nonmetallic screws
(b) GFCI protected
(c) a or b
(d) none of these

17. The metal mounting yoke of a replacement switch isn't required to be connected to an equipment grounding conductor if the wiring at the existing switch doesn't contain an equipment grounding conductor, and _____.

    (a) the switch faceplate is nonmetallic with nonmetallic screws
    (b) the replacement switch is GFCI protected
    (c) a or b
    (d) the circuit is AFCI protected

18. Snap switches in listed assemblies aren't required to be connected to an equipment grounding conductor if _____.

    (a) the device is provided with a nonmetallic faceplate that cannot be installed on any other type of device and the device does not have mounting means to accept other configurations of faceplates
    (b) the device is equipped with a nonmetallic yoke
    (c) all parts of the device that are accessible after installation of the faceplate are manufactured of nonmetallic material
    (d) all of these

19. A snap switch with integral nonmetallic enclosure complying with 300.15(E) is required to be connected to an equipment grounding conductor.

    (a) True
    (b) False

20. Snap switches installed in boxes shall have the _____ seated against the finished wall surface.

    (a) extension plaster ears
    (b) body
    (c) toggle
    (d) all of these

21. Nonmetallic boxes for switches shall be installed with a wiring method that provides or includes _____.

    (a) a grounded conductor
    (b) an equipment grounding conductor
    (c) an inductive balance
    (d) none of these

22. Metal enclosures for switches or circuit breakers shall be connected to the circuit _____.

    (a) grounded conductor
    (b) grounding conductor
    (c) equipment grounding conductor
    (d) any of these

23. Knife switches rated for more than 1,200A at 250V or less _____.

    (a) can be used only as isolating switches
    (b) shall not be opened under load
    (c) shall be placed so that gravity tends to close them
    (d) a and b

24. Alternating-current general-use snap switches are permitted to control _____.

    (a) resistive and inductive loads that do not exceed the ampere and voltage rating of the switch
    (b) tungsten-filament lamp loads that do not exceed the ampere rating of the switch at 120V
    (c) motor loads that do not exceed 80 percent of the ampere and voltage rating of the switch
    (d) all of these

25. Alternating-current or direct-current general-use snap switches may be used for control of inductive loads not exceeding _____ percent of the ampere rating of the switch at the applied voltage.

    (a) 50
    (b) 75
    (c) 90
    (d) 100

26. Snap switches rated _____ or less directly connected to aluminum conductors shall be listed and marked CO/ALR.

    (a) 15A
    (b) 20A
    (c) 25A
    (d) 30A

27. General-use _____ switches shall be used only to control permanently installed incandescent luminaires unless listed for control of other loads.

    (a) dimmer
    (b) fan speed control
    (c) timer
    (d) all of these

28. Switches shall be marked with _____.

    (a) current
    (b) voltage
    (c) maximum horsepower, if horsepower rated
    (d) all of these

29. A switching device with a marked OFF position shall completely disconnect all _____ conductors of the load it controls.

    (a) grounded
    (b) ungrounded
    (c) grounding
    (d) all of these

ARTICLE 406

Receptacles, Cord Connectors, and Attachment Plugs (Caps)

INTRODUCTION TO ARTICLE 406—RECEPTACLES, CORD CONNECTORS, AND ATTACHMENT PLUGS (CAPS)

This article covers the rating, type, and installation of receptacles, cord connectors, and attachment plugs (cord caps). It also addresses their grounding requirements. Some key points to remember include:

- Follow the grounding requirements of the specific type of device you're using.
- Provide GFCI protection where specified by 406.4(D)(3).
- Mount receptacles according to the requirements of 406.5, which are highly detailed.

QUESTIONS FOR ARTICLE 406— RECEPTACLES, CORD CONNECTORS, AND ATTACHMENT PLUGS (CAPS)

1. A child care facility is a building or structure, or portion thereof, used for educational, supervision, or personal care services for more than _____ children seven years in age or less.

   (a) two
   (b) three
   (c) four
   (d) six

2. Receptacles and cord connectors shall be rated not less than _____ at 125V, or at 250V, and shall be of a type not suitable for use as lampholders.

   (a) 10A
   (b) 15A
   (c) 20A
   (d) 30A

3. Receptacles rated _____ or less directly connected to aluminum conductors shall be listed and marked CO/ALR.

   (a) 15A
   (b) 20A
   (c) 25A
   (d) 30A

4. Receptacles incorporating an isolated grounding conductor connection intended for the reduction of electrical noise shall be identified by _____ on the face of the receptacle.

   (a) an orange triangle
   (b) a green triangle
   (c) the color orange
   (d) the engraved word ISOLATED

5. Isolated ground receptacles installed in nonmetallic boxes shall be covered with a nonmetallic faceplate, unless the box contains a feature or accessory that permits the effective grounding of the faceplate.

   (a) True
   (b) False

6. Receptacles and cord connectors having equipment grounding conductor contacts shall have those contacts connected to a(n) _____ conductor.

   (a) grounded
   (b) ungrounded
   (c) equipment grounding
   (d) neutral

7. Where a grounding means exists in the receptacle enclosure a(n) _____-type receptacle shall be used.

   (a) isolated ground
   (b) grounding
   (c) GFCI
   (d) dedicated

8. When replacing a nongrounding-type receptacle where attachment to an equipment grounding conductor does not exist in the receptacle enclosure, the receptacle can use a _____.

   (a) nongrounding-type receptacle
   (b) grounding receptacle
   (c) GFCI-type receptacle
   (d) a or c

9. When replacing receptacles in locations that would require GFCI protection under the current *NEC*, _____ receptacles shall be installed.

   (a) dedicated
   (b) isolated ground
   (c) GFCI-protected
   (d) grounding

10. Effective January 1, 2014, where a receptacle outlet is supplied by a branch circuit that requires arc-fault circuit interrupter protection [210.12(A)], a replacement receptacle at this outlet shall be _____.

    (a) a listed (receptacle) outlet branch circuit type arc-fault circuit interrupter receptacle
    (b) a receptacle protected by a listed (receptacle) outlet branch circuit type arc-fault circuit interrupter type receptacle
    (c) a receptacle protected by a listed combination type arc-fault circuit interrupter type circuit breaker
    (d) all of these

11. Listed tamper-resistant receptacles shall be provided where replacements are made at receptacle outlets that are required to be tamper resistant elsewhere in this *Code*.

    (a) True
    (b) False

12. Weather-resistant receptacles _____ where replacements are made at receptacle outlets that are required to be so protected elsewhere in the *Code*.

    (a) shall be provided
    (b) are not required
    (c) are optional
    (d) are not allowed

13. Receptacles mounted in boxes set back of the wall surface shall be installed so that the mounting _____ of the receptacle is held rigidly at the surface.

    (a) screws or nails
    (b) yoke or strap
    (c) faceplate
    (d) none of these

14. Receptacles mounted in boxes flush with the finished surface or projecting beyond it shall be installed so that the mounting yoke or strap of the receptacle is _____.

    (a) held rigidly against the box or box cover
    (b) mounted behind the wall surface
    (c) held rigidly at the finished surface
    (d) none of these

15. Receptacles mounted to and supported by a cover shall be secured by more than one screw unless listed and identified for securing by a single screw.

    (a) True
    (b) False

16. Receptacles in countertops and similar work surfaces in dwelling units shall not be installed _____.

(a) in the sides of cabinets
(b) in a face-up position
(c) on GFCI circuits
(d) on the kitchen small-appliance circuit

17. Receptacles shall not be grouped or ganged in enclosures unless the voltage between adjacent devices does not exceed _____.

(a) 100V
(b) 200V
(c) 300V
(d) 400V

18. Metal faceplates for receptacles shall be grounded.

(a) True
(b) False

19. Attachment plugs and cord connectors shall be listed and marked with the _____.

(a) manufacturer's name or identification
(b) voltage rating
(c) amperage rating
(d) all of these

20. Receptacles, cord connectors, and attachment plugs shall be constructed so that the receptacles or cord connectors do not accept an attachment plug with a different _____ or current rating than that for which the device is intended.

(a) voltage rating
(b) ampere interrupting capacity (AIC)
(c) temperature rating
(d) all of these

21. An outdoor receptacle in a location protected from the weather, or in another damp location, shall be installed in an enclosure that is weatherproof when the receptacle is _____.

(a) covered
(b) enclosed
(c) protected
(d) none of these

22. Receptacles installed outdoors, in a location protected from the weather or other damp locations, shall be in an enclosure that is _____ when the receptacle is covered.

(a) raintight
(b) weatherproof
(c) rainproof
(d) weathertight

23. A receptacle is considered to be in a location protected from the weather when located under roofed open porches, canopies, marquees, and the like, where it will not be subjected to _____.

(a) spray from a hose
(b) a direct lightning hit
(c) beating rain or water runoff
(d) falling or wind-blown debris

24. Nonlocking 15A and 20A, 125V and 250V receptacles installed in damp locations shall be listed as _____.

(a) raintight
(b) watertight
(c) weatherproof
(d) weather resistant

25. _____, 125V and 250V receptacles installed in a wet location shall have an enclosure that is weatherproof whether or not the attachment plug cap is inserted.

(a) 15A
(b) 20A
(c) a and b
(d) none of these

26. For other than one- or two-family dwellings, when 15A and 20A receptacles are installed in a wet location, the outlet box _____ must be listed for extra-duty use.

    (a) sleeve
    (b) hood
    (c) threaded entry
    (d) mounting

27. Where installed in a wet location, all _____ receptacle(s) shall be listed as weather-resistant.

    (a) 125V, 30A nonlocking
    (b) 250V, 15A nonlocking
    (c) 125V, 30A locking
    (d) 250V, 15A locking

28. 20A, 125V receptacles subject to _____ can have an enclosure that is weatherproof when the attachment plug is removed.

    (a) shower spray
    (b) beating rain
    (c) corrosive conditions
    (d) routine high-pressure spray

29. A 30A, 208V receptacle installed in a wet location, where the product intended to be plugged into it is not attended while in use, shall have an enclosure that is weatherproof with the attachment plug cap inserted or removed.

    (a) True
    (b) False

30. A receptacle shall not be installed within, or directly over, a bathtub or shower space.

    (a) True
    (b) False

31. A receptacle installed in an outlet box flush-mounted in a finished surface in a damp or wet location shall be made weatherproof by means of a weatherproof faceplate assembly that provides a _____ connection between the plate and the finished surface.

    (a) sealed
    (b) weathertight
    (c) sealed and protected
    (d) watertight

32. Grounding-type attachment plugs shall be used only with a cord having a(n) _____ conductor.

    (a) equipment grounding
    (b) isolated
    (c) computer circuit
    (d) insulated

33. In dwelling units, all nonlocking type 125V, 15A and 20A receptacles installed _____ shall be listed as tamper resistant.

    (a) in bedrooms
    (b) outdoors, at grade level
    (c) above counter tops
    (d) in all areas except as covered by exceptions

34. Nonlocking type 15A and 20A, 125V receptacles in a dwelling unit shall be listed as tamper resistant except _____.

    (a) receptacles located more than 5½ ft above the floor.
    (b) receptacles that are part of a luminaire or appliance.
    (c) a receptacle located within dedicated space for an appliance that in normal use is not easily moved from one place to another.
    (d) all of these

35. Nonlocking type 15A and 20A, 125V receptacles in a dwelling unit shall be listed as tamper resistant except nongrounding receptacles used for replacements for existing nongrounding receptacles as permitted in 406.4(D)(2)(a).

    (a) True
    (b) False

36. Nonlocking type 15A and 20A, 125V receptacles in _____ must be listed as tamper resistant.

    (a) restaurants
    (b) guest rooms and guest suites
    (c) office buildings
    (d) b and c

37. Nonlocking type 15A and 20A, 125V receptacles in _____ must be listed as tamper resistant.

    (a) theatres
    (b) arcades
    (c) child care facilities
    (d) major repair garages

ARTICLE
408

Switchboards and Panelboards

INTRODUCTION TO ARTICLE 408—SWITCHBOARDS AND PANELBOARDS

Article 408 covers the specific requirements for switchboards and panelboards that control power and lighting circuits. Some key points to remember:

- One objective of Article 408 is that the installation prevents contact between current-carrying conductors and people or equipment.
- The circuit directory of a panelboard must clearly identify the purpose or use of each circuit that originates in the panelboard.
- You must understand the detailed grounding and overcurrent protection requirements for panelboards.

QUESTIONS FOR ARTICLE 408— SWITCHBOARDS AND PANELBOARDS

1. Conductors and busbars on a switchboard or panelboard shall be located so as to be free from _____ and shall be held firmly in place.

   (a) obstructions
   (b) physical damage
   (c) a and b
   (d) none of these

2. Barriers shall be placed in all service switchboards such that no uninsulated, ungrounded service _____ or service terminal is exposed to inadvertent contact by persons or maintenance equipment while servicing load terminations.

   (a) busbar
   (b) conductors
   (c) cables
   (d) none of these

3. Each switchboard or panelboard used as service equipment shall be provided with a main bonding jumper within the panelboard, or within one of the sections of the switchboard, for connecting the grounded service-entrance conductor on its _____ side to the switchboard or panelboard frame.

   (a) load
   (b) supply
   (c) phase
   (d) high-leg

4. In switchboards and panelboards, load terminals for field wiring shall be so located that it is not necessary to reach across or beyond a(n) _____ ungrounded line bus in order to make connections.

   (a) insulated
   (b) uninsulated
   (c) grounded
   (d) high impedance

5. Panelboards supplied by a three-phase, 4-wire, delta-connected system shall have the phase with higher voltage-to-ground (high-leg) connected to the _____ phase.

    (a) A
    (b) B
    (c) C
    (d) any of these

6. A switchboard or panelboard containing a 4-wire, _____ system where the midpoint of one phase winding is grounded, shall be legibly and permanently field-marked to caution that one phase has a higher voltage-to-ground.

    (a) wye-connected
    (b) delta-connected
    (c) solidly grounded
    (d) ungrounded

7. A switchboard or panelboard containing an ungrounded electrical system is required to be legibly and permanently field-marked to caution that the system is ungrounded and include the _____.

    (a) contact information for the power supplier
    (b) contact information for emergency services
    (c) operating voltage between conductors
    (d) transformer impedance rating

8. Circuit directories can include labels that depend on transient conditions of occupancy.

    (a) True
    (b) False

9. The purpose or use of panelboard circuits and circuit _____, including spare positions, shall be legibly identified on a circuit directory located on the face or inside of the door of a panelboard, and at each switch or circuit breaker on a switchboard.

    (a) manufacturers
    (b) conductors
    (c) feeders
    (d) modifications

10. All switchboards and panelboards supplied by a feeder in _____ shall be marked as to the device or equipment where the power supply originates.

    (a) other than one- or two-family dwellings
    (b) all dwelling units
    (c) all nondwelling units
    (d) b and c

11. Noninsulated busbars shall have a minimum space of _____ between the bottom of a switchboard enclosure and busbars or other obstructions.

    (a) 6 in.
    (b) 8 in.
    (c) 10 in.
    (d) 12 in.

12. Conduits and raceways, including end fittings, shall not rise more than _____ above the bottom of a switchboard enclosure.

    (a) 3 in.
    (b) 4 in.
    (c) 5 in.
    (d) 6 in.

13. Unused openings for circuit breakers and switches in switchboards and panelboards shall be closed using _____ or other approved means that provide protection substantially equivalent to the wall of the enclosure.

    (a) duct seal and tape
    (b) identified closures
    (c) exothermic welding
    (d) sheet metal

14. Switchboards shall be placed so as to reduce to a minimum the probability of communicating _____ to adjacent combustible materials.

    (a) sparks
    (b) backfed
    (c) fire
    (d) all of these

15. For switchboards that are not totally enclosed, a space of _____ or more shall be provided between the top of the switchboard and any combustible ceiling.

    (a) 12 in.
    (b) 18 in.
    (c) 2 ft
    (d) 3 ft

16. Insulated conductors used within a switchboard shall be _____.

    (a) listed
    (b) flame-retardant
    (c) rated for the highest voltage it may contact
    (d) all of these

17. Switchboards that have any exposed live parts shall be installed in permanently _____ locations, and then only where under competent supervision and accessible only to qualified persons.

    (a) dry
    (b) mounted
    (c) supported
    (d) all of these

18. A panelboard shall be protected by an overcurrent device within the panelboard, or at any point on the _____ side of the panelboard.

    (a) load
    (b) supply
    (c) a or b
    (d) none of these

19. Panelboards equipped with snap switches rated at 30A or less shall have overcurrent protection not exceeding _____.

    (a) 30A
    (b) 50A
    (c) 100A
    (d) 200A

20. Plug-in-type circuit breakers that are back-fed shall be _____ by an additional fastener that requires more than a pull to release.

    (a) grounded
    (b) secured in place
    (c) shunt tripped
    (d) none of these

21. When equipment grounding conductors are installed in panelboards, a _____ shall be secured inside the cabinet.

    (a) grounded conductor
    (b) terminal lug
    (c) terminal bar
    (d) none of these

22. Each _____ conductor shall terminate within the panelboard at an individual terminal that is not used for another conductor.

    (a) grounded
    (b) ungrounded
    (c) grounding
    (d) all of these

23. Pilot lights, instruments, potential transformers, current transformers, and other switchboard devices with potential coils shall be supplied by a circuit that is protected by overcurrent devices rated _____.

    (a) 10A or less
    (b) 15A or less
    (c) 15A or more
    (d) 20A or less

24. A panelboard shall be provided with physical means to prevent the installation of more _____ devices than that number for which the panelboard was designed, rated, and listed.

    (a) overcurrent
    (b) equipment
    (c) circuit breaker
    (d) all of these

ARTICLE
410

Luminaires, Lampholders, and Lamps

INTRODUCTION TO ARTICLE 410—LUMINAIRES, LAMPHOLDERS, AND LAMPS

This article covers luminaires, lampholders, lamps, decorative lighting products, lighting accessories for temporary seasonal and holiday use, including portable flexible lighting products, and the wiring and equipment of such products and lighting installations. Even though Article 410 is highly detailed, it's broken down into 16 parts. The first five are sequential, and apply to all luminaires, lampholders, and lamps:

- General, Part I
- Location, Part II
- Boxes and Covers, Part III
- Supports, Part IV
- Equipment Grounding Conductors, Part V

This is mostly mechanical information, and it's not hard to follow or absorb. Part VI, Wiring, ends the sequence. The seventh, ninth, and tenth parts provide requirements for manufacturers to follow—use only equipment that conforms to these requirements. Part VIII provides requirements for installing lampholders. The rest of Article 410 addresses specific types of lighting.

Author's Comment: Article 411 addresses "Lighting Systems Operating at 30 Volts or Less."

QUESTIONS FOR ARTICLE 410— LUMINAIRES, LAMPHOLDERS, AND LAMPS

1. Article 410 covers luminaires, portable luminaires, lampholders, pendants, incandescent filament lamps, arc lamps, electric discharge lamps, and _____, and the wiring and equipment forming part of such products and lighting installations.

   (a) decorative lighting products
   (b) lighting accessories for temporary seasonal and holiday use
   (c) portable flexible lighting products
   (d) all of these

2. Closet storage space is defined as a volume bounded by the sides and back closet walls extending from the closet floor vertically to a height of _____ or the highest clothes-hanging rod at a horizontal distance of 2 ft from the sides and back of the closet walls.

   (a) 6 ft
   (b) 7 ft
   (c) 8 ft
   (d) 9 ft

3. Lighting track is a manufactured assembly and its length may not be altered by the addition or subtraction of sections of track.

   (a) True
   (b) False

4. Lighting track is a manufactured assembly designed to support and _____ luminaires that are capable of being readily repositioned on the track.

(a) connect
(b) protect
(c) energize
(d) all of these

5. Cleat-type lampholders located at least _____ above the floor can have exposed terminals.

(a) 3 ft
(b) 6 ft
(c) 8 ft
(d) 10 ft

6. A luminaire marked Suitable for Wet Locations _____ be permitted to be used in a damp location.

(a) shall
(b) shall not
(c) a or b
(d) none of these

7. Luminaires can be installed in a commercial cooking hood if the luminaire is identified for use within a _____ cooking hood.

(a) nonresidential
(b) commercial
(c) multifamily
(d) all of these

8. No parts of cord-connected luminaires, chain-, cable-, or cord-suspended luminaires, lighting track, pendants, or paddle fans shall be located within a zone measured 3 ft horizontally and _____ vertically from the top of the bathtub rim or shower stall threshold.

(a) 4 ft
(b) 6 ft
(c) 8 ft
(d) 10 ft

9. Luminaires located within the actual outside dimension of a bathtub and shower shall be marked for damp locations, or marked for wet locations where they are _____.

(a) below 7 ft in height
(b) below 6 ft 7 in. in height
(c) subject to shower spray
(d) not GFCI protected

10. Luminaires using a _____ lamp, that is subject to physical damage and installed in playing and spectator seating areas of indoor sports, mixed-use, or all-purpose facilities, shall be of the type that protects the lamp with a glass or plastic lens.

(a) mercury vapor
(b) metal halide
(c) fluorescent
(d) a or b

11. Lampholders installed over highly combustible material shall be of the _____ type.

(a) industrial
(b) switched
(c) unswitched
(d) residential

12. Unless an individual switch is provided for each luminaire located over combustible material, lampholders shall be located at least _____ above the floor, or shall be located or guarded so that the lamps cannot be readily removed or damaged.

(a) 3 ft
(b) 6 ft
(c) 8 ft
(d) 10 ft

13. The following types of luminaires can be installed in a clothes closet:

(a) A surface or recessed incandescent luminaire with completely enclosed light source.
(b) A surface or recessed fluorescent luminaire.
(c) A surface-mounted or recessed LED luminaire with a completely enclosed light source.
(d) all of these

14. Incandescent luminaires that have open lamps, and pendant-type luminaires, shall be permitted in clothes closets where proper clearance is maintained from combustible products.

    (a) True
    (b) False

15. Surface-mounted fluorescent luminaires in clothes closets shall be permitted on the wall above the door, or on the ceiling, provided there is a minimum clearance of _____ between the luminaire and the nearest point of a storage space.

    (a) 3 in.
    (b) 6 in.
    (c) 9 in.
    (d) 12 in.

16. In clothes closets, recessed incandescent or LED luminaires with a completely enclosed light source can be installed in the wall or the ceiling, provided there is a minimum clearance of _____ between the luminaire and the nearest point of a storage space.

    (a) 3 in.
    (b) 6 in.
    (c) 9 in.
    (d) 12 in.

17. Luminaires must maintain a minimum clearance from the closet storage space of _____.

    (a) 12 in. for surface-mounted incandescent or LED luminaires with a completely enclosed light source
    (b) 6 in. for surface-mounted fluorescent luminaires
    (c) 6 in. for recessed fluorescent luminaires or recessed incandescent or LED luminaires with a completely enclosed light source
    (d) all of these

18. The *NEC* allows a lighting outlet on the wall in a clothes closet when it is at least 6 in. away from storage space.

    (a) True
    (b) False

19. Surface-mounted fluorescent or LED luminaires are permitted within the closet storage space if identified for this use.

    (a) True
    (b) False

20. Coves for luminaires shall be located so that the lamps and equipment can be properly installed and _____.

    (a) maintained
    (b) protected from physical damage
    (c) tested
    (d) inspected

21. Electric-discharge and LED luminaires supported independently of the outlet box shall be connected to the branch circuit through _____.

    (a) raceways
    (b) Type MC, AC, MI, or NM cable
    (c) flexible cords
    (d) any of these

22. When electric-discharge and LED luminaires that are designed not to be supported solely by the outlet box are surface mounted over a concealed outlet box, the luminaire shall provide access to the wiring within the outlet box by means of suitable openings in the back of the luminaire.

    (a) True
    (b) False

23. The maximum weight of a luminaire permitted to be supported by the screw shell of a lampholder is _____.

    (a) 2 lb
    (b) 3 lb
    (c) 4 lb
    (d) 6 lb

24. Handholes in poles supporting luminaires shall not be required for poles _____ or less in height above finished grade, if the pole is provided with a hinged base.

(a) 5 ft
(b) 10 ft
(c) 15 ft
(d) 20 ft

25. Poles over 20 ft in height above grade, without a hinged base, that support luminaires shall _____.

(a) have an accessible handhole (sized 2 in. x 4 in.) with a cover suitable for use in wet locations
(b) have an equipment grounding terminal that is accessible from the handhole
(c) a and b
(d) none of these

26. Metal raceways shall be bonded to the metal pole with a(n) _____.

(a) grounding electrode
(b) grounded conductor
(c) equipment grounding conductor
(d) any of these

27. Luminaires attached to the framing of a suspended ceiling shall be secured to the framing member(s) by mechanical means such as _____.

(a) bolts
(b) screws
(c) rivets
(d) any of these

28. _____ clips identified for use with the type of ceiling-framing member(s) and luminaires shall be permitted to be used to secure luminaires to the ceiling-framing members.

(a) Marked
(b) Labeled
(c) Identified
(d) Listed

29. Outdoor luminaires and associated equipment can be supported by trees.

(a) True
(b) False

30. Exposed metal conductive parts of luminaires shall be _____.

(a) connected to an equipment grounding conductor
(b) painted
(c) removed
(d) a and b

31. Luminaires must be connected to an equipment grounding conductor of a type recognized in 250.118. If of the wire type, the circuit equipment grounding conductor must be sized in accordance with _____.

(a) Table 250.66
(b) Table 250.122
(c) Table 310.16
(d) a and c

32. Luminaires made of insulating material that are directly wired or attached to outlets supplied by a wiring method that does not provide a ready means for grounding attachment to an equipment grounding conductor shall be made of insulating material and shall have no exposed conductive parts.

(a) True
(b) False

33. Replacement luminaires can be installed in an outlet box that doesn't contain an equipment grounding conductor if an equipment grounding conductor is added from the luminaire and is connected to _____.

(a) the grounding electrode system or grounding electrode conductor
(b) the panelboard equipment grounding terminal
(c) the service neutral conductor within the service equipment enclosure
(d) any of these

34. Replacement luminaires aren't required to be connected to an equipment grounding conductor if no equipment grounding conductor exists at the outlet box and the luminaire is _____.

    (a) more than 20 years old
    (b) mounted to the box using nonmetallic fittings and screws
    (c) mounted more than 6 ft above the floor
    (d) GFCI protected

35. Luminaires shall be wired so that the _____ of each lampholder is connected to the same luminaire or circuit conductor or terminal.

    (a) stem
    (b) arm
    (c) supplemental protection
    (d) screw shell

36. Luminaires shall be wired with conductors having insulation suitable for the environmental conditions and _____ to which the conductors will be subjected.

    (a) temperature
    (b) voltage
    (c) current
    (d) all of these

37. Fixture wires used as pendant conductors for incandescent luminaires with intermediate or candelabra-base lampholders shall not be smaller than _____ AWG.

    (a) 22
    (b) 18
    (c) 16
    (d) 14

38. Splices and taps shall not be located within luminaire _____.

    (a) arms or stems
    (b) bases or screw shells
    (c) a and b
    (d) a or b

39. No _____ splices or taps shall be made within or on a luminaire.

    (a) unapproved
    (b) untested
    (c) uninspected
    (d) unnecessary

40. Wiring on luminaire chains and other movable parts shall be _____.

    (a) rated for 110°C
    (b) stranded
    (c) hard-usage rated
    (d) none of these

41. Luminaires that require adjustment or aiming after installation can be cord-connected without an attachment plug, provided the exposed cord is of the hard-usage type and is not longer than that required for maximum adjustment.

    (a) True
    (b) False

42. An electric-discharge or LED luminaire or listed assembly can be cord-connected if located _____ the outlet, the cord is visible for its entire length outside the luminaire, and the cord is not subject to strain or physical damage.

    (a) within
    (b) directly below
    (c) directly above
    (d) adjacent to

43. Luminaires can be used as a raceway for circuit conductors only when listed and marked for use as a raceway.

    (a) True
    (b) False

44. Luminaires identified for _____, with an integral outlet box per 410.21 shall be permitted to be used as a conductor raceway.

    (a) through-wiring
    (b) wet locations
    (c) Class 1, Division 1 locations
    (d) b and c

45. Luminaires designed for end-to-end assembly, or luminaires connected together by _____, can contain a 2-wire branch circuit, or one multiwire branch circuit, supplying the connected luminaires. One additional 2-wire branch circuit supplying one or more of the connected luminaires is permitted.

    (a) rigid metal conduit
    (b) recognized wiring methods
    (c) flexible wiring methods
    (d) EMT

46. Branch-circuit conductors within _____ of a ballast shall have an insulation temperature rating not lower than 90°C (194°F).

    (a) 1 in.
    (b) 3 in.
    (c) 6 in.
    (d) 8 in.

47. Luminaires shall be marked with the maximum lamp wattage, manufacturer's _____, trademark, or other suitable means of identification.

    (a) address
    (b) name
    (c) phone number
    (d) none of these

48. Portable luminaires shall be wired with _____ recognized by 400.4, and have an attachment plug of the polarized or grounding type.

    (a) flexible cable
    (b) flexible cord
    (c) nonmetallic flexible cable
    (d) nonmetallic flexible cord

49. Lampholders of the screw-shell type shall be installed for use as lampholders only.

    (a) True
    (b) False

50. Lampholders installed in wet locations shall be listed for use in _____ locations.

    (a) damp
    (b) wet
    (c) dry
    (d) any of these

51. Lampholders installed in damp locations shall be listed for use in _____ locations.

    (a) damp
    (b) wet
    (c) dry
    (d) a or b

52. Lampholders shall be constructed, installed, or equipped with shades or guards so that _____ isn't subjected to temperatures in excess of 90°C (194°F).

    (a) ferrous material
    (b) the shade or guard
    (c) combustible material
    (d) a or b

53. Luminaires installed in _____ shall comply with 410.115 through 410.122.

    (a) recessed cavities in walls or ceilings
    (b) suspended ceilings
    (c) Class I classified locations
    (d) a and b

54. A recessed luminaire shall be installed so that adjacent combustible material will not be subjected to temperatures in excess of _____°C.

    (a) 75
    (b) 90
    (c) 125
    (d) 150

55. Recessed incandescent luminaires shall have _____ protection and shall be identified as thermally protected.

    (a) physical
    (b) corrosion
    (c) thermal
    (d) all of these

56. A recessed luminaire not identified for contact with insulation shall have all recessed parts spaced not less than _____ from combustible materials, except for points of support.

    (a) ¼ in.
    (b) ½ in.
    (c) 1¼ in.
    (d) 6 in.

57. Type IC recessed luminaires are permitted to make contact with combustible material at _____.

    (a) recessed parts
    (b) points of support
    (c) portions passing through or finishing off the opening in the building structure
    (d) all of these

58. Thermal insulation shall not be installed above or within _____ of the recessed luminaries' enclosure, wiring compartment, ballast, transformer, LED driver, or power supply unless it is a Type IC luminaire.

    (a) ½ in.
    (b) 3 in.
    (c) 6 in.
    (d) 12 in.

59. The minimum distance that an outlet box containing tap supply conductors is permitted to be placed from a recessed luminaire is _____.

    (a) 1 ft
    (b) 2 ft
    (c) 3 ft
    (d) 4 ft

60. The raceway or cable for tap conductors to recessed luminaires shall have a minimum length of _____

    (a) 6 in.
    (b) 12 in.
    (c) 18 in.
    (d) 24 in.

61. Ballasts for fluorescent lighting installed indoors shall have _____ protection.

    (a) AFCI
    (b) supplementary
    (c) integral thermal
    (d) none of these

62. Luminaires containing a metal halide lamp (other than a thick glass PAR lamp) shall be provided with a containment barrier that encloses the lamp, or shall be provided with a physical means that only allows the use of a(n) _____.

    (a) Type O lamp
    (b) Type CB lamp
    (c) a or b
    (d) inert gas

63. In indoor locations other than dwellings and associated accessory buildings, fluorescent luminaires that utilize double-ended lamps and contain ballast(s) and can be serviced in place shall have a disconnecting means either internal or external to each luminaire.

    (a) True
    (b) False

64. For existing installed luminaires in indoor locations, other than dwellings and associated accessory structures, a disconnecting means _____ in fluorescent luminaires that utilize double-ended lamps (typical fluorescent lamps) at the time a ballast is replaced.

    (a) shall be installed
    (b) is not required to be added
    (c) shall not be installed
    (d) can be a screw terminal

65. In indoor locations other than dwellings and associated accessory structures, fluorescent luminaires that utilize double-ended lamps (typical fluorescent lamps) and contain ballasts that can be serviced in place must have a disconnecting means except for _____.

    (a) emergency illumination required in 700.16
    (b) cord and plug connected luminaires with accessible plugs and receptacles
    (c) industrial establishments with restricted public access and written procedures and conditions of maintenance and supervision
    (d) all of these

66. If more than one luminaire is installed on a branch circuit that isn't of the multiwire type, a disconnecting means isn't required for every luminaire when the light switch for the space ensures that some of the luminaires in the space will still provide illumination.

    (a) True
    (b) False

67. When connected to multiwire branch circuits, the fluorescent luminaire disconnect must simultaneously break all circuit conductors of the ballast, including the neutral conductor.

    (a) True
    (b) False

68. When the fluorescent luminaire disconnecting means for fluorescent luminaires that utilize double-ended lamps (typical fluorescent lamps) is external to the luminaire, it shall be _____.

    (a) accessible to qualified persons
    (b) a single device
    (c) located in sight from the luminaire
    (d) all of these

69. Surface-mounted luminaires with a ballast shall have a minimum clearance of _____ from combustible low-density cellulose fiberboard, unless the luminaire is marked for surface mounting on combustible low-density cellulose fiberboard.

    (a) ½ in.
    (b) 1 in.
    (c) 1½ in.
    (d) 2 in.

70. Electric-discharge luminaires having an open-circuit voltage exceeding _____ shall not be installed in or on dwelling occupancies.

    (a) 120V
    (b) 250V
    (c) 600V
    (d) 1,000V

71. Lighting track fittings can be equipped with general-purpose receptacles.

    (a) True
    (b) False

72. The connected load on lighting track is permitted to exceed the rating of the track under some conditions.

    (a) True
    (b) False

73. A 120V section of lighting track that is continuously loaded shall not exceed 12 ft in length, in accordance with 220.43(B).

    (a) True
    (b) False

74. Track lighting shall not be installed _____.

    (a) where likely to be subjected to physical damage
    (b) in wet or damp locations
    (c) a and b
    (d) none of these

75. Lighting track shall not be installed less than _____ above the finished floor except where protected from physical damage or where the track operates at less than 30V rms, open-circuit voltage.

    (a) 4 ft
    (b) 5 ft
    (c) 5½ ft
    (d) 6 ft

76. Lighting track shall not be installed within the zone measured 3 ft horizontally and _____ vertically from the top of the bathtub rim or shower stall threshold.

    (a) 2 ft
    (b) 3 ft
    (c) 4 ft
    (d) 8 ft

77. _____ identified for use on lighting track shall be designed specifically for the track on which they are to be installed.

    (a) Fittings
    (b) Receptacles
    (c) Devices
    (d) all of these

78. Lighting track shall have two supports for a single section of _____ or shorter in length and each individual section of not more than 4 ft attached to it shall have one additional support, unless the track is identified for supports at greater intervals.

    (a) 2 ft
    (b) 4 ft
    (c) 6 ft
    (d) 8 ft

79. Decorative lighting and similar accessories used for holiday lighting and similar purposes shall be _____.

    (a) marked
    (b) listed
    (c) arc fault protected
    (d) GFCI protected

ARTICLE 411

Lighting Systems Operating at 30V or Less

INTRODUCTION TO ARTICLE 411—LIGHTING SYSTEMS OPERATING AT 30V OR LESS

Article 411 provides the requirements for lighting systems operating at 30V or less, which are often found in such applications as landscaping, kitchen over-the-counter lighting, commercial display lighting, and museums. Don't let the half-page size of Article 411 give you the impression that 30V lighting isn't something you need to be concerned about. These systems are limited in their voltage, but the current rating can be as high as 25A, which means they're still a potential source of fire. Installation of these systems is widespread and becoming more so.

Many of these systems now use LEDs, and 30V halogen lamps are also fairly common. All 30V lighting systems have an ungrounded secondary circuit supplied by an isolating transformer. These systems have restrictions that effect where they can be located, and they can have a maximum supply breaker size of 25A.

QUESTIONS FOR ARTICLE 411—LIGHTING SYSTEMS OPERATING AT 30 VOLTS OR LESS

1. A lighting system covered by Article 411 shall have a power supply rated not more than _____ and not more than 30V.

   (a) 15A
   (b) 20A
   (c) 25A
   (d) 30A

2. Lighting systems operating at 30V or less shall be listed or assembled with listed components.

   (a) True
   (b) False

3. Lighting systems operating at 30V or less can be concealed or extended through a building wall, floor or ceiling without regard to the wiring method used.

   (a) True
   (b) False

4. Lighting systems operating at 30V or less shall not be installed within _____ ft of pools, spas, fountains, or similar locations.

   (a) 5 ft
   (b) 6 ft
   (c) 10 ft
   (d) 20 ft

5. Exposed secondary circuits of lighting systems operating at 30V or less shall be _____.

   (a) installed in a Chapter 3 wiring method
   (b) supplied by a Class 2 power source and shall use Class 2 cable in accordance with Article 725
   (c) at least 7 ft above the finished floor unless listed for a lower installation height
   (d) any of these

ARTICLE
422

Appliances

INTRODUCTION TO ARTICLE 422—APPLIANCES

Article 422 covers electric appliances used in any occupancy. The meat of this article is contained in Parts II and III. Parts IV and V are primarily for manufacturers, but you should examine appliances for compliance before installing them. If the appliance has a label from a recognized labeling authority (for example, UL), it complies [90.7].

QUESTIONS FOR ARTICLE 422—APPLIANCES

1. A vending machine is defined as any self-service device that dispenses products or merchandise without the necessity of replenishing the device between each vending operation and designed to require insertion of a _____.

    (a) coin or paper currency
    (b) token or card
    (c) key or payment by other means
    (d) all of these

2. Branch-circuit conductors to individual appliances shall not be sized _____ than required by the appliance markings.

    (a) larger
    (b) smaller

3. Individual circuits for nonmotor-operated appliances that are continuously loaded shall have the branch-circuit rating sized not less than _____ percent of the appliance marked ampere rating, unless otherwise listed.

    (a) 80
    (b) 100
    (c) 125
    (d) 150

4. If a protective device rating is marked on an appliance, the branch-circuit overcurrent device rating shall not exceed _____ percent of the protective device rating marked on the appliance.

    (a) 50
    (b) 80
    (c) 100
    (d) 115

5. Infrared lamps for commercial and industrial heating appliances shall have overcurrent protection not exceeding _____.

    (a) 30A
    (b) 40A
    (c) 50A
    (d) 60A

6. If a branch circuit supplies a single nonmotor-operated appliance, the rating of overcurrent protection shall not exceed _____ if the overcurrent protection rating is not marked and the appliance is rated 13.30A or less.

    (a) 15A
    (b) 20A
    (c) 25A
    (d) 30A

7. If a branch circuit supplies a single nonmotor-operated appliance, the rating of overcurrent protection shall not exceed _____ percent of the appliance rated current if the overcurrent protection rating is not marked and the appliance is rated over 13.30A.

   (a) 100
   (b) 125
   (c) 150
   (d) 160

8. Central heating equipment, other than fixed electric space-heating equipment, shall be supplied by a(n) _____ branch circuit.

   (a) multiwire
   (b) individual
   (c) multipurpose
   (d) small-appliance

9. Fixed storage-type water heater having a capacity of _____ gallons or less shall be considered a continuous load for the purposes of sizing branch circuits.

   (a) 60
   (b) 75
   (c) 90
   (d) 120

10. A waste disposal can be cord-and-plug-connected, but the cord shall not be less than 18 in. or more than _____ in length.

    (a) 30 in.
    (b) 36 in.
    (c) 42 in.
    (d) 48 in.

11. The length of the cord for a dishwasher or trash compactor shall not be longer than _____, measured from the rear of the appliance.

    (a) 2 ft
    (b) 4 ft
    (c) 6 ft
    (d) 8 ft

12. Wall-mounted ovens and counter-mounted cooking units shall be permitted to be _____.

    (a) permanently connected
    (b) cord-and-plug-connected
    (c) a or b
    (d) none of these

13. Each appliance shall have a means that _____ disconnects all ungrounded circuit conductors.

    (a) sequentially
    (b) automatically
    (c) simultaneously
    (d) all of these

14. For permanently connected appliances rated over _____ the branch-circuit circuit breaker can serve as the disconnecting means where the circuit breaker is within sight from the appliance, or is capable of being locked in the open position with a permanently installed locking provision that remains in place with or without the lock installed.

    (a) 200 VA
    (b) 300 VA
    (c) 400 VA
    (d) 500 VA

15. For motor-operated appliances rated over _____, a switch or circuit breaker located within sight from the motor-operated appliance can serve as the appliance disconnect.

    (a) 1/8 hp
    (b) ¼ hp
    (c) 15A
    (d) b and c

16. If an appliance of more than 1/8 hp is provided with a unit switch that complies with 422.34(A), (B), (C), or (D), the switch or circuit breaker serving as the other disconnecting means shall be permitted to be out of sight from the appliance.

    (a) True
    (b) False

17. For cord-and-plug-connected appliances, _____ plug and receptacle is permitted to serve as the disconnecting means.

    (a) a labeled
    (b) an accessible
    (c) a metal enclosed
    (d) none of these

18. For cord-and-plug-connected household electric ranges, an attachment plug and receptacle connection at the rear base of the range can serve as the disconnecting means, if it is _____.

    (a) less than 40A
    (b) a flush-mounted receptacle
    (c) GFCI protected
    (d) accessible by the removal of a drawer

19. Appliances that have a unit switch with a marked _____ position that disconnects all the ungrounded conductors can serve as the appliance disconnecting means.

    (a) on
    (b) off
    (c) on/off
    (d) all of these

20. Cord-and-plug connected vending machines manufactured or remanufactured on or after January 1, 2005 shall include a ground-fault circuit interrupter as an integral part of the attachment plug or in the power-supply cord within 12 in. of the attachment plug. Older vending machines not incorporating integral GFCI protection shall _____.

    (a) be remanufactured
    (b) be disabled
    (c) be connected to a GFCI-protected outlet
    (d) be connected to an AFCI-protected circuit

21. Electric drinking fountains shall be _____ protected.

    (a) GFCI
    (b) AFCI
    (c) a or b
    (d) none of these

22. Each electric appliance shall be provided with a(n) _____ giving the identifying name and the rating in volts and amperes, or in volts and watts.

    (a) pamphlet
    (b) nameplate
    (c) auxiliary statement
    (d) owner's manual

ARTICLE 424

Fixed Electric Space-Heating Equipment

INTRODUCTION TO ARTICLE 424—FIXED ELECTRIC SPACE-HEATING EQUIPMENT

Many people are surprised to see how many pages Article 424 has. This is a nine-part article on fixed electric space heaters. Why so much text for what seems to be a simple application? The answer is that Article 424 covers a variety of applications—heaters come in various configurations for various uses. Not all of these parts are for the electrician in the field—the requirements in Part IV are for manufacturers.

Fixed space heaters (wall-mounted, ceiling-mounted, or free-standing) are common in many utility buildings and other small structures, as well as in some larger structures. When used to heat floors, space-heating cables address the thermal layering problem typical of forced-air systems—so it's likely you'll encounter them. Duct heaters are very common in large office and educational buildings. These provide a distributed heating scheme. Locating the heater in the ductwork, but close to the occupied space, eliminates the waste of transporting heated air through sheet metal routed in unheated spaces, so it's likely you'll encounter those as well.

QUESTIONS FOR ARTICLE 424—FIXED ELECTRIC SPACE-HEATING EQUIPMENT

1. Fixed electric space-heating equipment and motors shall be considered a _____ load for branch circuit sizing.

   (a) noncontinuous
   (b) intermittent
   (c) continuous
   (d) none of these

2. If a permanently installed electric baseboard heater has factory-installed receptacle outlets, the receptacle is permitted to be connected to the heater circuits.

   (a) True
   (b) False

3. Fixed electric space-heating equipment requiring supply conductors with insulation rated over _____ shall be clearly and permanently marked.

   (a) 60°C
   (b) 75°C
   (c) 90°C
   (d) all of these

4. Fixed electric space-heating equipment shall be installed to provide the _____ spacing between the equipment and adjacent combustible material, unless it is listed for direct contact with combustible material.

   (a) required
   (b) minimum
   (c) maximum
   (d) safest

5. Means shall be provided to simultaneously disconnect the _____ of all fixed electric space-heating equipment from all ungrounded conductors.

   (a) heater
   (b) motor controller(s)
   (c) supplementary overcurrent device(s)
   (d) all of these

6. A unit switch with a marked _____ position that is part of a fixed space heater, and disconnects all ungrounded conductors, shall be permitted to serve as the required disconnecting means.

   (a) on
   (b) closed
   (c) off
   (d) none of these

7. Electric space-heating equipment employing resistance-type heating elements rated more than _____ shall have the heating elements subdivided.

   (a) 24A
   (b) 36A
   (c) 48A
   (d) 60A

8. Resistance-type heating elements in electric space-heating equipment shall be protected at not more than _____.

   (a) 24A
   (b) 36A
   (c) 48A
   (d) 60A

9. Electric space-heating cables shall be furnished complete with factory-assembled nonheating leads at least _____ in length.

   (a) 6 in.
   (b) 18 in.
   (c) 3 ft
   (d) 7 ft

10. On electric space-heating cables, blue leads indicate a cable rated for use on a nominal circuit voltage of _____.

    (a) 120V
    (b) 208V
    (c) 240V
    (d) 277V

11. Conductors located above an electric space heated ceiling are considered to be operating in an ambient temperature of _____.

    (a) 20°C
    (b) 30°C
    (c) 50°C
    (d) 86°C

12. Electric space-heating cables shall not extend beyond the room or area in which they _____.

    (a) provide heat
    (b) originate
    (c) terminate
    (d) are connected

13. Electric space-heating cables shall not be installed over cabinets whose clearance from the ceiling is less than the minimum _____ dimension of the cabinet to the nearest cabinet edge that is open to the room or area.

    (a) horizontal
    (b) vertical
    (c) overall
    (d) depth

14. The minimum clearance between an electric space-heating cable and an outlet box used for surface luminaires shall not be less than _____.

    (a) 6 in.
    (b) 8 in.
    (c) 14 in.
    (d) 18 in.

15. Ground-fault circuit-interrupter protection shall be provided for cables installed in electrically heated floors of _____.

    (a) bathrooms
    (b) hydromassage bathtub locations
    (c) kitchens
    (d) all of these

16. Duct heater controller equipment shall have a disconnecting means installed within _____ the controller except as allowed by 424.19(A).

    (a) 25 ft of
    (b) sight from
    (c) the side of
    (d) none of these

17. When installing duct heaters, sufficient clearance shall be maintained to permit replacement and adjustment of controls and heating elements.

    (a) True
    (b) False

18. A heating panel is a complete assembly provided with a junction box or length of flexible conduit for connection to a(n) _____.

    (a) wiring system
    (b) service
    (c) branch circuit
    (d) approved conductor

Motors, Motor Circuits, and Controllers

INTRODUCTION TO ARTICLE 430—MOTORS, MOTOR CIRCUITS, AND CONTROLLERS

Article 430 contains the specific rules for conductor sizing, overcurrent protection, control circuit conductors, controllers, and disconnecting means for electric motors. The installation requirements for motor control centers are covered in Part VIII, and air-conditioning and refrigeration equipment are covered in Article 440.

Article 430 is one of the longest articles in the *NEC*. It's also one of the most complex, but motors are also complex equipment. They're electrical and mechanical devices, but what makes motor applications complex is the fact that they're inductive loads with a high-current demand at start-up that's typically six, or more, times the running current. This makes overcurrent protection for motor applications necessarily different from the protection employed for other types of equipment. So don't confuse general overcurrent protection with motor protection—you must calculate and apply them differently using the rules in Article 430.

You might be uncomfortable with the allowances for overcurrent protection found in this article, such as protecting a 10 AWG conductor with a 60A overcurrent protection device, but as you learn to understand how motor protection works, you'll understand why these allowances aren't only safe, but necessary.

QUESTIONS FOR ARTICLE 430—MOTORS, MOTOR CIRCUITS, AND CONTROLLERS

1. For general motor applications, the motor branch-circuit short-circuit and ground-fault protection device shall be sized based on the _____ values.

   (a) motor nameplate
   (b) NEMA standard
   (c) *NEC* Table
   (d) Factory Mutual

2. The motor _____ currents listed in Tables 430.247 through 430.250 shall be used to determine the ampacity of motor-circuit conductors and short-circuit and ground-fault protection devices.

   (a) nameplate
   (b) full-load
   (c) power factor
   (d) service factor

3. A motor for general use shall be marked with a time rating of _____.

   (a) continuous
   (b) 5 or 15 minutes
   (c) 30 or 60 minutes
   (d) any of these

4. Motor controllers and terminals of control circuit devices shall be connected with copper conductors unless identified for use with a different conductor.

   (a) True
   (b) False

5. Torque requirements for motor control circuit device terminals shall be a minimum of _____ lb-in. (unless otherwise identified) for screw-type pressure terminals used for 14 AWG and smaller copper conductors.

   (a) 7
   (b) 9
   (c) 10
   (d) 15

6. Where motors are provided with terminal housings, the housings shall be of _____ and of substantial construction.

   (a) steel
   (b) iron
   (c) metal
   (d) copper

7. A motor terminal housing enclosing rigidly mounted motor terminals shall have a minimum of _____ between line terminals for a 230V motor.

   (a) ¼ in.
   (b) 3/8 in.
   (c) ½ in.
   (d) 5/8 in.

8. Motors shall be located so that adequate _____ is provided and so that maintenance, such as lubrication of bearings and replacing of brushes, can be readily accomplished.

   (a) space
   (b) ventilation
   (c) protection
   (d) all of these

9. Open motors having commutates or collector rings shall be located or protected so that sparks cannot reach adjacent combustible material. This shall not prohibit the installation of these motors _____.

   (a) on wooden floors
   (b) over combustible fiber
   (c) under combustible material
   (d) none of these

10. In determining the highest rated motor for purposes of 430.24, the highest rated motor shall be based on the rated full-load current as selected _____.

   (a) from the motor nameplate
   (b) from Tables 430.247, 430.248, 430.249, and 430.250
   (c) from taking the horsepower times 746 watts
   (d) using the largest horsepower motor

11. Branch-circuit conductors supplying a single continuous-duty motor shall have an ampacity not less than _____ rating.

   (a) 125 percent of the motor's nameplate current
   (b) 125 percent of the motor's full-load current as determined by 430.6(A)(1)
   (c) 125 percent of the motor's full locked-rotor
   (d) 80 percent of the motor's full-load current

12. Conductors supplying several motors shall not be sized smaller than _____ percent of the full-load current rating of the highest rated motor plus the sum of the full-load current ratings of all other motors in the group, plus the ampacity or other loads.

   (a) 80
   (b) 100
   (c) 125
   (d) 150

13. Feeder tap conductors supplying motor circuits, with an ampacity at least one-third that of the feeder, shall not exceed _____ in length.

   (a) 10 ft
   (b) 15 ft
   (c) 20 ft
   (d) 25 ft

14. Overload devices are intended to protect motors, motor control apparatus, and motor branch-circuit conductors against _____.

   (a) excessive heating due to motor overloads
   (b) excessive heating due to failure to start
   (c) short circuits and ground faults
   (d) a and b

15. A separate overload device used to protect continuous-duty motors rated more than 1 hp shall be selected to trip at no more than _____ percent of the motor nameplate full-load current rating if marked with a service factor of 1.15 or greater.

    (a) 110
    (b) 115
    (c) 120
    (d) 125

16. When an overload device sized in accordance with 430.32(A)(1) and (B)(1) is not sufficient to start the motor, higher-size sensing elements shall be permitted if the trip current does not exceed _____ percent of the motor nameplate full-load current rating, when the motor is marked with a service factor of 1.12.

    (a) 100
    (b) 110
    (c) 120
    (d) 130

17. Motor overload protection shall not be shunted or cut out during the starting period if the motor is _____.

    (a) not automatically started
    (b) automatically started
    (c) manually started
    (d) none of these

18. Unless overload protection is provided by other approved means, the minimum number of overload units required for a three-phase ac motor is _____.

    (a) one
    (b) two
    (c) three
    (d) any of these

19. Overload relays and other devices for motor overload protection that are not capable of _____ shall be protected by fuses, circuit breakers, or motor short-circuit protector.

    (a) opening short circuits
    (b) clearing overloads
    (c) opening ground faults
    (d) a or c

20. A motor _____ device that can restart a motor automatically after overload tripping shall not be installed if automatic restarting of the motor can result in injury to persons.

    (a) short-circuit
    (b) ground-fault
    (c) overcurrent
    (d) overload

21. If a(n) _____ shutdown is necessary to reduce hazards to persons, the overload sensing devices can be connected to a supervised alarm instead of causing immediate interruption of the motor circuit.

    (a) emergency
    (b) normal
    (c) orderly
    (d) none of these

22. The maximum rating or setting of an inverse time breaker used as the motor branch-circuit short-circuit and ground-fault protective device for a single-phase motor is _____ percent of the full-load current given in Table 430.248.

    (a) 125
    (b) 175
    (c) 250
    (d) 300

23. The motor branch-circuit short-circuit and ground-fault protective device shall be capable of carrying the _____ current of the motor.

    (a) varying
    (b) starting
    (c) running
    (d) continuous

24. Where the motor short-circuit and ground-fault protection devices determined by Table 430.52 do not correspond to the standard sizes or ratings, a higher rating that does not exceed the next higher standard ampere rating shall be permitted.

    (a) True
    (b) False

25. A motor can be provided with combined overcurrent protection using a single protective device to provide branch-circuit _____ where the rating of the device provides the overload protection specified in 430.32.

    (a) short-circuit protection
    (b) ground-fault protection
    (c) motor overload protection
    (d) all of these

26. A feeder supplying fixed motor load(s) shall have a protective device with a rating or setting _____ branch-circuit short-circuit and ground-fault protective device for any motor in the group, plus the sum of the full-load currents of the other motors of the group.

    (a) not greater than the largest rating or setting of the
    (b) 125 percent of the largest rating of any
    (c) equal to the largest rating of any
    (d) none of these

27. Overcurrent protection for motor control circuits shall not exceed _____ percent if the conductor is based on Table 310.15(B)(17) and does not extend beyond the motor control equipment enclosure.

    (a) 100
    (b) 150
    (c) 300
    (d) 400

28. Motor control circuit conductors that extend beyond the motor control equipment enclosure shall have short-circuit and ground-fault protection sized not greater than _____ percent of value specified in Table 310.15(B)(16) for 60°C conductors.

    (a) 100
    (b) 150
    (c) 300
    (d) 400

29. Motor control circuit transformers, with a primary current rating of less than 2A, can have the primary protection device set at no more than _____ percent of the rated primary current rating.

    (a) 150
    (b) 200
    (c) 400
    (d) 500

30. Motor control circuits shall be arranged so they will be disconnected from all sources of supply when the disconnecting means is in the open position.

    (a) True
    (b) False

31. If the motor control circuit transformer is located in the controller enclosure, the transformer shall be connected to the _____ side of the control circuit disconnecting means.

    (a) line
    (b) load
    (c) adjacent
    (d) none of these

32. The branch-circuit protective device can serve as the controller for a stationary motor rated at _____ or less that is normally left running and cannot be damaged by overload or failure to start.

    (a) 1/8 hp
    (b) ¼ hp
    (c) 3/8 hp
    (d) ½ hp

33. The motor controller shall have horsepower ratings at the application voltage not _____ than the horsepower rating of the motor.

    (a) lower than
    (b) higher than
    (c) equal to
    (d) none of these

34. A _____ rated in amperes shall be permitted as a controller for all motors.

    (a) branch-circuit inverse time circuit breaker
    (b) molded case switch
    (c) a and b
    (d) none of these

35. For stationary motors of 2 hp or less and 300V or less on ac circuits, the controller can be an ac-rated only general-use snap switch where the motor full-load current rating is not more than _____ percent of the rating of the switch.

    (a) 50
    (b) 60
    (c) 70
    (d) 80

36. A motor controller shall open all conductors to the motor where not used as a disconnecting means.

    (a) True
    (b) False

37. Each motor shall be provided with an individual controller.

    (a) True
    (b) False

38. A _____ shall be located in sight from the motor location and the driven machinery location.

    (a) controller
    (b) protection device
    (c) disconnecting means
    (d) all of these

39. The motor disconnecting means shall not be required to be in sight from the motor and the driven machinery location, provided _____.

    (a) the controller disconnecting means is capable of being individually locked in the open position
    (b) the provisions for locking are permanently installed on, or at, the switch or circuit breaker used as the controller disconnecting means
    (c) locating the motor disconnecting means within sight of the motor is impractical or introduces additional or increased hazards to people or property
    (d) all of these

40. The disconnecting means for the controller and motor shall open all ungrounded supply conductors.

    (a) True
    (b) False

41. The disconnecting means for a motor controller shall be designed so that it does not _____ automatically.

    (a) open
    (b) close
    (c) restart
    (d) shut down

42. The motor disconnecting means for a motor shall _____ whether it is in the open (off) or closed (on) position.

    (a) plainly indicate
    (b) provide current
    (c) be in the upper position
    (d) none of these

43. Where more than one motor disconnecting means is provided in the same motor branch circuit, at least one of the disconnecting means shall be readily accessible.

    (a) True
    (b) False

44. A motor disconnecting means can be a _____.

    (a) listed molded case circuit breaker
    (b) listed motor-circuit switch rated in horsepower
    (c) listed molded case switch
    (d) any of these

45. If a motor disconnecting means is a motor-circuit switch, it shall be rated in _____.

    (a) horsepower
    (b) watts
    (c) amperes
    (d) locked-rotor current

46. A branch-circuit overcurrent device can serve as the disconnecting means for a stationary motor of 1/8 hp or less.

    (a) True
    (b) False

47. A horsepower-rated _____ having a horsepower rating not less than the motor rating shall be permitted to serve as the disconnecting means.

    (a) attachment plug and receptacle
    (b) flanged surface inlet and cord connector
    (c) automatic controller
    (d) a or b

48. The disconnecting means for motor circuits rated 600 volts, nominal, or less shall have an ampere rating not less than _____ percent of the full-load current rating of the motor.

    (a) 80
    (b) 100
    (c) 115
    (d) 125

49. The disconnecting means for a torque motor shall have an ampere rating of at least _____ percent of the motor nameplate current.

    (a) 100
    (b) 115
    (c) 125
    (d) 175

50. A switch or circuit breaker can be used as both the controller and disconnecting means if it _____.

    (a) opens all ungrounded conductors
    (b) is protected by an overcurrent device in each ungrounded conductor
    (c) is manually operable, or both power and manually operable
    (d) all of these

51. An oil switch can be used as both the motor controller and disconnecting means on a circuit whose rating _____ or 100A.

    (a) does not exceed 240V
    (b) does not exceed 300V
    (c) does not exceed 600V
    (d) exceeds 600V

52. Exposed live parts of motors and controllers operating at _____ or more between terminals shall be guarded against accidental contact by enclosure or by location.

    (a) 24V
    (b) 50V
    (c) 60V
    (d) 150V

ARTICLE 440

Air-Conditioning and Refrigeration Equipment

INTRODUCTION TO ARTICLE 440—AIR-CONDITIONING AND REFRIGERATION EQUIPMENT

This article applies to electrically driven air-conditioning and refrigeration equipment. The rules in this article add to, or amend, the rules in Article 430 and other articles.

Each equipment manufacturer has the motor for a given air-conditioning unit built to its own specifications. Cooling and other characteristics are different from those of nonhermetic motors. For each motor, the manufacturer has worked out all of the details and supplied the correct protection, conductor sizing, and other information on the nameplate. So when wiring an air conditioner, trust the information on the nameplate and don't try to over-complicate the situation. The math for sizing the overcurrent protection and conductor minimum ampacity has already been done for you.

QUESTIONS FOR ARTICLE 440— AIR-CONDITIONING AND REFRIGERATION EQUIPMENT

1. Article 440 applies to electric motor-driven air-conditioning and refrigerating equipment that has a hermetic refrigerant motor-compressor.

   (a) True
   (b) False

2. The _____ current for a hermetic refrigerant motor-compressor is the current resulting when the motor-compressor is operated at the rated load, rated voltage, and rated frequency of the equipment it serves.

   (a) full-load current
   (b) nameplate rating
   (c) selection current
   (d) rated-load current

3. The rules of _____ shall apply to air-conditioning and refrigerating equipment that does not incorporate a hermetic refrigerant motor-compressor.

   (a) Article 422
   (b) Article 424
   (c) Article 430
   (d) all of these

4. Equipment such as _____ shall be considered appliances, and the provisions of Article 422 apply in addition to Article 440.

   (a) room air conditioners
   (b) household refrigerators and freezers
   (c) drinking water coolers and beverage dispensers
   (d) all of these

5. A disconnecting means that serves a hermetic refrigerant motor-compressor shall have an ampere rating of at least _____ percent of the nameplate rated-load current or branch-circuit selection current, whichever is greater.

   (a) 80
   (b) 100
   (c) 115
   (d) 125

6. An attachment plug and receptacle can serve as the disconnecting means for cord-connected _____.

    (a) room air conditioners
    (b) household refrigerators and freezers
    (c) drinking water coolers and beverage dispensers
    (d) all of these

7. The disconnecting means for air-conditioning and refrigerating equipment shall be _____ from the air-conditioning or refrigerating equipment.

    (a) readily accessible
    (b) within sight
    (c) a or b
    (d) a and b

8. Disconnecting means for air-conditioning or refrigerating equipment can be installed _____ the air-conditioning or refrigerating equipment, but not on panels that are designed to allow access to the equipment, and not over the equipment nameplate.

    (a) on
    (b) within
    (c) a or b
    (d) none of these

9. Where the air conditioner disconnecting means is not within sight from the equipment, the provision for locking or adding a lock to the disconnecting means shall be on the switch or circuit breaker and remain in place _____ the lock installed.

    (a) with
    (b) without
    (c) with or without
    (d) none of these

10. Short-circuit and ground-fault protection for an individual air-conditioner motor-compressor shall not exceed _____ percent of the motor-compressor rated-load current or branch-circuit protection current, whichever is greater.

    (a) 80
    (b) 125
    (c) 175
    (d) 250

11. Branch-circuit conductors supplying a single air-conditioner motor-compressor shall have an ampacity not less than _____ percent of either the motor-compressor rated-load current or the branch-circuit selection current, whichever is greater.

    (a) 100
    (b) 125
    (c) 150
    (d) 200

12. Conductors supplying more than one air-conditioner motor-compressor shall have an ampacity not less than the sum of the rated load or branch-circuit current ratings, whichever is larger, of all the air-conditioner motor-compressors plus the full-load currents of any other motors, plus _____ percent of the highest motor or motor compressor rating in the group.

    (a) 25
    (b) 50
    (c) 80
    (d) 100

13. A hermetic motor-compressor controller shall have a _____ current rating not less than the respective nameplate rating(s) on the compressor.

    (a) continuous-duty full-load
    (b) locked-rotor
    (c) a or b
    (d) a and b

14. The rating of the attachment plug and receptacle shall not exceed _____ at 250V for a cord-and-plug-connected air-conditioner motor-compressor.

    (a) 15A
    (b) 20A
    (c) 30A
    (d) 40A

15. The total rating of a cord-and-plug-connected room air conditioner, connected to the same branch circuit which supplies lighting units, other appliances, or general-use receptacles, shall not exceed _____ percent of the branch-circuit rating.

    (a) 40
    (b) 50
    (c) 70
    (d) 80

16. An attachment plug and receptacle can serve as the disconnecting means for a single-phase room air conditioner rated 250 volts or less if _____.

    (a) the manual controls on the room air conditioner are readily accessible and located within 1.8 m (6 ft) of the floor
    (b) an approved manually operable disconnecting means is installed in a readily accessible location within sight from the room air conditioner
    (c) a or b
    (d) a and b

17. When supplying a room air conditioner rated 120V, the length of a flexible supply cord shall not exceed _____.

    (a) 4 ft
    (b) 6 ft
    (c) 8 ft
    (d) 10 ft

INTRODUCTION TO ARTICLE 445—GENERATORS

This article contains the electrical installation, and other requirements, for generators. These requirements include such things as where generators can be installed, nameplate markings, conductor ampacity, and disconnecting means.

Generators are basically motors that operate in reverse—they produce electricity when rotated, instead of rotating when supplied with electricity. Article 430, which covers motors, is the longest article in the *NEC*. Article 445, which covers generators, is one of the shortest. At first, this might not seem to make sense. But you don't need to size and protect conductors to a generator. You do need to size and protect them to a motor.

Generators need overload protection, and it's necessary to size the conductors that come from the generator. But these considerations are much more straightforward than the equivalent considerations for motors. Before you study Article 445, take a moment to read the definition of "Separately Derived System" in Article 100.

QUESTIONS FOR ARTICLE 445—GENERATORS

1. Article 445 contains installation and other requirements for generators.

   (a) True
   (b) False

2. Each generator shall be provided with a _____ listing the manufacturer's name, the rated frequency, power factor, number of phases (if of alternating current), and its rating in kilowatts or kilovolt-amperes.

   (a) list
   (b) faceplate
   (c) nameplate
   (d) sticker

3. Constant-voltage generators, except ac generator exciters, shall be protected from overcurrent by _____ or other acceptable overcurrent protective means suitable for the conditions of use.

   (a) inherent design
   (b) circuit breakers
   (c) fuses
   (d) any of these

4. The ampacity of ungrounded conductors from the generator terminals to the first distribution device containing overcurrent protection shall not be less than _____ percent of the nameplate rating of the generator.

   (a) 75
   (b) 115
   (c) 125
   (d) 140

5. Separately derived system generators must have the _____ conductor sized not smaller than required to carry the maximum unbalanced current as determined by 220.61.

    (a) neutral
    (b) grounding
    (c) a and b
    (d) none of these

6. Generators must have a disconnecting means that is lockable in the open position, except where:

    (a) The driving means for the generator can be readily shut down.
    (b) The generator isn't arranged to operate in parallel with another generator or other source of voltage.
    (c) a and b
    (d) a or b

ARTICLE 450

Transformers

INTRODUCTION TO ARTICLE 450—TRANSFORMERS

Article 450 opens by saying, "This article covers the installation of all transformers." Then it lists eight exceptions. So what does Article 450 really cover? Essentially, it covers power transformers and most kinds of lighting transformers.

A major concern with transformers is preventing overheating. The *Code* doesn't completely address this issue. Article 90 explains that the *NEC* isn't a design manual, and it assumes that the person using the *Code* has a certain level of expertise. Proper transformer selection is an important part of preventing transformer overheating.

The *NEC* assumes you've already selected a transformer suitable to the load characteristics. For the *Code* to tell you how to do that would push it into the realm of a design manual. Article 450 then takes you to the next logical step—providing overcurrent protection and the proper connections. But this article doesn't stop there; 450.9 provides ventilation requirements, and 450.13 contains accessibility requirements.

Part I of Article 450 contains the general requirements such as guarding, marking, and accessibility, Part II contains the requirements for different types of transformers, and Part III covers transformer vaults.

QUESTIONS FOR ARTICLE 450—TRANSFORMERS

1. The primary overcurrent protection for a transformer rated 600V, nominal, or less, with no secondary protection and having a primary current rating of over 9A must be set at not more than _____ percent.

   (a) 125
   (b) 167
   (c) 200
   (d) 300

2. A secondary tie of a transformer is a circuit operating at _____, nominal, or less, between phases that connects two power sources or power-supply points.

   (a) 600V
   (b) 1,000V
   (c) 12,000V
   (d) 35,000V

3. Transformers with ventilating openings shall be installed so that the ventilating openings _____.

   (a) are a minimum 18 in. above the floor
   (b) are not blocked by walls or obstructions
   (c) are aesthetically located
   (d) are vented to the exterior of the building

4. Transformers and transformer vaults shall be readily accessible to qualified personnel for inspection and maintenance, except _____.

   (a) dry-type transformers 600V or less, located in the open on walls, columns, or structures
   (b) dry-type transformers rated not more than 50 kVA/ 600V installed in hollow spaces of buildings not permanently closed in by structure
   (c) a or b
   (d) none of these

5. For transformers, other than Class 2 and Class 3, a means is required to disconnect all transformer ungrounded primary conductors. The disconnecting means must be located within sight of the transformer unless the _____.

    (a) disconnect location is field-marked on the transformer
    (b) disconnect is lockable
    (c) disconnect is nonfusible
    (d) a and b

ARTICLE
480

Storage Batteries

INTRODUCTION TO ARTICLE 480—STORAGE BATTERIES

The stationary battery is the heart of any uninterruptible power supply. Article 480 addresses stationary batteries for commercial and industrial grade power supplies, not the small, "point of use" UPS boxes.

Stationary batteries are also used in other applications, such as emergency power systems. Regardless of the application, if it uses stationary batteries then Article 480 applies.

Lead-acid stationary batteries fall into two general categories: flooded, and valve regulated (VRLA). These differ markedly in such ways as maintainability, total cost of ownership, and scalability. The *NEC* doesn't address these differences, as they're engineering issues and not fire safety or electrical safety issues [90.1].

The *Code* doesn't address such design issues as optimum tier height, distance between tiers, determination of charging voltage, or string configuration. Nor does it address battery testing, monitoring, or maintenance. All of these involve highly specialized areas of knowledge, and are required for optimizing operational efficiency. Standards other than the *NEC* address these issues.

What the *Code* does address, in Article 480, are issues related to preventing electrocution and the ignition of the gases that all stationary batteries (even "sealed" ones) emit.

QUESTIONS FOR ARTICLE 480— STORAGE BATTERIES

1. The provisions of Article _____ apply to stationary storage battery installations.

    (a) 450
    (b) 460
    (c) 470
    (d) 480

2. A battery system includes storage batteries, battery chargers, and can include inverters, converters, and associated electrical equipment.

    (a) True
    (b) False

3. Nominal battery voltage, as it relates to storage batteries, is defined as the voltage of a battery based on the _____ of cells in the battery.

    (a) number
    (b) type
    (c) a and b
    (d) a or b

4. Nominal battery voltage is typically _____.

    (a) 2V per cell for lead-acid systems
    (b) 1.20V for per cell for alkali systems
    (c) 4V per cell for lithium-ion systems
    (d) all of these

5. Wiring and equipment supplied from storage batteries must be in accordance with Chapters 1 through 4 of the *NEC* unless otherwise permitted by 480.4.

    (a) True
    (b) False

6. A disconnecting means is required within sight of the storage battery for all ungrounded battery system conductors operating at over _____ nominal.

    (a) 20V
    (b) 30V
    (c) 40V
    (d) 50V

7. A _____ disconnecting means is required within sight of the storage battery for all ungrounded battery system conductors operating at over 50V nominal.

    (a) accessible
    (b) readily accessible
    (c) safety
    (d) all of these

8. A vented alkaline-type battery, as it relates to storage batteries, operating at less than 250V shall be installed with not more than _____ cells in the series circuit of any one tray.

    (a) 10
    (b) 12
    (c) 18
    (d) 20

9. Racks (rigid frames designed to support battery cells or trays) must be made of one of the following:

    (a) Metal, treated to be resistant to deteriorating action by the electrolyte and provided with nonconducting or continuous insulating material members directly supporting the cells.
    (b) Fiberglass.
    (c) Other suitable nonconductive materials.
    (d) Any of these

10. Provisions shall be made for sufficient diffusion and ventilation of the gases from a storage battery to prevent the accumulation of a(n) _____ mixture.

    (a) corrosive
    (b) explosive
    (c) toxic
    (d) all of these

11. The required working space requirements of 110.26 are measured from the edge of the battery _____.

    (a) terminals
    (b) enclosure
    (c) rack
    (d) any of these

12. Each vented cell of a battery, as it relates to storage batteries, shall be equipped with _____ that is(are) designed to prevent destruction of the cell due to ignition of gases within the cell by an external spark or flame under normal operating conditions.

    (a) pressure relief
    (b) a flame arrester
    (c) fluid level indicators
    (d) none of these

Please use the 2011 *Code* book to answer the following questions, which are based on the 2011 *NEC*.

Workbook Final Exam A

1. When the opening to an outlet, junction, or switch point is less than 8 in. in any dimension, each conductor shall be long enough to extend at least _____ outside the opening of the enclosure.

   (a) 0 in.
   (b) 3 in.
   (c) 6 in.
   (d) 12 in.

2. A recessed luminaire not identified for contact with insulation shall have all recessed parts spaced not less than _____ from combustible materials, except for points of support.

   (a) ¼ in.
   (b) ½ in.
   (c) 1¼ in.
   (d) 6 in.

3. A motor terminal housing enclosing rigidly mounted motor terminals shall have a minimum of _____ between line terminals for a 230V motor.

   (a) ¼ in.
   (b) 3/8 in.
   (c) ½ in.
   (d) 5/8 in.

4. Grounding electrodes of the rod type less than _____ in diameter shall be listed.

   (a) ½ in.
   (b) 5/8 in.
   (c) ¾ in.
   (d) none of these

5. A cable, raceway, or box installed under metal-corrugated sheet roof decking shall be supported so the top of the cable, raceway, or box is not less than _____ from the lowest surface of the roof decking to the top of the cable, raceway, or box.

   (a) ½ in.
   (b) 1 in.
   (c) 1½ in.
   (d) 2 in.

6. The minimum working space on a circuit that is 120 volts-to-ground, with exposed live parts on one side and no live or grounded parts on the other side of the working space, is _____.

   (a) 1 ft
   (b) 3 ft
   (c) 4 ft
   (d) 6 ft

7. Branch-circuit conductors within _____ of a ballast shall have an insulation temperature rating not lower than 90°C (194°F).

   (a) 1 in.
   (b) 3 in.
   (c) 6 in.
   (d) 8 in.

8. The load for electric clothes dryers in a dwelling unit shall be _____ watts or the nameplate rating, whichever is larger, per dryer.

   (a) 1,500
   (b) 4,500
   (c) 5,000
   (d) 8,000

9. A dwelling unit containing three 120V small-appliance branch circuits has a calculated load of _____ VA for the small appliance circuits.

   (a) 1,500
   (b) 3,000
   (c) 4,500
   (d) 6,000

10. Surface-type cabinets, cutout boxes, and meter socket enclosures in damp or wet locations shall be mounted so there is at least _____ airspace between the enclosure and the wall or supporting surface.

    (a) 1/16 in.
    (b) ¼ in.
    (c) 1¼ in.
    (d) 6 in.

11. Noncombustible surfaces that are broken or incomplete around boxes employing a flush-type cover or faceplate shall be repaired so there will be no gaps or open spaces larger than _____ at the edge of the box.

    (a) 1/16 in.
    (b) 1/8 in.
    (c) ¼ in.
    (d) ½ in.

12. For motor-operated appliances rated over _____, a switch or circuit breaker located within sight from the motor operated appliance can serve as the appliance disconnect.

    (a) 1/8 hp
    (b) ¼ hp
    (c) 15A
    (d) b and c

13. In general, the minimum size conductor permitted for use in parallel installations is _____ AWG.

    (a) 10
    (b) 4
    (c) 1
    (d) 1/0

14. At least one receptacle outlet shall be installed within 18 in. of the top of a show window for each _____, or major fraction thereof, of show-window area measured horizontally at its maximum width.

    (a) 10 ft
    (b) 12 ft
    (c) 18 ft
    (d) 24 ft

15. The minimum clearance for overhead feeder conductors that pass over track rails of railroads is _____.

    (a) 10 ft
    (b) 12 ft
    (c) 24.50 ft
    (d) 30 ft

16. A bare 4 AWG copper conductor installed horizontally near the bottom or vertically, and within that portion of a concrete foundation or footing that is in direct contact with the earth can be used as a grounding electrode when the conductor is at least _____ in length.

    (a) 10 ft
    (b) 15 ft
    (c) 20 ft
    (d) 25 ft

17. Feeder tap conductors supplying motor circuits, with an ampacity at least one-third that of the feeder, shall not exceed _____ in length.

    (a) 10 ft
    (b) 15 ft
    (c) 20 ft
    (d) 25 ft

18. Open individual conductors shall not be smaller than _____ AWG copper for spans up to 50 ft in length and _____ AWG copper for a longer span, unless supported by a messenger wire.

    (a) 10, 8
    (b) 8, 8
    (c) 6, 8
    (d) 6, 6

19. The disconnecting means for a torque motor shall have an ampere rating of at least _____ percent of the motor nameplate current.

    (a) 100
    (b) 115
    (c) 125
    (d) 175

20. Motor control circuit conductors that extend beyond the motor control equipment enclosure shall have short-circuit and ground-fault protection sized not greater than _____ percent of value specified in Table 310.15(B)(16) for 60°C conductors.

    (a) 100
    (b) 150
    (c) 300
    (d) 400

21. A separate overload device used to protect continuous-duty motors rated more than 1 hp shall be selected to trip at no more than _____ percent of the motor nameplate full-load current rating if marked with a service factor of 1.15 or greater.

    (a) 110
    (b) 115
    (c) 120
    (d) 125

22. Metal cable trays containing only non power conductors such as communication, data, signal, conductors and cables must be electrically continuous, through listed connections or the use of an insulated stranded bonding jumper not smaller than _____.

    (a) 12 AWG
    (b) 10 AWG
    (c) 6 AWG
    (d) 4 AWG

23. An equipment bonding jumper can be installed on the outside of a raceway, providing the length of the equipment bonding jumper is not more than _____ and the equipment bonding jumper is routed with the raceway.

    (a) 12 in.
    (b) 24 in.
    (c) 36 in.
    (d) 72 in.

24. Conductor adjustment factors shall not apply to conductors in raceways having a length not exceeding _____.

    (a) 12 in.
    (b) 24 in.
    (c) 36 in.
    (d) 48 in.

25. Luminaires must maintain a minimum clearance from the closet storage space of _____.

    (a) 12 in. for surface-mounted incandescent or LED luminaires with a completely enclosed light source
    (b) 6 in. for surface-mounted fluorescent luminaires
    (c) 6 in. for recessed fluorescent luminaires or recessed incandescent or LED luminaires with a completely enclosed light source
    (d) all of these

26. Branch-circuit conductors supplying a single continuous-duty motor shall have an ampacity not less than _____ rating.

    (a) 125 percent of the motor's nameplate current
    (b) 125 percent of the motor's full-load current as determined by 430.6(A)(1)
    (c) 125 percent of the motor's full locked-rotor
    (d) 80 percent of the motor's full-load current

27. Where installed in a wet location, all _____ receptacle(s) shall be listed as weather-resistant.

    (a) 125V, 30A nonlocking
    (b) 250V, 15A nonlocking
    (c) 125V, 30A locking
    (d) 250V, 15A locking

28. The feeder/service calculated load for a multifamily dwelling containing nine 12 kW ranges is _____.

    (a) 13,000W
    (b) 14,700W
    (c) 16,000W
    (d) 24,000W

29. Underground service conductors that supply power to limited loads of a single branch circuit shall not be smaller than _____.

    (a) 14 AWG copper
    (b) 14 AWG aluminum
    (c) 12 AWG copper
    (d) 12 AWG aluminum

30. The working space in front of the electric equipment shall not be less than _____ wide, or the width of the equipment, whichever is greater.

    (a) 15 in.
    (b) 30 in.
    (c) 40 in.
    (d) 60 in.

31. The voltage between conductors in a surface metal raceway shall not exceed _____ unless the metal has a thickness of not less than 0.04 in. nominal.

    (a) 150V
    (b) 300V
    (c) 600V
    (d) 1,000V

32. For installations that supply only limited loads of a single branch circuit, the service disconnecting means shall have a rating not less than _____.

    (a) 15A
    (b) 20A
    (c) 25A
    (d) 30A

33. The standard ampere ratings for fuses includes _____.

    (a) 1A
    (b) 6A
    (c) 601A
    (d) all of these

34. A minimum working space depth of _____ to live parts operating at 277 volts-to-ground is required where there are exposed live parts on one side and no live or grounded parts on the other side.

    (a) 2 ft
    (b) 3 ft
    (c) 4 ft
    (d) 6 ft

35. Interior metal water piping located not more than _____ from the point of entrance to the building shall be permitted to be used as a conductor to interconnect electrodes that are part of the grounding electrode system.

    (a) 2 ft
    (b) 4 ft
    (c) 5 ft
    (d) 6 ft

36. The length of the cord for a dishwasher or trash compactor shall not be longer than _____, measured from the rear of the appliance.

    (a) 2 ft
    (b) 4 ft
    (c) 6 ft
    (d) 8 ft

37. The total volume occupied by two internal cable clamps, six 12 AWG conductors, and a single-pole switch is _____.

    (a) 2.00 cu in.
    (b) 4.50 cu in.
    (c) 14.50 cu in.
    (d) 20.25 cu in.

38. In dwelling unit bathrooms, not less than one 15A or 20A, 125V receptacle outlet must be installed within _____ from the outside edge of each bathroom basin.

    (a) 20 in.
    (b) 3 ft
    (c) 4 ft
    (d) 6 ft

39. Live parts of electrical equipment operating at _____ or more shall be guarded against accidental contact by approved enclosures or by suitable permanent, substantial partitions, or screens arranged so that only qualified persons have access to the space within reach of the live parts.

    (a) 20V
    (b) 30V
    (c) 50V
    (d) 100V

40. The smallest size fixture wire permitted by the *NEC* is _____ AWG.

    (a) 22
    (b) 20
    (c) 18
    (d) 16

41. Service-entrance cables mounted in contact with a building shall be supported at intervals not exceeding _____.

    (a) 24 in.
    (b) 30 in.
    (c) 3 ft
    (d) 4 ft

42. Electric space-heating equipment employing resistance-type heating elements rated more than _____ shall have the heating elements subdivided.

    (a) 24A
    (b) 36A
    (c) 48A
    (d) 60A

43. The size of the grounding electrode conductor for a building or structure supplied by a feeder shall not be smaller than that identified in _____, based on the largest ungrounded supply conductor.

    (a) 250.66
    (b) 250.122
    (c) Table 310.15(B)(16)
    (d) none of these

44. Nominal battery voltage is typically _____.

    (a) 2V per cell for lead-acid systems
    (b) 1.20V for per cell for alkali systems
    (c) 4V per cell for lithium-ion systems
    (d) all of these

45. Unless an individual switch is provided for each luminaire located over combustible material, lampholders shall be located at least _____ above the floor, or shall be located or guarded so that the lamps cannot be readily removed or damaged.

    (a) 3 ft
    (b) 6 ft
    (c) 8 ft
    (d) 10 ft

46. The dedicated equipment space for electrical equipment that is required for panelboards installed indoors is measured from the floor to a height of _____ above the equipment, or to the structural ceiling, whichever is lower.

    (a) 3 ft
    (b) 6 ft
    (c) 12 ft
    (d) 30 ft

47. At least one receptacle outlet not more than _____ above a balcony, deck or porch shall be installed within the perimeter at each balcony, deck or porch of a dwelling unit.

    (a) 3 ft
    (b) 6½ ft
    (c) 8 ft
    (d) 24 in.

48. Overhead feeder conductors to a building shall have a vertical clearance of final spans above, or within _____ measured horizontally from the platforms, projections, or surfaces from which they might be reached.

    (a) 3 ft
    (b) 6 ft
    (c) 8 ft
    (d) 10 ft

49. Overhead service conductors installed over roofs shall have a vertical clearance of _____ above the roof surface, unless a lesser distance is permitted by an exception.

    (a) 3 ft
    (b) 8 ft
    (c) 12 ft
    (d) 15 ft

50. Overhead service conductors to a building shall maintain a vertical clearance of final spans above, or within, _____ measured horizontally from the platforms, projections, or surfaces from which they might be reached.

    (a) 3 ft
    (b) 6 ft
    (c) 8 ft
    (d) 10 ft

51. Type MC cable installed horizontally through wooden or metal framing members are considered secured and supported where such support doesn't exceed _____ intervals.

    (a) 3 ft
    (b) 4 ft
    (c) 6 ft
    (d) 8 ft

52. Conductor ampacity shall be determined using the _____ column of Table 310.15(B)(16) for circuits rated 100A or less or marked for 14 AWG through 1 AWG conductors, unless the equipment terminals are listed for use with conductors that have higher temperature ratings.

    (a) 30°C
    (b) 60°C
    (c) 75°C
    (d) 90°C

53. The feeder conductor ampacity shall not be less than that of the service-entrance conductors where the feeder conductors carry the total load supplied by service conductors with an ampacity of _____ or less.

    (a) 30A
    (b) 55A
    (c) 60A
    (d) 100A

54. Infrared lamps for commercial and industrial heating appliances shall have overcurrent protection not exceeding _____.

    (a) 30A
    (b) 40A
    (c) 50A
    (d) 60A

55. Listed outlet boxes to support ceiling-suspended fans that weigh more than _____lb shall have the maximum allowable weight marked on the box.

    (a) 35 lb
    (b) 50 lb
    (c) 60 lb
    (d) 70 lb

56. No parts of cord-connected luminaires, chain-, cable-, or cord-suspended luminaires, lighting track, pendants, or paddle fans shall be located within a zone measured 3 ft horizontally and _____ vertically from the top of the bathtub rim or shower stall threshold.

    (a) 4 ft
    (b) 6 ft
    (c) 8 ft
    (d) 10 ft

57. A wall-mounted luminaire weighing not more than _____ can be supported to a device box or plaster ring with no fewer than two No. 6 or larger screws.

    (a) 4 lb
    (b) 6 lb
    (c) 8 lb
    (d) 10 lb

58. A demand factor of _____ percent applies to a multifamily dwelling with ten units if the optional calculation method is used.

    (a) 43
    (b) 50
    (c) 60
    (d) 75

59. The provisions of Article _____ apply to stationary storage battery installations.

    (a) 450
    (b) 460
    (c) 470
    (d) 480

60. Alternating-current or direct-current general-use snap switches may be used for control of inductive loads not exceeding _____ percent of the ampere rating of the switch at the applied voltage.

    (a) 50
    (b) 75
    (c) 90
    (d) 100

61. Branch circuits that supply lighting units that have ballasts, autotransformers, or LED drivers shall have the calculated load based on _____ of the units, not to the total wattage of the lamps.

    (a) 50 percent of the rating
    (b) 80 percent of the rating
    (c) the total ampere rating
    (d) 150 percent of the rating

62. For equipment rated 1,200A or more and over 6 ft wide that contains overcurrent devices, switching devices, or control devices, there shall be one entrance to and egress from the required working space not less than 24 in. wide and _____ high at each end of the working space.

    (a) 5½ ft
    (b) 6 ft
    (c) 6½ ft
    (d) any of these

63. What is the minimum size copper supply side bonding jumper for a service raceway containing 4/0 THHN aluminum conductors?

    (a) 6 AWG aluminum
    (b) 4 AWG aluminum
    (c) 4 AWG copper
    (d) 3 AWG copper

64. When installing PVC conduit underground without concrete cover, there shall be a minimum of _____ of cover.

    (a) 6 in.
    (b) 12 in.
    (c) 18 in.
    (d) 22 in.

65. What is the minimum cover requirement for Type UF cable supplying power to a 120V, 15A GFCI-protected circuit outdoors under a driveway of a one-family dwelling?

    (a) 6 in.
    (b) 12 in.
    (c) 16 in.
    (d) 24 in.

66. Type AC cable shall be secured at intervals not exceeding 4½ ft and within _____ of every outlet box, cabinet, conduit body, or fitting.

    (a) 6 in.
    (b) 8 in.
    (c) 10 in.
    (d) 12 in.

67. Noninsulated busbars shall have a minimum space of _____ between the bottom of a switchboard enclosure and busbars or other obstructions.

    (a) 6 in.
    (b) 8 in.
    (c) 10 in.
    (d) 12 in.

68. The raceway or cable for tap conductors to recessed luminaires shall have a minimum length of _____.

    (a) 6 in.
    (b) 12 in.
    (c) 18 in.
    (d) 24 in.

69. When bare conductors are installed with insulated conductors, their ampacities shall be limited to _____.

    (a) 60°C
    (b) 75°C
    (c) 90°C
    (d) the lowest temperature rating for any of the insulated conductors

70. For Type NM and NMC cable, the conductor ampacity used for ambient temperature correction [310.15(B)(2)(a)], conductor bundling adjustment [310.15(B)(3)(a)], or both, is based on the 90ºC conductor insulation rating [310.15(B)(2)], provided the adjusted or corrected ampacity doesn't exceed that for a _____ rated conductor.

    (a) 60°C
    (b) 75°C
    (c) 90°C
    (d) 120°C

71. The ampacity of 18 TFFN is _____.
    (a) 6A
    (b) 8A
    (c) 10A
    (d) 14A

72. The ampacity of ungrounded conductors from the generator terminals to the first distribution device containing overcurrent protection shall not be less than _____ percent of the nameplate rating of the generator.
    (a) 75
    (b) 115
    (c) 125
    (d) 140

73. THWN insulated conductors are rated _____.
    (a) 75°C
    (b) for wet locations
    (c) a and b
    (d) not enough information

74. Overhead service conductors shall have a horizontal clearance of _____ from a pool.
    (a) 8 ft
    (b) 10 ft
    (c) 12 ft
    (d) 14 ft

75. A disconnecting means that serves a hermetic refrigerant motor-compressor shall have an ampere rating of at least _____ percent of the nameplate rated-load current or branch-circuit selection current, whichever is greater.
    (a) 80
    (b) 100
    (c) 115
    (d) 125

76. If the circuit's overcurrent device exceeds _____, the conductor ampacity must have a rating not less than the rating of the overcurrent device.
    (a) 800A
    (b) 1,000A
    (c) 1,200A
    (d) 2,000A

77. Panelboards supplied by a three-phase, 4-wire, delta-connected system shall have the phase with higher voltage-to-ground (high-leg) connected to the _____ phase.
    (a) A
    (b) B
    (c) C
    (d) any of these

78. Joints between lengths of ENT, couplings, fittings, and boxes shall be made by _____.
    (a) a qualified person
    (b) set screw fittings
    (c) an approved method
    (d) exothermic welding

79. The space above a hung ceiling used for environmental air-handling purposes is an example of _____, and the wiring limitations of _____ apply.
    (a) a specifically fabricated duct used for environmental air, 300.22(B)
    (b) other space used for environmental air (plenum), 300.22(C)
    (c) a supply duct used for environmental air, 300.22(B)
    (d) none of these

80. The following types of luminaires can be installed in a clothes closet:
    (a) A surface or recessed incandescent luminaire with completely enclosed light source.
    (b) A surface or recessed fluorescent luminaire.
    (c) A surface-mounted or recessed LED luminaire with a completely enclosed light source.
    (d) all of these

81. Which of the following statements about Type S fuses are true?
    (a) Adapters shall fit Edison-base fuseholders.
    (b) Adapters are designed to be easily removed.
    (c) Type S fuses shall be classified as not over 125V and 30A.
    (d) a and c

82. All 15A and 20A, 125V receptacles installed within 6 ft of the outside edge of a sink in locations other than dwelling units must be _____.
    (a) AFCI protected
    (b) GFCI protected
    (c) tamperproof
    (d) a and b

83. For a separate building or structure supplied by a separately derived system when overcurrent protection isn't provided for the supply conductors to the building/structure as permitted by 240.21(C)(4), the installation must be _____ in accordance with 250.30(A).

    (a) AFCI protected
    (b) grounded and bonded
    (c) isolated
    (d) all of these

84. Power distribution blocks installed in metal wireways shall _____.

    (a) allow for sufficient wire-bending space at terminals
    (b) not have uninsulated exposed live parts
    (c) a or b
    (d) a and b

85. When a feeder supplies _____ in which equipment grounding conductors are required, the feeder shall include or provide an equipment grounding conductor.

    (a) an equipment disconnecting means
    (b) electrical systems
    (c) branch circuits
    (d) electric-discharge lighting equipment

86. Many terminations and equipment are marked with _____.

    (a) an etching tool
    (b) a removable label
    (c) a tightening torque
    (d) the manufacturer's initials

87. Receptacles incorporating an isolated grounding conductor connection intended for the reduction of electrical noise shall be identified by _____ on the face of the receptacle.

    (a) an orange triangle
    (b) a green triangle
    (c) the color orange
    (d) the engraved word ISOLATED

88. Where Type NM cable passes through factory or field openings in metal members, it shall be protected by _____ bushings or _____ grommets that cover metal edges.

    (a) approved
    (b) identified
    (c) listed
    (d) none of these

89. Splices and taps shall not be located within luminaire _____.

    (a) arms or stems
    (b) bases or screw shells
    (c) a and b
    (d) a or b

90. FMC shall be supported and secured _____.

    (a) at intervals not exceeding 4½ ft
    (b) within 8 in. on each side of a box where fished
    (c) where fished
    (d) at intervals not exceeding 6 ft

91. LFMC shall be supported and secured _____.

    (a) at intervals not exceeding 4½ ft
    (b) within 8 in. on each side of a box where fished
    (c) where fished
    (d) at intervals not exceeding 6 ft

92. Circuit breakers shall be capable of being closed and opened by manual operation. Operation by other means, such as electrical or pneumatic, shall be permitted if means for _____ operation are also provided.

    (a) automated
    (b) timed
    (c) manual
    (d) shunt trip

93. Conductors shall be _____ unless otherwise provided.

    (a) bare
    (b) stranded
    (c) of copper
    (d) of aluminum

94. The standard length of RMC shall _____.

    (a) be 10 ft
    (b) include a coupling on each length
    (c) be threaded on each end
    (d) all of these

95. To prevent moisture from entering service equipment, service-entrance conductors shall _____.

    (a) be connected to service-drop conductors below the level of the service head
    (b) have drip loops formed on the individual service-entrance conductors
    (c) a or b
    (d) a and b

96. Service conductors supplying a building or other structure shall not _____ of another building or other structure.

    (a) be installed on the exterior walls
    (b) pass through the interior
    (c) a and b
    (d) none of these

97. Electrically conductive materials that are likely to _____ in ungrounded systems shall be connected together and to the supply system grounded equipment in a manner that creates a low-impedance path for ground-fault current that is capable of carrying the maximum fault current likely to be imposed on it.

    (a) become energized
    (b) require service
    (c) be removed
    (d) be coated with paint or nonconductive materials

98. On a 4-wire, delta-connected system where the midpoint of one phase winding is grounded, the conductor having the higher phase voltage-to-ground shall be durably and permanently marked by an outer finish that is _____ in color.

    (a) black
    (b) red
    (c) blue
    (d) orange

99. A means external to enclosures for connecting intersystem _____ conductors shall be provided at service equipment or metering equipment enclosure and disconnecting means of buildings or structures supplied by a feeder.

    (a) bonding
    (b) ungrounded
    (c) secondary
    (d) a and b

100. Flexible cords and cables shall be protected by _____ where passing through holes in covers, outlet boxes, or similar enclosures.

    (a) bushings
    (b) fittings
    (c) a or b
    (d) none of these

101. Bends in PVC conduit shall be made only _____.

    (a) by hand forming the bend
    (b) with bending equipment identified for the purpose
    (c) with a truck exhaust pipe
    (d) by use of an open flame torch

102. Galvanized steel, stainless steel and red brass RMC can be installed in concrete, in direct contact with the earth, or in areas subject to severe corrosive influences when protected by _____ and judged suitable for the condition.

    (a) ceramic
    (b) corrosion protection
    (c) backfill
    (d) a natural barrier

103. Each multiwire branch circuit shall be provided with a means that will simultaneously disconnect all _____ conductors at the point where the branch circuit originates.

    (a) circuit
    (b) grounded
    (c) grounding
    (d) ungrounded

104. For grounded systems, electrical equipment and conductive material likely to become energized, shall be installed in a manner that creates a _____ from any point on the wiring system where a ground fault may occur to the electrical supply source.

    (a) circuit facilitating the operation of the overcurrent device
    (b) low-impedance path
    (c) path capable of safely carrying the ground-fault current likely to be imposed on it
    (d) all of these

105. The independent support wires for supporting electrical wiring methods in a fire-rated ceiling assembly shall be distinguishable from fire-rated suspended-ceiling framing support wires by _____.

    (a) color
    (b) tagging
    (c) other effective means
    (d) any of these

Please use the 2011 *Code* book to answer the following questions, which are based on the 2011 *NEC*.

Workbook Final Exam B

1. Electric utilities may include entities that install, operate, and maintain _____.

   (a) communications systems (telephone, CATV, Internet, satellite, or data services)
   (b) electric supply systems (generation, transmission, or distribution systems)
   (c) local area network wiring on the premises
   (d) a or b

2. Bonding jumpers for service raceways shall be used around impaired connections such as _____.

   (a) concentric knockouts
   (b) eccentric knockouts
   (c) reducing washers
   (d) any of these

3. Lighting track is a manufactured assembly designed to support and _____ luminaires that are capable of being readily repositioned on the track.

   (a) connect
   (b) protect
   (c) energize
   (d) all of these

4. The ampacities listed in the Tables of Article 310.15(B)(6) do not take _____ into consideration.

   (a) continuous loads
   (b) voltage drop
   (c) insulation
   (d) wet locations

5. A hermetic motor-compressor controller shall have a _____ current rating not less than the respective nameplate rating(s) on the compressor.

   (a) continuous-duty full-load
   (b) locked-rotor
   (c) a or b
   (d) a and b

6. The difference in construction between Type NM cable and Type NMC cable is that Type NMC cable is _____, which Type NM is not.

   (a) corrosion resistant
   (b) flame-retardant
   (c) fungus-resistant
   (d) a and c

7. Raceways, cable trays, cablebus, auxiliary gutters, cable armor, boxes, cable sheathing, cabinets, elbows, couplings, fittings, supports, and support hardware shall be of materials suitable for _____.

   (a) corrosive locations
   (b) wet locations
   (c) the environment in which they are to be installed
   (d) none of these

8. An outdoor receptacle in a location protected from the weather, or in another damp location, shall be installed in an enclosure that is weatherproof when the receptacle is _____.

   (a) covered
   (b) enclosed
   (c) protected
   (d) none of these

9. Letters used to designate the number of conductors within a cable are _____.

   (a) D - Two insulated conductors laid parallel
   (b) M - Two or more insulated conductors twisted spirally
   (c) T - Two or more insulated conductors twisted in parallel
   (d) a and b

10. When replacing receptacles in locations that would require GFCI protection under the current *NEC*, _____ receptacles shall be installed.

    (a) dedicated
    (b) isolated ground
    (c) GFCI-protected
    (d) grounding

11. Type MC Cable listed for _____ is permitted to be installed underground under a building without installation in a raceway.

    (a) direct burial
    (b) damp and wet locations
    (c) rough service
    (d) b and c

12. In a multiple-occupancy building, each occupant shall have access to his or her own _____.

    (a) disconnecting means
    (b) building drops
    (c) building-entrance assembly
    (d) lateral conductors

13. If a(n) _____ shutdown is necessary to reduce hazards to persons, the overload sensing devices can be connected to a supervised alarm instead of causing immediate interruption of the motor circuit.

    (a) emergency
    (b) normal
    (c) orderly
    (d) none of these

14. In indoor locations other than dwellings and associated accessory structures, fluorescent luminaires that utilize double-ended lamps (typical fluorescent lamps) and contain ballasts that can be serviced in place must have a disconnecting means except for _____.

    (a) emergency illumination required in 700.16
    (b) cord-and-plug connected luminaires with accessible plugs and receptacles
    (c) industrial establishments with restricted public access and written procedures and conditions of maintenance and supervision
    (d) all of these

15. ENT and fittings can be_____, provided fittings identified for this purpose are used.

    (a) encased in poured concrete
    (b) embedded in a concrete slab on grade where the tubing is placed on sand or approved screenings
    (c) a or b
    (d) none of these

16. A(n) _____ shall be used to connect the grounding terminal of a grounding-type receptacle to a grounded box.

    (a) equipment bonding jumper
    (b) grounded conductor jumper
    (c) a or b
    (d) a and b

17. Grounding-type attachment plugs shall be used only with a cord having a(n) _____ conductor.

    (a) equipment grounding
    (b) isolated
    (c) computer circuit
    (d) insulated

18. Auxiliary grounding electrodes can be connected to the _____.

    (a) equipment grounding conductor
    (b) grounded conductor
    (c) a and b
    (d) none of these

19. When LFNC is used to connect equipment requiring flexibility after installation, a separate _____ shall be installed.

    (a) equipment grounding conductor
    (b) expansion fitting
    (c) flexible nonmetallic connector
    (d) none of these

20. Which of the following metal parts shall be protected from corrosion?

    (a) Ferrous metal raceways.
    (b) Ferrous metal elbows.
    (c) Ferrous boxes.
    (d) all of these

21. Unused openings other than those intended for the operation of equipment, intended for mounting purposes, or permitted as part of the design for listed equipment shall be _____.

    (a) filled with cable clamps or connectors only
    (b) taped over with electrical tape
    (c) repaired only by welding or brazing in a metal slug
    (d) effectively closed to afford protection substantially equivalent to the wall of the equipment

22. Smooth-sheath Type MC cable with an external diameter not greater than ¾ in. shall have a bending radius not more than _____ times the cable external diameter.

    (a) five
    (b) 10
    (c) 12
    (d) 13

23. In dwelling units, when determining the spacing of receptacle outlets, _____ on exterior walls shall not be considered wall space.

    (a) fixed panels
    (b) fixed glass
    (c) sliding panels
    (d) all of these

24. PVC conduit and fittings for use above ground shall have the following characteristics _____.

    (a) flame retardant
    (b) resistance to low temperatures and sunlight
    (c) resistance to distortion from heat
    (d) all of these

25. Chapters 1 through 4 of the *NEC* apply _____.

    (a) generally to all electrical installations
    (b) only to special occupancies and conditions
    (c) only to special equipment and material
    (d) all of these

26. Which of the following switches must indicate whether they are in the open (off) or closed (on) position?

    (a) General-use switches.
    (b) Motor-circuit switches.
    (c) Circuit breakers.
    (d) all of these

27. When the disconnecting means for a building supplied by a feeder is a power-operated switch or circuit breaker, it shall be able to be opened by hand in the event of a _____.

    (a) ground fault
    (b) short circuit
    (c) power surge
    (d) power failure

28. A switching device with a marked OFF position shall completely disconnect all _____ conductors of the load it controls.

    (a) grounded
    (b) ungrounded
    (c) grounding
    (d) all of these

29. Plug-in-type circuit breakers that are back-fed shall be _____ by an additional fastener that requires more than a pull to release.

    (a) grounded
    (b) secured in place
    (c) shunt tripped
    (d) none of these

30. No _____ shall be attached to any terminal or lead so as to reverse designated polarity.

    (a) grounded conductor
    (b) grounding conductor
    (c) ungrounded conductor
    (d) grounding connector

31. Metal raceways shall be bonded to the metal pole with a(n) _____.

    (a) grounding electrode
    (b) grounded conductor
    (c) equipment grounding conductor
    (d) any of these

32. Receptacles mounted in boxes flush with the finished surface or projecting beyond it shall be installed so that the mounting yoke or strap of the receptacle is _____.

    (a) held rigidly against the box or box cover
    (b) mounted behind the wall surface
    (c) held rigidly at the finished surface
    (d) none of these

33. Electric space-heating cables shall not be installed over cabinets whose clearance from the ceiling is less than the minimum _____ dimension of the cabinet to the nearest cabinet edge that is open to the room or area.

    (a) horizontal
    (b) vertical
    (c) overall
    (d) depth

34. If a motor disconnecting means is a motor-circuit switch, it shall be rated in _____.

    (a) horsepower
    (b) watts
    (c) amperes
    (d) locked-rotor current

35. Article 200 contains the requirements for _____.

    (a) identification of terminals
    (b) grounded conductors in premises wiring systems
    (c) identification of grounded conductors
    (d) all of these

36. Each service disconnecting means shall be permanently _____ to identify it as a service disconnect.

    (a) identified
    (b) positioned
    (c) marked
    (d) none of these

37. Wireways can pass transversely through a wall _____.

    (a) if the length passing through the wall is unbroken
    (b) if the wall is of fire-rated construction
    (c) in hazardous (classified) locations
    (d) if the wall is not of fire-rated construction

38. Cable tray systems shall not be used _____.

    (a) in hoistways
    (b) where subject to severe physical damage
    (c) in hazardous (classified) locations
    (d) a or b

39. Flexible cord used in listed extension cord sets shall be considered protected against overcurrent when used _____.

    (a) in indoor installations
    (b) in unclassified locations
    (c) within the extension cord's listing requirements
    (d) within 50 ft of the branch-circuit panelboard

40. Cable trays shall _____.

    (a) include fittings or other suitable means for changes in direction and elevation
    (b) have side rails or equivalent structural members
    (c) be made of corrosion-resistant material or protected from corrosion as required by 300.6
    (d) all of these

41. Raceways shall be _____ between outlet, junction, or splicing points prior to the installation of conductors.

    (a) installed complete
    (b) tested for ground faults
    (c) a minimum of 80 percent complete
    (d) none of these

42. Exposed secondary circuits of lighting systems operating at 30V or less shall be _____.

    (a) installed in a Chapter 3 wiring method
    (b) supplied by a Class 2 power source and shall use Class 2 cable in accordance with Article 725
    (c) at least 7 ft above the finished floor unless listed for a lower installation height
    (d) any of these

43. The additional service disconnecting means for fire pumps, emergency systems, legally required standby, or optional standby services, shall be installed remote from the one to six service disconnecting means for normal service to minimize the possibility of _____ interruption of supply.

    (a) intentional
    (b) accidental
    (c) simultaneous
    (d) prolonged

44. Where installed to reduce electrical noise for electronic equipment, a metal raceway can terminate to a(n) _____ nonmetallic fitting(s) or spacer on the electronic equipment. The metal raceway shall be supplemented by an internal insulated equipment grounding conductor.

    (a) listed
    (b) labeled
    (c) identified
    (d) marked

45. When a building is supplied with a(n) _____ fire sprinkler system, ENT shall be permitted to be used within walls, floors, and ceilings, exposed or concealed, in buildings exceeding three floors above grade.

    (a) listed
    (b) identified
    (c) NFPA 13-2010
    (d) none of these

46. Where exposed to the direct rays of the sun, insulated conductors and jacketed cables installed in cable trays shall be _____ as being sunlight resistant.

    (a) listed
    (b) approved
    (c) identified
    (d) none of these

47. For raceways terminating at a cable tray, a(n) _____ cable tray clamp or adapter shall be used to securely fasten the raceway to the cable tray system.

    (a) listed
    (b) approved
    (c) identified
    (d) none of these

48. Where Type NM cables pass through cut or drilled slots or holes in metal members, the cable shall be protected by _____ which are installed in the opening prior to the installation of the cable and which securely cover all metal edges.

    (a) listed bushings
    (b) listed grommets
    (c) plates
    (d) a or b

49. Where nonmetallic wiring methods are subject to exposure to chemical solvents or vapors, they shall be inherently resistant to chemicals based upon their being _____.

    (a) listed for the chemical
    (b) identified for the chemical
    (c) a and b
    (d) a or b

50. Threadless couplings and connectors used with RMC in wet locations shall be _____.

    (a) listed for wet locations
    (b) listed for damp locations
    (c) nonabsorbent
    (d) weatherproof

51. Equipment grounding conductors, grounding electrode conductors, and bonding jumpers shall be connected by _____.

    (a) listed pressure connectors
    (b) terminal bars
    (c) exothermic welding
    (d) any of these

52. A panelboard shall be protected by an overcurrent device within the panelboard, or at any point on the _____ side of the panelboard.

    (a) load
    (b) supply
    (c) a or b
    (d) none of these

53. Unless identified for use in the operating environment, no conductors or equipment shall be _____ having a deteriorating effect on the conductors or equipment.

    (a) located in damp or wet locations
    (b) exposed to fumes, vapors, liquids or gases
    (c) exposed to excessive temperatures
    (d) all of these

54. The motor controller shall have horsepower ratings at the application voltage not _____ than the horsepower rating of the motor.

    (a) lower than
    (b) higher than
    (c) equal to
    (d) none of these

55. When LFMC is used to connect equipment where flexibility is necessary to minimize the transmission of vibration from equipment of for equipment requiring movement after installation, a(n) _____ conductor shall be installed.

(a) main bonding
(b) grounded
(c) equipment grounding
(d) none of these

56. Bends in LFNC shall be made so that the conduit will not be damaged and the internal diameter of the conduit will not be effectively reduced. Bends can be made _____.

(a) manually without auxiliary equipment
(b) with bending equipment identified for the purpose
(c) with any kind of conduit bending tool that will work
(d) by the use of an open flame torch

57. Attachment plugs and cord connectors shall be listed and marked with the _____.

(a) manufacturer's name or identification
(b) voltage rating
(c) amperage rating
(d) all of these

58. Luminaires using a _____ lamp, that is subject to physical damage and installed in playing and spectator seating areas of indoor sports, mixed-use, or all-purpose facilities, shall be of the type that protects the lamp with a glass or plastic lens.

(a) mercury vapor
(b) metal halide
(c) fluorescent
(d) a or b

59. For a single separately derived system, the grounding electrode conductor connects the grounded conductor of the derived system to the grounding electrode at the same point on the separately derived system where the _____ is connected.

(a) metering equipment
(b) transfer switch
(c) system bonding jumper
(d) largest circuit breaker

60. Replacement luminaires aren't required to be connected to an equipment grounding conductor if no equipment grounding conductor exists at the outlet box and the luminaire is _____.

(a) more than 20 years old
(b) mounted to the box using nonmetallic fittings and screws
(c) mounted more than 6 ft above the floor
(d) GFCI protected

61. Type UF cable shall not be used in _____.

(a) motion picture studios
(b) storage battery rooms
(c) hoistways
(d) all of these

62. The motor _____ currents listed in Tables 430.247 through 430.250 shall be used to determine the ampacity of motor circuit conductors and short-circuit and ground-fault protection devices.

(a) nameplate
(b) full-load
(c) power factor
(d) service factor

63. Utilization equipment weighing less than 6 lb can be supported to any box or plaster ring secured to a box, provided the equipment is secured with at least two _____ or larger screws.

(a) No. 6
(b) No. 8
(c) No. 10
(d) self tapping

64. At existing buildings or structures, an intersystem bonding termination is not required if other acceptable means of bonding exits. An external accessible means for bonding communications systems together can be by the use of _____.

(a) nonflexible metallic raceway
(b) an exposed grounding electrode conductor
(c) a connection to grounded raceway or equipment approved by the authority having jurisdiction
(d) any of these

65. Tap connections to a common grounding electrode conductor for multiple separately derived systems may be made to a copper or aluminum busbar that is _____.

    (a) not over ½ in. x 4 in.
    (b) not over ¼ in. x 2 in.
    (c) at least ¼ in. x 2 in.
    (d) a and c

66. Nominal battery voltage, as it relates to storage batteries, is defined as the voltage of a battery based on the _____ of cells in the battery.

    (a) number
    (b) type
    (c) a and b
    (d) a or b

67. Conductors and busbars on a switchboard or panelboard shall be located so as to be free from _____ and shall be held firmly in place.

    (a) obstructions
    (b) physical damage
    (c) a and b
    (d) none of these

68. A unit switch with a marked _____ position that is part of a fixed space heater, and disconnects all ungrounded conductors, shall be permitted to serve as the required disconnecting means.

    (a) on
    (b) closed
    (c) off
    (d) none of these

69. Where the circuit breaker handles are operated vertically, the up position of the handle shall be the _____.

    (a) on position
    (b) off position
    (c) tripped position
    (d) any of these

70. Overload relays and other devices for motor overload protection that are not capable of _____ shall be protected by fuses, circuit breakers, or motor short-circuit protector.

    (a) opening short circuits
    (b) clearing overloads
    (c) opening ground faults
    (d) a or c

71. Cable wiring methods shall not be used as a means of support for _____.

    (a) other cables
    (b) raceways
    (c) nonelectrical equipment
    (d) all of these

72. A panelboard shall be provided with physical means to prevent the installation of more _____ devices than that number for which the panelboard was designed, rated, and listed.

    (a) overcurrent
    (b) equipment
    (c) circuit breaker
    (d) all of these

73. Vegetation such as trees shall not be used for support of _____.

    (a) overhead conductor spans
    (b) surface wiring methods
    (c) luminaires
    (d) electric equipment

74. Hazards often occur because of _____.

    (a) overloading of wiring systems by methods or usage not in conformity with the *NEC*
    (b) initial wiring not providing for increases in the use of electricity
    (c) a and b
    (d) none of these

75. Conductors in ferrous metal raceways and enclosures shall be arranged so as to avoid heating the surrounding ferrous metal by alternating-current induction. To accomplish this, the _____ conductor(s) shall be grouped together.

    (a) phase
    (b) grounded
    (c) equipment grounding
    (d) all of these

76. Listed FMC and LFMC shall contain an equipment grounding conductor if the raceway is installed for the reason of _____.

    (a) physical protection
    (b) flexibility after installation
    (c) minimizing transmission of vibration from equipment
    (d) b or c

77. The service conductors shall be connected to the service disconnecting means by _____ or other approved means.

    (a) pressure connectors
    (b) clamps
    (c) solder
    (d) a or b

78. A snap switch that does not have means for connection to an equipment grounding conductor shall be permitted for replacement purposes only where the wiring method does not include an equipment grounding conductor and the switch is _____.

    (a) provided with a faceplate of nonconducting, noncombustible material with nonmetallic screws
    (b) GFCI protected
    (c) a or b
    (d) none of these

79. All conductors of a circuit, including the grounded and equipment grounding conductors, shall be contained within the same _____, unless otherwise permitted elsewhere in the *Code*.

    (a) raceway
    (b) cable
    (c) trench
    (d) all of these

80. Electric-discharge and LED luminaires supported independently of the outlet box shall be connected to the branch circuit through _____.

    (a) raceways
    (b) Type MC, AC, MI, or NM cable
    (c) flexible cords
    (d) any of these

81. The disconnecting means for air-conditioning and refrigerating equipment shall be _____ from the air-conditioning or refrigerating equipment.

    (a) readily accessible
    (b) within sight
    (c) a or b
    (d) a and b

82. Nonlocking type 15A and 20A, 125V receptacles in a dwelling unit shall be listed as tamper resistant except _____.

    (a) receptacles located more than 5½ ft above the floor
    (b) receptacles that are part of a luminaire or appliance
    (c) a receptacle located within dedicated space for an appliance that in normal use is not easily moved from one place to another
    (d) all of these

83. Metal wireways are sheet metal troughs with _____ for housing and protecting electric conductors and cable.

    (a) removable covers
    (b) hinged covers
    (c) a or b
    (d) none of these

84. Wiring methods permitted for service-entrance conductors include _____.

    (a) rigid metal conduit
    (b) electrical metallic tubing
    (c) PVC conduit
    (d) all of these

85. Luminaires designed for end-to-end assembly, or luminaires connected together by _____, can contain a 2-wire branch circuit, or one multiwire branch circuit, supplying the connected luminaires. One additional 2-wire branch circuit supplying one or more of the connected luminaires is permitted.

    (a) rigid metal conduit
    (b) recognized wiring methods
    (c) flexible wiring methods
    (d) EMT

86. Conduits or raceways through which moisture may contact live parts shall be _____ at either or both ends.

    (a) sealed
    (b) plugged
    (c) bushed
    (d) a or b

87. Flexible metal conduit shall not be required to be _____ where fished between access points through concealed spaces in finished buildings or structures and supporting is impracticable.

    (a) secured
    (b) supported
    (c) complete
    (d) (a) and (b)

88. Fixture wires are used to connect luminaires to the _____ conductors supplying the luminaires.

    (a) service
    (b) branch-circuit
    (c) feeder
    (d) none of these

89. Lightning protection system ground terminals _____ be bonded to the building grounding electrode system.

    (a) shall
    (b) shall not
    (c) shall be permitted to
    (d) none of these

90. When the *Code* uses "_____," it means the identified actions are allowed but not required, and they may be options or alternative methods.

    (a) shall
    (b) shall not
    (c) shall be permitted
    (d) a or b

91. Each cable entering a cutout box _____.

    (a) shall be secured to the cutout box
    (b) can be sleeved through a chase
    (c) shall have a maximum of two cables per connector
    (d) all of these

92. Direct-buried conductors, cables, or raceways, which are subject to movement by settlement or frost, shall be arranged to prevent damage to the _____ or to equipment connected to the raceways.

    (a) siding of the building mounted on
    (b) landscaping around the cable or raceway
    (c) the enclosed conductors
    (d) expansion fitting

93. Receptacle outlets installed for a specific appliance in a dwelling unit, such as laundry equipment, shall be located within _____ of the intended location of the appliance.

    (a) sight
    (b) 3 ft
    (c) 6 ft
    (d) none of these

94. The following systems shall be installed in accordance with the *NEC* requirements:

    (a) Signaling.
    (b) Communications.
    (c) Electrical conductors, equipment, and raceways.
    (d) all of these

95. A device or utilization equipment wider than a single 2 in. device box shall have _____ volume allowances provided for each gang required for mounting.

    (a) single
    (b) double
    (c) triple
    (d) none of these

96. For other than one- or two-family dwellings, when 15A and 20A receptacles are installed in a wet location, the outlet box _____ must be listed for extra-duty use.

    (a) sleeve
    (b) hood
    (c) threaded entry
    (d) mounting

97. Where it is unlikely that two or more noncoincident loads will be in use simultaneously, only the _____ loads used at one time is required to be used in computing the total load to a feeder.

(a) smaller of the
(b) largest of the
(c) difference between the
(d) none of these

98. A surface extension can be made from the cover of a box where the cover is designed so it is unlikely to fall off or be removed if its securing means becomes loose. The wiring method shall be _____ for a length sufficient to permit removal of the cover and provide access to the box interior, and arranged so that any grounding continuity is independent of the connection between the box and cover.

(a) solid
(b) flexible
(c) rigid
(d) cord

99. Short-radius conduit bodies such as capped elbows, and service-entrance elbows that enclose conductors 6 AWG and smaller shall not contain _____.

(a) splices
(b) taps
(c) devices
(d) any of these

100. Where combination surface metal raceways are used for both signaling conductors and lighting and power circuits, the different systems shall be run in separate compartments identified by _____ of the interior finish.

(a) stamping
(b) imprinting
(c) color coding
(d) any of these

101. In an FMC installation, _____ connectors shall not be concealed.

(a) straight
(b) angle
(c) grounding-type
(d) none of these

102. Conductors, splices or terminations in a handhole enclosure shall be listed as _____.

(a) suitable for wet locations
(b) suitable for damp locations
(c) suitable for direct burial in the earth
(d) none of these

103. A grounded conductor shall not be connected to normally noncurrent-carrying metal parts of equipment on the _____ side of the system bonding jumper of a separately derived system except as otherwise permitted in Article 250.

(a) supply
(b) grounded
(c) high-voltage
(d) load

104. Circuit breakers used to switch high-intensity discharge lighting circuits shall be listed and marked as _____.

(a) SWD
(b) HID
(c) a or b
(d) a and b

105. A building or structure that is supplied by a feeder shall have the interior metal water piping system bonded with a conductor sized in accordance with _____.

(a) Table 250.66
(b) Table 250.122
(c) Table 310.15(B)(16)
(d) none of these